Dedication

To three enchanting people: Zeke, Natalia, Isaiah

About the author

Norton Paley has over 25 years of corporate experience in general management, marketing management and product development at McGraw-Hill Inc, John Wiley & Sons and Alexander-Norton Inc. He has authored seven books, including:

- The Strategic Marketing Planner
- Action Guide to Marketing Planning and Strategy
- Marketing for the Non-marketing Executive: An Integrated Management Resource Guide
- The Marketing Strategy Desktop Guide
- Pricing Strategies and Practices
- Marketing Principles and Tactics Everyone Must Know
- The Manager's Guide to Competitive Strategies, 2nd Ed.

In addition to advising management on competitive strategies and strategic planning, Paley also has extensive global experience lecturing to managers at such firms as American Express, Cargill (worldwide), Chevron Chemical, Babcock & Wilcox, Dow Chemical (worldwide), W.R. Grace & Co., Prentice-Hall, Ralston-Purina, Hoechst, and McDonnell-Douglas. Also, he participated in lecture tours in the Republic of China and Mexico.

His byline columns have appeared in *The Management Review and Sales & Marketing Management.*

CONTENTS

THREE
Business Problem Solver: The Strategic Business Plan in Action

FOUR
Checklists for Developing Competitive Strategies

FIVE
Help Topics

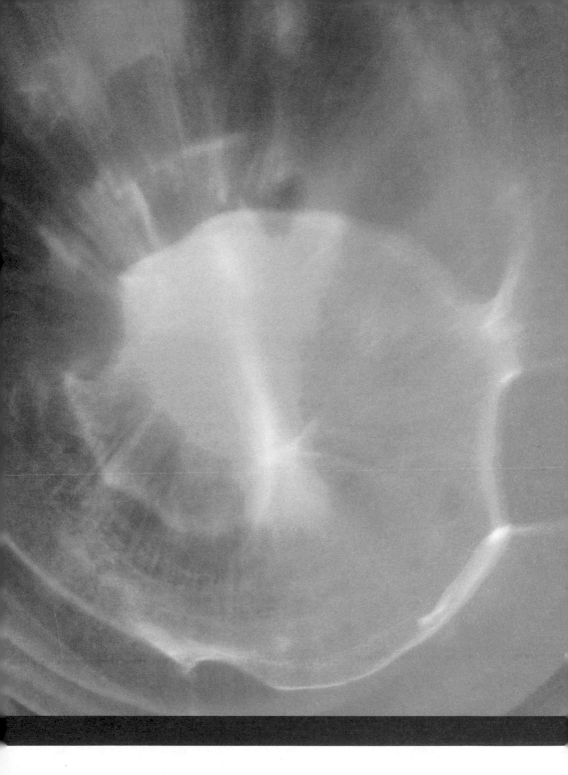

Introduction

Introduction

Why plan? There are many compelling reasons. Included among them are the following:

"Two thirds of rapid-growth firms have written business plans. Firms with written plans grow faster, achieve a higher proportion of revenues from new products and services, and enable CEO's to manage more critical business functions than those firms whose plans are unwritten.

Additionally, growth firms with a written business plan have increased their revenues 69 percent faster over the past five years than those without a written plan."

From a survey by PricewaterhouseCoopers

"Strategic Planning – It's Back! Reengineering? Cost-cutting? Been there, done that. Now, strategy is king."

Headline from a Business Week cover story. The story points out the following key issues as outcomes of the planning process:

- Strategy planning is again a major focus for higher revenues and profits – and to hatch new products, expand existing business, and create new markets.

- Business strategy is the single most important management issue and will remain so for the next five years.

- Democratizing the strategy planning process is handled by turning it over to teams of line and staff managers from different disciplines.

"The plan is nothing; planning is everything."

Former U.S. President and General Dwight D. Eisenhower

The previous comments consist of two dimensions: First, a written plan defines the business mission, lists objectives and strategies, and provides details about products and services. Implicit in the physical makeup of the plan are the numerous details about tactics to reach customers in geographically and culturally dispersed markets, using the seemingly limitless potential of the Internet.

The second dimension, which is firmly embedded in Eisenhower's comment, defines planning as a mental process. This is the juncture where experience, skill and insight converge to envision the future. It is the point in time to prioritize objectives; shape imaginative strategies; deploy people, material and financial resources for maximum impact; and assign levels of authority and responsibility to trained individuals who can skillfully implement the plan.

Further, giving a human face to this dimension is leadership, which energizes the morale of the rank and file to push forward in an increasing competitive environment. Often, it is the singular factor in deciding the success or failure of the business plan.

Therefore, the principle reason to develop a plan is to bind those two dimensions together into a cohesive and managerial whole, to make sense of the organizational and marketplace arenas, and to create order out of what can easily deteriorate into disorder.

In some organizations plans are known as strategic plans, strategic business plans, corporate plans, or strategic market plans. Whichever label you select, what remains significant is that there is a defined structure to develop a plan and a thinking (planning) mode to engage the mental process. In turn, that process requires you to envision the future and implement resourceful approaches to activate the vision.

The title, *Strategic Business Plan*, will be used in this book to highlight *strategic*, which emphasizes the long-term focus of the plan, and *business*, which defines the pragmatic, action-oriented part of the plan that is all-inclusive, detailed, and suggests that every function contributes to the financial health and competitive vitality of the organization.

The following case illustrates a broad application of strategic business planning.

Case example

Dow Chemical executives conducted a strategic planning session during the 1990s that examined in depth each of their diverse businesses. The aim: set a firm direction for the organization in a changing competitive environment. Looking as far as they could into the 21st Century, they concluded that Dow's total concentration of resources would be directed to chemicals.

Further, as long as the company could retain global leadership in its various markets, it would avoid diversification, which was prevalent among Dow's competitors. Implementing the new strategy meant selling off such well-known consumer products as Ziploc bags and Saran Wrap.

In place of those divested business units, extensive acquisitions were made, including Union Carbide and numerous other chemical companies. Once all the divesting, acquiring and consolidating of assets, people and businesses were completed, a comprehensive restructuring of Dow was set in motion to bring the diverse units into a cohesive force to achieve the strategic objectives of the plan.

Among the changes: Dow formed a Web-based buying consortium with other large companies, which resulted in huge savings. It also established a Web strategy to improve interactions with its customers through, 'My Account at Dow'. This feature established the interactive Internet connection for customers to conveniently place orders, track orders and handle billings.

The centerpiece of the restructuring – and the essential component to effective leadership – was Dow's enhanced ability to control its geographically dispersed businesses located throughout North America, Europe, Latin America, and the Pacific Rim. Dow streamlined its corporate structure so that layers of management from the CEO at its headquarters in Midland, Michigan to the most junior employees at an off-site location were reduced from its former 12 layers to a mere five.

Also germane to the grand plan was the rapid transfer of information through the purchase of 38,000 PCs and terminals, so that everybody was online. One and all received appropriate information, and communications could take place rapidly and accurately – both in and out of the company.

That move improved the efficient transfer of knowledge and information to employees throughout its far-flung empire, so that individuals could make rational decisions based on real-time conditions. In effect, the system created a virtual managerial forum for conducting a cohesive global meeting.

While Dow represents a large organization's approach to deal with the future, the very same planning process can apply to a smaller organization or individual business unit. That is, the physical plan in and of itself is not the magic elixir. As previously pointed out, it is the mental process that goes into planning that yields favorable outcomes. Meaning:

> The plan is but a structured format containing a series of questions or a list of directions. It is the mode of *planning* that stretches your thinking into the future, analyzes events and statistics, makes judgments, formulates ideas and converts them into action.

Within that context, planning engages the mind to think about and act on such pragmatic questions as:

- How do you maintain control of individuals who are geographically separated and where directives from higher-ups are often imprecise?

- How do you integrate the skilled individuals and the not so-skilled to work in harmony at the critical junctures of acting with speed to exploit a favorable market opportunity?

- How do you reach an acceptable balance in deploying personnel, so that the more aggressive individuals act boldly but not impulsively; and the more reticent ones act with some bravado, yet don't retreat prematurely under competitive pressure?

- How do you shape a winning strategy and deploy your resources to achieve your target objectives?

Perhaps the most stunning example that addresses many of the above questions, and in particular how individuals exhibit different sets of skills, is the shocking demise of many dot.coms during the economic turbulence of 2000-01. At the onset of the Internet revolution, venture capitalists were clambering to fund millions to any entrepreneur with the guts and an idea for a company.

In the aftermath of the failures, however, the mood changed dramatically and the demand from those same money backers switched to experienced management talent as the key requisite to rescue floundering companies and fund new startups.

While some experienced executives from the Old Economy companies were somewhat conservative and slow to act, they knew enough to deploy resources based on hard estimates of the marketplace and not wishful thinking. They could calculate the financial consequences of their strategic and tactical decisions. They grasped the need to balance growth with meeting financial targets. They fully recognized the value of a motivated workforce as intellectual capital. And they knew how to develop a strategically focused business plan with a vision that projected beyond Monday-morning obstacles.

In contrast, the entrepreneur was often viewed as inexperienced, impulsive, and driven by a 'damn the torpedoes, full speed ahead' attitude. However, in many instances entrepreneurs did demonstrate outstanding technical expertise, intuitive spark and inner-directed fearlessness.

Above all, they exhibited the fiery passion and personality traits endemic to fast-track individuals. Thus, blending experienced leaders with pure entrepreneurs could result in an effective balance and an efficient utilization of talents.

Expectations

Consequently, embracing the Strategic Business Plan, along with acquiring the mental process of *planning*, permits you to handle similar situations with a high level of managerial competence. The process also allows you to estimate the strengths and weaknesses of your organization or business unit. You can measure the tangible results of your analysis and form rational judgments about individuals and their management styles.

In turn, you can determine the level of skills required to achieve planning objectives and pinpoint the areas of training to shore-up personnel performance. Further, you can identify the types of market intelligence that would increase the accuracy of your decisions.

When completed, the plan is perhaps the most comprehensive and useful people-to-people communications vehicle of all. The effective plan clarifies a corporate vision and the objectives and strategies that may otherwise be distorted through verbal communications and the telegraphic language typically used in e-mail. When thoughtfully read and fully internalized by individuals, the plan transmits guidelines to personnel on how to actively participate at significant business events where on-the-spot decisions are needed.

Also, the document reduces the level of vaguely communicated directions, particularly where there is an impasse; and it generally decreases the level of misunderstanding up and down the organizational chart. Thus, the plan, when viewed against a backdrop of long-term strategic goals and strategies, lessens the intensity of miscommunications and misinterpretations.

Additionally, the plan results in an organizational design, a system of controls and a logical approach to optimize the grouping of personnel based on complementary sets of skills.

Implementation

The quality and thereby the effectiveness of the plan, however, depends on the personal commitment to planning, the level of support by senior management and the skill of individuals writing the plan. Also, probably most important to the planning process: the willingness and courage to move beyond the pressing problems of today and take a thoughtful look into the foreseeable future, where fresh opportunities prevail, new markets materialize, trends surface and breakthrough technologies offer enticing new possibilities.

While pragmatic issues do exist and short-term earnings by necessity remain top-of-mind, nonetheless, by definition the effective manager looks beyond the immediate and plans for the future – even if the future is defined as 12, 24, or 36 months.

While the erratic behavior of a marketplace offers no guarantees of success, in pragmatic terms even where your plans are made and the strategies diligently implemented, all that you can reasonably expect from your best efforts is that the competitive edge falls in your favor. Should some objectives and strategies lack total accuracy, consider the opportunistic effect where your competitor has done little or ineffectual planning. Consequently, following the proverbial seat-of-the-pants approach, your rival would react to every news headline and scatter resources without direction. Certainly, the competitive odds would be on your side.

A business plan, therefore, should contain a strategic focus as well as a tactical implementation. The long-term view keeps you concentrated on your company's mission or strategic direction and as long as there are valid assumptions backed by reliable assessments, it should hold you on course.

Flexibility also plays an active part, primarily at the shorter-term tactical level, where there is greater need for alertness to take advantage of tangible opportunities – as long as they link to your longer-term objectives.

There is still another major benefit of planning: taking advantage of a competitor who is not prepared. Meaning: There is no honor in braving repeated market battles with competitors and falling prey to harmful price wars and other profit-draining promotional actions. Instead, the respect goes to those managers who avoid sustained and careless expenditures of resources, while achieving their desired objectives.

Outcomes of Planning

The following list summarizes the positive outcomes of immersing yourself, and those with whom you interact, in the planning process. Acquiring the skills to develop resourceful plans, which is the purpose of this book, will enhance your ability to:

- Make market estimates and thereby calculate your chances of success.
- Identify your competitor's strategies and counter them before they materialize.
- Resolve internal difficulties before they arise.
- Recognize customers' needs and buying behavior, and then translate the findings into new market and product opportunities.
- Create strategies and tactics that result in a sustainable competitive advantage.
- Concentrate your strength against a competitor's weaknesses.
- Manage personnel with greater efficiency.
- Assess your company and employees' states of readiness.

- Select the markets in which to concentrate your resources.

- Make strategic decisions with greater precision.

- Energize your group or organization to take advantage of the immense global opportunities.

In all, developing competence in planning helps you to win – to win markets and customers, to win a profitable and sustainable market position, to win over competitors.

Getting the Most Out of This Book

As you work through each of the six chapters of this book, you will continuously improve your knowledge of planning. You will find application checks, real company examples and case studies embedded throughout the book to help you link new skills back to your job.

1. The Strategic Business Plan (SBP) – Strategic Section

Using a real company to illustrate the planning techniques (only the name is disguised for confidentiality), you will begin the step-by-step process to see how the long-term strategic portion of the SBP is formed.

2. The Strategic Business Plan – Tactical Section

Continuing with the case example, you will learn how to develop a 1-year tactical section of your SBP and how to link it to the strategic section.

3. Business Problem Solver: the Strategic Business Plan in Action

Actual case examples show how successful companies solved severe competitive problems – and won. Should your company face similar problems, you will find action strategies you can utilize within your own organization. Also, for each case example, references are made to the particular sections of the SBP that address those problems.

4. Checklists for Developing Competitive Strategies

Where you need to evaluate the potential of a market or use a system to generate competitive strategies, several evaluation checklists provide added precision to you SBP.

5. Help Topics

This convenient reference consists of comprehensive guidelines to assist you in the planning process outlined in Parts 1 and 2. For easy use, the topics are keyed to the applicable SBP section. Also, beyond their specific applications to the plan, you will find the Help Topics immensely practical as a general resource in designing business-building strategies and sharpening your management skills.

6. Appendix

This part contains planning forms and guidelines to develop your own customized SBP.

Customizing Your Plan

While maintaining the basic structure of the SBP, you are free to alter the forms to accommodate for the unique vocabulary and issues related to your company and industry. You can even add special forms, software, or spreadsheets required by your organization and thereby make the SBP a permanent part of your operation.

Finally, there is one caution in using the SBP format

Don't short-circuit the plan by skipping sections or altering the sequence in which the plan is prepared. The process is shown as a logical progression that leads you step-by-step from section to section, from the broad strategic focus to the narrow tactical implementation. The intent is to free up your mind to think broadly about your product or service, convert your thinking into a business perspective, and then follow through with decisive action.

You are now ready to proceed to Part 1 and learn how to prepare a realistic SBP that you can confidently submit to upper-level management, or to a bank for a loan, or for any other reason such as forming an alliance with a prospective partner.

As you go through the process, remember you are not alone. You have a good deal of assistance throughout this book to help you sharpen your planning skills. With planning as the defining requirement for the 21st Century manager, honing those skills can serve you profitably over the course of your career.

Good luck and successful planning.

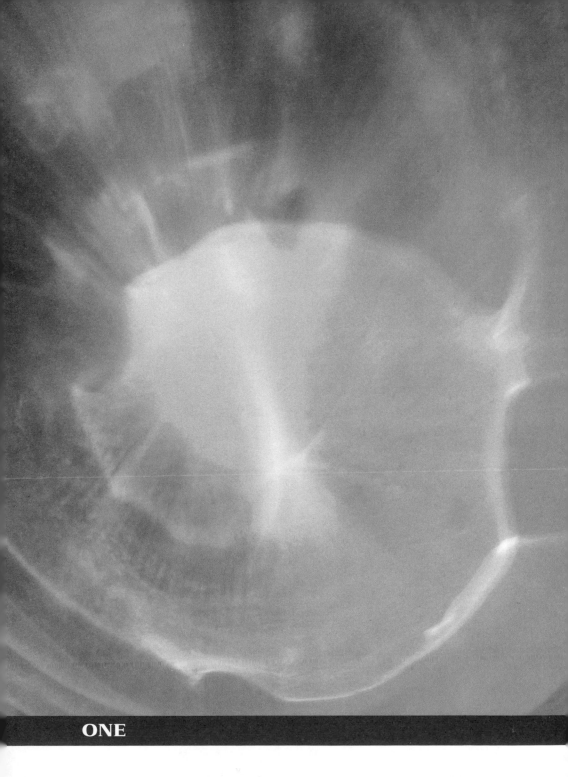

The Strategic Business Plan (SBP)
– Strategic Section

ONE

The Strategic Business Plan (SBP) – Strategic Section

Overview

Now that you have viewed the compelling reasons for developing a reliable plan and surveyed the numerous outcomes you can expect from a SBP, you are ready to develop your own plan that would give you a competitive edge.

To obtain optimum results from a SBP requires following a process, which is diagrammed in Figure 1.1. (Each section of the SBP diagram will be highlighted as the material is discussed in the text.) As you examine the flowchart, notice that the top row of boxes represents the *strategic* portion of the plan and covers a 3 to 5-year timeframe.

The bottom row of boxes displays the *tactical* 1-year plan. Although these sections – strategic and tactical – are discussed in separate chapters for ease of explanation, in actual form it is the merging of the strategic plan and the tactical plan into one unified SBP that makes it a complete format.

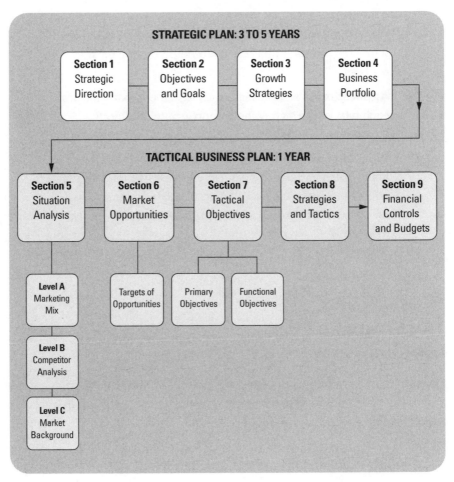

FIGURE 1.1. **STRATEGIC BUSINESS PLAN**

You will find that following the SBP process will add an organized and disciplined approach to your thinking. Yet the process in no way confines your thinking or creativity. Instead, it enhances your inventiveness and extends a strategic vision that elevates the creative process. In turn, that vision can pay off in abundant opportunities expressed through markets, products, and services.

This chapter addresses the strategic portion of the SBP (Figure 1.1, Sections 1-4.) The following chapter addresses the tactical plan (Figure 1.1, Sections 5-9.) To make the most comfortable learning experience for you, the following format is used for each section:

- **Planning Guidelines**: Each section of the SBP is defined with point-by-point directions to help you master the process.

- **Application**: A sample plan of an actual company illustrates each part of the plan. Where appropriate, additional commentary is added to more fully explain their usage.

- **Working Draft**: As you go through each section, you can make notes and develop your own draft. When completed, you can transfer the notes and any subsequent updates to an extra set of planning forms in the Appendix.

The Strategic Plan: Looking Forward 3 to 5 Years

The strategic plan (top row of boxes in Figure 1.1) represents the managerial process for developing and maintaining a strategic fit between the organization and changing market opportunities. It relies on developing the following sections:

1. a strategic direction or mission statement,
2. objectives and goals,
3. growth strategies,
4. a business portfolio.

Section 1: Strategic Direction

Let's begin with the first box, Section 1. This is where you create a strategic direction for your company, business unit, product, or service. It is also known as a mission or vision statement.

Planning Guidelines

You can use the following questions to provide an organized approach to developing a strategic direction. Your thoughtful answers will help shape the ideal vision of what your company, business unit, or product/service will look like over the next 3 to 5 years. More precisely, it should echo your – and your teams – long-range outlook, as long as it is consistent with overall corporate objectives and policies.

As you think about your strategic direction, consider the following six questions:

1. What are our organization's distinctive areas of expertise?
2. What business should we be in over the next 3 to 5 years?
3. What segments or categories of customers will we serve?
4. What additional functions are we likely to fulfill for customers as we see the market evolve?
5. What new technologies will we require to satisfy future customer/ market needs?
6. What changes are taking place in markets, consumer behavior, competition, environment, culture and the economy that will impact our company?

The point of this exercise is that the responsibility for defining a strategic direction no longer belongs exclusively to upper management. Also, there are a host of internal and external issues that can affect your SBP.

For best results, managers from various departments – marketing/sales, product development, manufacturing, finance and logistics – should contribute to defining the strategic direction of the business or individual product.

Let's examine each of the questions:

1. What are our organization's distinctive areas of expertise?

This question refers to your organization's (or business unit's) competencies. You can develop your answer by evaluating the following:

- Relative competitive strengths of your product or service based on customer satisfaction, profitability and market share.
- Relationships with distributors and/or end-use customers.
- Existing production capabilities.
- Size of your sales-force.
- Financial strength.
- R&D expenditures.
- Amount of customer or technical service provided.

Further, where time and resources permit, you can delve into the question by conducting an extensive strengths/weaknesses analysis that serves as a marketing audit. (See Part 4 for a practical format to conduct the analysis.)

2. What business should we be in over the next 3 to 5 years?

The major work in this area of strategic thinking is attributed to Harvard Business School Professor Theodore Levitt[1], in his classic article, 'Marketing Myopia'. Using the railroads as a prime example, Levitt cited how railroads declined in use during the 20th Century as technology advanced and as executives defined that industry too narrowly. He explains that to continue growing, companies must determine customers' needs and wants and not rely simply on the longevity of their products.

According to Levitt, a myopic view is grounded on the following four beliefs that begin in a manager's mind and permeates an organization:

(1) growth is guaranteed by an expanding and affluent population, (2) there is no competitive substitute for the industry's major product, (3) excessive belief in mass production and rapidly declining unit costs as output rises, and (4) preoccupation with a product that lends itself to experimentation and manufacturing cost improvement.

1. T. Levitt, 'Marketing Myopia,' Harvard Business Review (Sept./Oct. 1975), p.28

The key point: looking out the window toward inevitable change, not into a mirror that reflects existing patterns, characterizes the market-driven vs. the product-driven organization.

Table 1.1 illustrates how organizations in a variety of industries express their identity between two orientations: The product-driven or inward-directed orientation, which Levitt calls *myopic* and is characterized by the famous comment of Henry Ford, "Give them any color they want as long as it's black". In stark contrast, a former IBM executive describes an outward market-driven or customer-oriented approach as, "This is the year of the customer".

Note in Table 1.1 how the differing orientations would change the character of an organization and, in turn, become the underpinnings of a company's (or business units) strategic direction.

Product-Driven Orientation	Market-Driven Orientation
Railroad company	Transportation company
Oil company	Energy company
Baby food manufacturer	Child care business
Cosmetics company	Beauty, fashion, health company
Computer manufacturing company	Information processing company
Electrical wire manufacturer	Energy transfer business
Vacuum cleaner manufacturer	Cleaner environment business
Valve company	Fluid control company

TABLE 1.1. **COMPANY IDENTITY AS REFLECTED BY ORIENTATION**

To continue growing, therefore, managers must create a viable strategic direction that looks critically at marketable trends and connects them with customers' needs and wants. Doing so avoids relying on the longevity of existing products to sustain company growth.

The implications of how you strategically position your business for the future determines the breadth of existing and new product lines and the range of existing and new markets served. If you are too narrow (myopic in Levitt's terms) in defining your business, the resulting product and market mix will be generally narrow and possibly too confining for growth.

On the other hand, defining your business too broadly can result in spreading capital, people and other resources beyond the capabilities of the organization. You can create a comfortable balance by positioning your business somewhere between the extremes of the two orientations.

Therefore, first examine the culture, skills and resources of your organization. Second, consider such factors as customer needs, business functions to be enhanced or added, and types of new technologies you need to compete successfully. The answers will emerge through the question and answer process suggested in this section.

3. What segments or categories of customers will we serve?

Customers exist at various levels in the supply chain and in different segments of the market. At the end of the chain are end-use consumers with whom you may or may not come in direct contact.

Other customers within the distribution channel serve as intermediaries and typically perform several functions. Intermediaries include distributors who take possession of the products and often serve as a warehousing facility.

Still, other intermediaries repackage products and maintain inventory control systems to serve the next level of distribution, and there are value-added resellers that provide customer service, technical advice, computer software, or educational programs to differentiate their products from those of competitors.

Examining the existing and future needs at each level of distribution helps you project the types of customers you want to target for the 3- to 5-year period covered by the strategic portion of your SBP. Similarly, you will want to review various segments and target those that will provide the best opportunities over the planning period.

4. What additional functions are we likely to fulfill for customers as we see the market evolve?

As competitive intensity increases worldwide, each intermediary customer along the supply chain is increasingly pressured to maintain a competitive advantage. This guideline question asks you to determine what functions or capabilities are needed to solve customers' problems.

More precisely, you are looking beyond your immediate customer and reaching out further into the distribution channel to identify those functions that would solve your customers' *customers'* problems. Such functions might include providing computerized inventory control, after-sales technical support, quality control programs, just-in-time delivery, or financial assistance. Overall, this question relates to the 'myopia' issue that defines the business in terms of customer needs.

5. What new technologies will we require to satisfy future customer/market needs?

Within the framework of the previous question and the practices of your industry, examine the impact of technologies to satisfy your customers' needs. Look at where your company ranks with the various technologies and types of software used for product design and productivity, manufacturing, and distribution systems. Look, too, at the continuing changes in information technology (IT) and business intelligence with its resulting effects on product innovation and market competitiveness.

Also appraise such emerging technologies as expert diagnostic systems for problem-solving and the rapidly changing communications systems to manage and protect an increasingly wireless enterprise.

6. What changes are taking place in markets, onsumer behavior, competition, environment, culture and the economy that will impact on our company?

This form of external analysis permits you to sensitize yourself to those critical issues that relate to markets, customers, competition and the industry. They can range from local economic conditions to broad governmental regulations. As you will see, all can impact on your SBP.

Answering these six questions allows you to make a long-term visionary inquiry that becomes the underpinnings of your strategic direction. That is, as long as it complements the overall policies of your organization. As will be shown in a later section of the SBP, the strategic direction permits you to accurately define market expansion, product development and service offerings.

What follows is an application of a strategic direction for a single product line within a diversified global healthcare organization. The statement comes directly from its actual SBP. To maintain the company's anonymity, we will call it ZNI-Tech Corp.

One division of the company manufactures hypodermic products for the healthcare field. ZNI will be used to illustrate applications throughout the SBP. Only enough of the actual plan is provided to illustrate the guidelines. For security reasons, minor changes were made in the plan to further disguise the actual identity of the company. Also, commentary is added where needed to further clarify the application.

Application

Our strategic direction is to meet the needs of consumers and healthcare providers for drug-delivery devices by offering a full line of hypodermic products and product systems. Our leadership position will be maintained through internal research and development, licensing of technology, and/or acquisition options to provide alternative administration and monitoring systems.

COMMENTARY

ZNI's primary product is the hypodermic needle. The strategic direction could have stated simply that the company is a manufacturer of hypodermic needles. That would have been far too 'myopic' and restrictive for growing and maintaining a dominant competitive position.

The broader interpretations of 'drug delivery devices' and 'product systems' certainly incorporate ZNI's core business of hypodermic needles. The important issue, however, is that it excites the mind to create fresh opportunities for product designers to develop new products and services.

For example, devices exist and are under development that eliminates the necessity for needles. Instead, delivering drugs to the body can be accomplished through new forms of pills and internally implanted pumps with sensors to control the release of the drug within the body.

Other devices that look like writing pens with drug-filled cartridges are alternatives to the syringe and needle. And still other product systems incorporate monitoring devices to measure medical effectiveness of the drug and automatically calculate the amount of dosages required for an individual patient.

With a measure of creativity even broader considerations of the strategic direction could impact on markets, products, technologies and services. These include: safe disposal systems for needles and syringes linked to increasing environmental concerns; product configurations by types of diseases, geographic location, culture, and demographics within a target population segment; and systems that calculate for the severity of an illness and its contagious impact on unprotected groups.

Therefore, by conceiving a broader interpretation of a business – from railroad to transportation – helps avoid the negative impact of a shrinking market position due to older technologies. Taking time to develop a well-thought out strategic direction provides an organized framework to extend your thinking to what your company or product line can or should become within an achievable timeframe of 3 to 5 years.

Although the example used here represents a division of a company, the same thought process is appropriate for a product line within a mid-size organization – and certainly within a small single-product company.

Look again at ZNI's strategic direction. In addition to product systems and services, the statement refers to a 'leadership position'. ZNI's existing position certainly could be maintained through internal R&D, however, the broader thinking also opens a pathway to new products, devices, systems, and services through licensing of technology, acquisition, joint ventures, and a variety of other forms of strategic alliances.

Working Draft

You are now ready to write your own first draft of a strategic direction. Initially, avoid the myopic, narrow approach and think as broadly as you can, using the six-guideline questions and the Help Topics in Part 5. Then, adjust your position within the range of narrow to broad direction, and write a statement that provides a realistic strategic direction for your company, business unit, or individual product.

As you reflect on the above questions and examples, also consider the leadership and culture of your organization. Is it passive, conservative, or aggressive? What value systems and patterns of behavior tend to govern the long-term and day-to-day management decisions? Look, too, at available resources: Are there adequate funds available? Are the human resource skills adequate?

Serious deficiencies in your organization may prevent you from realizing your strategic direction. As you will see later in the planning process, you can correct some deficiencies by developing SBP objectives that address organizational and human resource factors to help you sharpen your vision.

Note, too, while ZNI's strategic direction is written in one paragraph, you can write yours in one sentence or two paragraphs. That means, write it in a format and to whatever length to communicate to your management a clear statement to cover 3 to 5 years.

Now begin to write your own working draft of a strategic direction. First, answer the following questions and then compress the output into a single statement, as illustrated in the ZNI application.

1. What are our organization's distinctive areas of expertise?

2. What business should our firm be in over the next 3 to 5 years?

How will it differ from what exists today?

3. What segments or categories of customers will we serve?

4. What additional functions are we likely to fulfill for customers as we see the market evolve?

5. What new technologies will we require to satisfy future customer/ market needs?

6. What changes are taking place in markets, consumer behavior, competition, environment, culture and the economy that will impact our company?

Our strategic direction _____

_____

_____

_____

_____

Section 2: Objectives and Goals

Planning Guidelines

State your objectives and goals both quantitatively and non-quantitatively. Your primary guideline is that they have a strategic focus with a timeframe of 3 to 5 years. Further, your objectives should have a direct impact on your business and correlate with your strategic direction.

This time period is reasonable for most businesses: short enough to be realistic and achievable in an increasingly volatile marketplace; long enough to be visionary about the impact of new technologies, changing customer behavioral patterns, the global marketplace, emerging competitors and changing demographics.

Quantitative Objectives

Indicate, in precise statements, major performance expectations such as sales growth (dollars/units), market share, return on investment, profit and any other quantitative objectives required by your management. In this section of the SBP the objectives are generally broad and relate to the total business or to a few major segments. (In the tactical phase these will be more specific by products and markets.)

Non-Quantitative Objectives

In addition, consider non-quantitative objectives as setting a foundation from which to build on to your organization's existing strengths and eliminate its internal weaknesses. In turn, your objectives should help you realize your strategic direction. Objectives could span diverse areas from organizational design, distribution networks and strategy teams, to new product development.

Use the following examples to trigger additional objectives for your business. Above all, make your objectives specific, actionable, realistic and focused on achieving a sustainable competitive advantage. Keep them in line with the full scope of your strategic direction.

UPGRADING DISTRIBUTION CHANNELS

This objective relates to the supply chain, which includes any intermediary between your organization and the end user (including distributors, dealers and brokers). Upgrading could include management and sales training, technical support, installing inventory control systems, or even providing financial assistance.

EXPANDING SECONDARY DISTRIBUTION

As an extension of the above objective, you may need to expand into new geographic segments, such as geographic areas that lack adequate distribution or sales representation. This objective is especially important when you cannot release the sales-force from existing responsibilities and your only viable alternative is to expand through independent distributors.

Also, your organization may need additional linkages in the distribution channel. For example, although direct contact from manufacturer to distributor exists, there could be an opportunity to expand further into the distribution channel by contacting resellers at the next level of distribution.

CONSOLIDATING A SEGMENT POSITION

As a protective measure to consolidate a leadership position, objectives could include: securing long-term sales contracts with key accounts, penetrating strategically important geographic territories by adding more sales and service personnel, or gaining maximum commitment from major distributors through technology transfer and financial assistance. Such objectives would help consolidate your market position and bar entry by aggressive competitors.

BUILDING 'SPECIALTY PRODUCT' PENETRATION

This objective considers both offensive and defensive moves. First, an offensive objective means developing a specialty product dedicated to penetrating a new market segment not held – or lightly defended – by a competitor.

Second, a defensive objective means protecting a dominant position. For instance, developing a specialty product that duplicates or imitates the competitive product, thereby eliminating the uniqueness of the competitor's innovation. Still another defensive objective is to introduce an interim specialty product to 'buy time' until the next major product innovation is introduced.

ESTABLISHING OR IMPROVING BUSINESS INTELLIGENCE SYSTEMS

While this objective emphasizes organizing the inflow of information to identify noteworthy changes in the environment, industry and customers, the primary focus remains on competitors.

Specifically, the intent here is to assess the future impact of the following factors on your business:

1. **Competitors' size** – categorized by market share, growth rate, and profitability.

2. **Competitors' objectives** – rated by both quantitative (sales, profits, ROI) and non-quantitative (product innovation; market leadership; and international, national, and regional distribution.)

3. **Competitors' strategies** – analyzed by internal strategies (manufacturing capabilities, delivery, marketing expertise) and external strategies (distribution network, field support, market coverage, and ability to defend or build market share.)

4. **Competitors' organization** – examined by the leadership, organizational design, culture, management systems and people skills.

5. **Competitors' cost structure** – examined by pricing flexibility, ease or difficulty of exiting a market, and attitudes toward short-term versus long-term profitability.

6. **Competitors' overall strengths and weaknesses** – identified by their internal systems and any market positions vulnerable to attack.

The total assessment serves as a window through which to develop a clear image of the actions you need to sustain a competitive advantage.

FOCUSING TRAINING ACTIONS

This objective considers internal and external training. Internal training reaches various levels of functional managers who need to interact with specific markets, customers and product applications. Such functions include product management, customer service, technical support and the sales-force.

External training serves distributors' sales-forces, service organizations and customers. In this context, the primary aim of training is to maintain a competitive advantage through programs that assist customers in such areas as customizing services for their customers and finding creative approaches that add value to otherwise basic, undifferentiated products or services.

LAUNCHING NEW AND REPOSITIONING OLD PRODUCTS

Products are 'new' when they are perceived as new by the marketplace.

Therefore, it is appropriate for this objective to consider not only launching totally new products, but also reintroducing older products that have been differentiated through new applications, new packaging, or value-added services.

UPGRADING FIELD SERVICES

The range of field services include checking levels of inventory, providing technical service, or placing a customer-service individual at a customer's location for an indefinite period.

IMPROVING MARKETING MIX MANAGEMENT

The marketing mix consists of product or service, price, promotion and distribution. There is generally a dominant component within the mix that acts as the driving force in achieving a competitive advantage. Determining the optimum mix means you involve functional managers from such diverse functions as finance, sales, manufacturing, R&D and distribution to shape the marketing mix objectives. (A checklist for evaluating your marketing mix against that of your competitor is included in Part 4.)

Application

ZNI-Tech's Objectives and Goals

QUANTITATIVE OBJECTIVES

	200X (Year 1) (000)	200X (Year 2) (000)	200X (Year 3) (000)
Gross Sales ($)	8,260	8,720	8,833
Returns	339	375	363
Cost of Sales	2,545	2,632	2,387
Gross Profit	5,376	5,713	6,083
Expenses			
Shipping	273	333	329
Selling	532	857	704
General and Administrative	392	299	251
Total Expenses	1,197	1,489	1,284
Operating Income	4,179	4,224	4,799

COMMENTARY

The quantitative objectives illustrated above comprise ZNI's actual format. Additional quantitative objectives would include share of market, return on investment, cash flow, or return on sales. Some organizations require extensive amounts of financial information in the SBP. Others require only a minimal amount, such as sales, units and profit margins. Your SBP should complement the financial format suggested by the financial manager or your next management level.

The following sample objectives are non-quantitative (or qualitative.) You must distinguish between the quantitative objectives of the plan (illustrated above) and the non-quantitative objectives suggested in the guidelines of this section. In some instances quantification can be included with an objective for clarification, as noted in one of the following objectives:

Non-quantitative Objectives

1. Maintain ZNI's low-cost producer status while introducing new improvements to existing products.

2. Aggressively maintain our dominant market-share position in all market segments.

3. Maintain sufficient manufacturing capacity to absorb our competitors' market share in existing segments as well as serve new and emerging segments.

4. Launch new products to strengthen our leadership position in drug delivery devices.

5. Maintain a level of 78% retail distribution and 53% retail market share for hypodermic products.

6. Increase trade distribution and block entry of competitors into the home-care segment of the market.

Notice the strong parallel of ZNI's objectives with its strategic direction. Phrases that describe the strategic direction include 'full line of hypodermic needles' and 'leadership position'. ZNI's objectives address those phrases. Again, the strategic direction provides a 'vision' to project what the future can look like; objectives provide the precise outcomes.

Note, too, how these objectives have long-term strategic implications. Where possible, you can add quantitative information for each objective. However, it is not always necessary in this strategic section of the SBP.

The key point is that this planning format permits flexibility to accommodate to the practices of individual organizations. Quantitative details can be added later in the plan, usually in the growth strategy section and certainly at the tactical one-year portion of the SBP.

Working Draft

Now write a draft of your quantitative and non-quantitative objectives for a 3 to 5 year period.

QUANTITATIVE OBJECTIVES

Use or modify the table below or incorporate a format used in your organization.

	200X (Year 1)	200X (Year 2)	200X (Year 3)
Gross Sales ($)			
Returns			
Cost of Sales			
Gross Profit			
Expenses			
Shipping			
Selling			
General and Administrative			
Total Expenses			
Operating Income			

Non-quantitative Objectives (Add, delete, or modify to suit your needs.)

Upgrade distribution channels. _____

_____

Expand secondary distribution. _____

_____

Consolidate a segment position. _____

_____

Build 'specialty product' penetration. _____

_____

Establish or improve business intelligence systems. _____

_____

Focus training actions._____

_____

Launch new and reposition old products. _____

_____

Upgrade field services. _____

_____

Improve marketing mix management._____

_____

Section 3: Growth Strategies

Planning Guidelines

This section outlines the process you can use to secure your objectives and goals. Think of *strategies* as actions to achieve your longer-term objectives; *tactics* as actions to achieve shorter-term objectives. Since this section's timeframe covers 3 to 5 years, strategies are indicated here. The one-year portion, illustrated later in the plan, identifies tactics.

For best results in developing realistic growth strategies, base your decisions after analyzing your organization's internal capabilities. These include looking at such areas as performance, strategy, strategic priorities, costs, product portfolio, financial resources and strengths/weaknesses. (For a comprehensive discussion on each topic go to Part 5, Help Topic – *Looking At Your Company*.)

Overall, however, your thinking about strategies boils down to actions among the following:

- Growth and mature markets.
- Long-term brand or product positioning.
- Product quality.
- Market share growth potential.
- Distribution channel options.
- Product, price, and promotion mix.
- Spending strategies.
- Specific marketing, sales, R&D, manufacturing strengths to be exploited.

In practice, where you have broad-based, long-term objectives, you should develop multiple strategies for each objective. Among those objectives where it is difficult to be specific or where little information is on-hand, you can use general strategy statements. For example:

- Form a committee to investigate an emerging market segment on the Continent.
- Hire an outside consultant to conduct a feasibility study about a new laser technology.

- Locate a new distribution center to expand market coverage in the north.
- Specific actions for each would be detailed in the tactical portion of the SBP.

As for planning formats: You can vary them according to your individual or team's style. For instance, you have the option of merging the objectives and strategies sections by restating each objective from Section 2 and listing its corresponding strategies, as illustrated in the following *Application*. Another option is to write a general strategy statement followed by a detailed listing of subordinate objectives and strategies.

What follows is a general strategy statement derived from ZNI's actual SBP, along with a selection of three of the six objectives from the previous section, together with related strategies.

Application

GENERAL STRATEGY

ZNI-Tech will maintain industry leadership by addressing the full range of consumer and health care provider needs related to drug delivery devices.

These needs include not only the marketing of delivery devices which are virtually painless, easy to read and conveniently used, but also programs and educational services to aid in the achievement of normal bodily functions to maintain overall good health. These additional services will meet user needs both at the time of diagnosis and in the continuing treatment of the problem.

A dominant position in the drug delivery device market will be maintained by developing market segmentation opportunities through continued product differentiation and innovation.

OBJECTIVE 1

Maintain ZNI's low-cost producer status while introducing new improvements to existing products.

Strategies

- Reduce costs by 32.5% before 200X. Maintaining low cost producer status gives our company the widest strategic flexibility in dealing with competitive assaults on our franchise. Potential areas of cost reduction:

  - Overhead reductions, 4.5%
  - Waste reductions, 7.0%
  - High speed needle line, 6.5%
  - Sales territory redesign, 8.0%
  - Quality improvement and reduction in repair service, 4.0%
  - Packaging improvement, 2.5%
  - **Total: 32.5%**

- Improve existing products through improved dosage control and improved packaging to maintain a competitive advantage.

OBJECTIVE 2

Aggressively maintain our dominant market share position in all market segments.

Strategies

- Develop the Supra-Fine 111 needle to maintain superior product quality and performance versus competition, as it relates to injection comfort.

- Increase spending levels on consumer/trade support programs to provide added-value to product offerings, thereby decreasing attractiveness of lower-priced alternatives while maintaining brand loyalty.

- Maintain broadest retail distribution and highest service levels to gain retailer support in promoting our brands and carrying adequate inventory levels.

- Continue health care educational programs to gain professional recommendations at time of diagnosis and thereby maintain brand loyalty among users.

OBJECTIVE 3

Launch new products to strengthen our leadership position in drug delivery devices.

Strategies

- Introduce a 40-unit syringe to address the needs of users on multiple dose therapy. Converting users to a 40-unit syringe will insulate this group against competitive initiatives.

- Develop and introduce a disposable pen-cartridge injection system to further segment the market and thereby reduce the competitive points of entry.

- Become a full-line supplier of drug delivery devices by broadening product offerings through internal research and development, joint venture, licensing and acquisitions.

COMMENTARY

Recall the overall planning guideline: The primary output of the SBP includes strategies to achieve competitive advantage. As noted in the above examples, ZNI's strategies cover a wide range of activities and incorporate a variety of functions within the organization.

Accordingly, you can see the practicality of involving as many functional managers as possible in developing your SBP. Not only will their ideas prove helpful, they will also internalize the strategies and be more motivated to implement them.

In turn, implementation is accomplished through each manager's functional plan that evolves from the SBP. The result: Managers' participation from manufacturing, product development, finance, sales and distribution make the SBP come alive.

Working Draft

Now, develop a rough draft of strategies for each of your objectives.

Objective 1:_____

_____

Strategy: _____

_____

Objective 2: _____

_____

Strategy: _____

_____

Objective 3: _____

_____

Strategy: _____

_____

Section 4: Business Portfolio Plan

Planning Guidelines

The business portfolio provides for an organized listing of *existing* products and markets and *new* products and markets. Following a logical progression, it is based on the strategic direction, objectives and goals, and growth strategies outlined in previous sections.

Key point: the content of your portfolio mirrors your strategic direction. That is, the broader the dimension of your strategic direction, the more expansive the range of products and markets in the portfolio. Conversely, the narrower the dimension of your strategic direction, the more limited the content of products and markets.

Use the following format and guidelines to develop your own business portfolio:

EXISTING PRODUCTS/EXISTING MARKETS (MARKET PENETRATION)

Simply list those products you currently offer to existing customer groups or market segments. In an appendix of the SBP, you can document sales, profits, market share data, competitive position and other pertinent information. From such information you can determine if your level of penetration is adequate and if possibilities exist for further growth.

For example, even minor changes in market and customer buying patterns may create fresh opportunities to increase market penetration by focusing in such areas as improving product quality, instituting just-in-time delivery, increasing technical support, improving customer service, or installing computerized inventory control systems.

After identifying new opportunities, it may be necessary for you to revisit Section 3 (Growth Strategies) and list actions you would take to implement the opportunities.

NEW PRODUCTS/EXISTING MARKETS (PRODUCT DEVELOPMENT)

Use this section to extend your thinking about new products to existing markets, in keeping with the strategic direction you created for your business. Again, recall the guideline that the broader the dimension of your strategic direction the broader the possibilities for the content of your portfolio.

If the definition of your business is too narrow, you may be limited in what you can list in this part of your portfolio. You still have the opportunity to go back to the strategic direction and recast it. You thereby open the possibilities for product expansion – if that is consistent with the overall aims of senior management and available resources.

In this section you are looking for new products that you can sell to current customer segments. These may include the specialty products discussed earlier or all new products.

What is a new product? Recall the definition that a new product is *new* when it is *perceived* as new by the customer. Therefore, product development could include added features, improved quality, new packaging, extended warranties and other value-added items wrapped around existing core products. And, of course, product development includes totally new products based on advances in technologies.

EXISTING PRODUCTS/NEW MARKETS (MARKET DEVELOPMENT)

Another growth direction is to take your current products into new markets. Therefore, explore possibilities for market development by identifying emerging, neglected, or poorly served segments in which existing products can be utilized.

A classic case is 3M's Scotch Brand Tape that has been market-extended for use in offices, schools, homes, packaging and scores of industrial applications. Another classic product, nylon, illustrates market development with applications of the product over the past 60 years in such diverse products as parachutes, clothes, tires and carpets.

The possibilities are exciting. Yet caution is advised. Where, then, is the balance? How far afield should you go from your basic markets?

Again, go back to your strategic direction as a guiding beacon to direct your thinking. Think about those questions you answered to derive your strategic direction:

- What business should my firm be in over the next three to five years?
- What customer segments will we serve?
- What additional functions are we likely to fulfill for customers?
- What changes are taking place in markets and the environment?
- How will our organization participate in that future?

Here, too, it is extremely valuable to involve the next level of management in assessing risks and providing guidance on expansion. The risk in this instance is not with products. The products already exist. The risk is in the re-deployment – and possible dispersion – of the sales-force from its primary markets. Or, it is the possible distraction of other functions of the organization from their focus on core products and markets. A further consideration is the added investment required to develop or enter new markets.

It is also valuable to use a strategy team to help make such assessments. Since the team members represent diverse functions of the business, they would take responsibility for implementing the strategies through their respective functions. (Go to Part 5, Help Topic – *Strategy Teams.*)

NEW PRODUCTS/NEW MARKETS (DIVERSIFICATION)

This portion of the business portfolio is visionary, since it involves developing new products to meet the needs of new and yet untapped markets. New technologies, global markets, and new strategic alliances provide the framework from which this section evolves. These factors will assist you in participating in new markets, rather than riding existing businesses into maturity and then to decline.

Once again, interpret your strategic direction in its broadest context. Do not seek diversification for its own sake. Rather, the whole purpose of the exercise is for you to develop an organized framework for meaningful expansion.

Also, you will find that the other parts of the portfolio feed this portion. In practice, the number of new products into new markets will be the smallest part of the portfolio, because they carry the greatest risk. Yet organizations such as 3M, Intel, Motorola, Sony and General Electric will fill this portion of the portfolio extensively.

Known for their high levels of R&D, those visionary companies commit themselves entirely to future growth and leadership in their respective markets. This pattern exists more so than in those organizations making commodity products, as well as with firms that lack the strategic vision to find their place in the future.

The grid in Figure 1.2 is a useful format to create your business portfolio of products and markets, both existing and new.

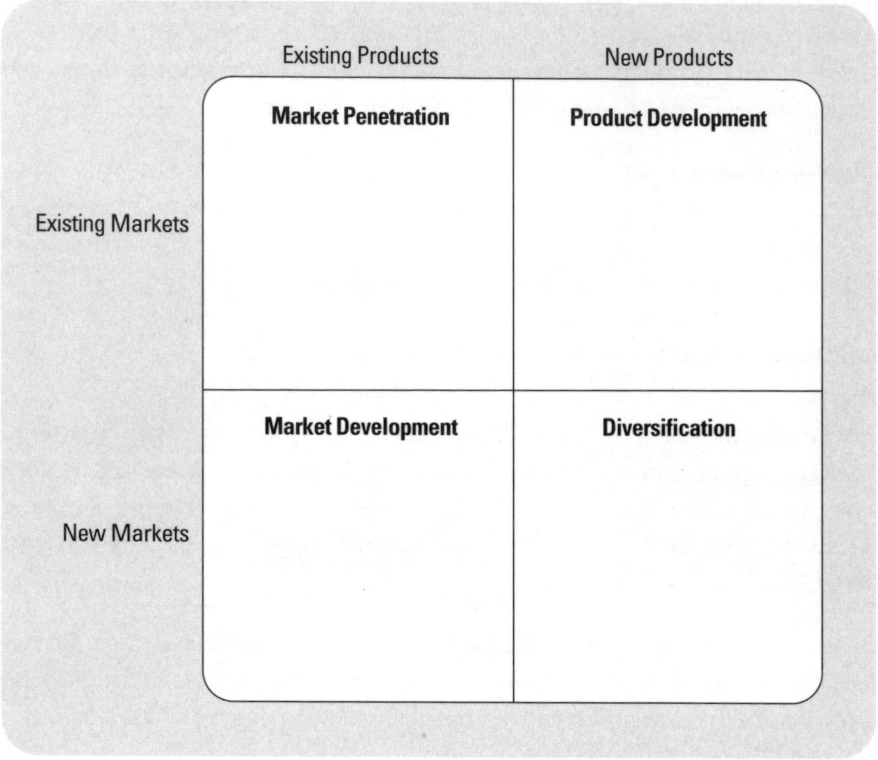

	Existing Products	New Products
Existing Markets	**Market Penetration**	**Product Development**
New Markets	**Market Development**	**Diversification**

FIGURE 1.2: **BUSINESS PORTFOLIO**

Application

	ZNI's Existing Products	ZNI's New Products

Existing Markets	• 24-Guage Hypodermic Needle
	• Diabetes
	• Allergy
	• Hospital
	• Clinics
	• Homecare
		• 32-Guage Hypodermic Needle
		• SupraFine III Needles
		• 40-Guage Syringe/
		  Multiple-Dose
		  Therapy System

New Markets	• Aids
	  – Urban Markets
	  – Ethnic Populations
	  – Demographic Segments
	• Pacific Rim Countries
		• Disposable Pen – Cartridge
		  Injection System
		• Implanted Injection Pumps
		  With Sensors

FIGURE 1.3: ZNI-TECH'S BUSINESS PORTFOLIO

COMMENTARY

To illustrate the makeup of this section, ZNI's business portfolio (Figure 1.3) is only a partial representation of products and markets from its actual plan. Supporting information on sales, units, profits, market share and other quantitative information would be included in an appendix of the SBP.

Also, ZNI's actual portfolio lists additional diseases for which hypodermic systems are needed. These, too, would be placed in the appropriate quadrant. The information on population, ethnic, geographic and demographic factors also breaks down into sub-segments, which would drive new packaging, methods of treatment, educational programs and types of distribution.

In practice, you will find all four sections of the SBP are interconnected. For instance: (1) The strategic direction gives scope to your thinking by providing a company or product with a vision; (2) objectives permit you to list in quantitative and non-quantitative terms what you want to achieve; (3) growth strategies indicate how you will reach your objectives; (4) the business portfolio shows the effect of all the proceeding work in the form of products and markets.

The interconnection also occurs as you add a new market or product to the portfolio. In that case you may need to return to the strategy section and identify how to develop the product and launch it into the market. Consequently, you are constantly creating opportunities and fine-tuning your SBP.

Working Draft

Now develop your rough draft of a Business Portfolio Plan, using the grid in Figure 1.2 to categorize existing products/existing markets, new products/ existing markets, existing products/new markets, and new products/new markets.

The Business Portfolio completes the strategic portion of the SBP. Now you are ready to proceed to Part 2 and the tactical one-year plan.

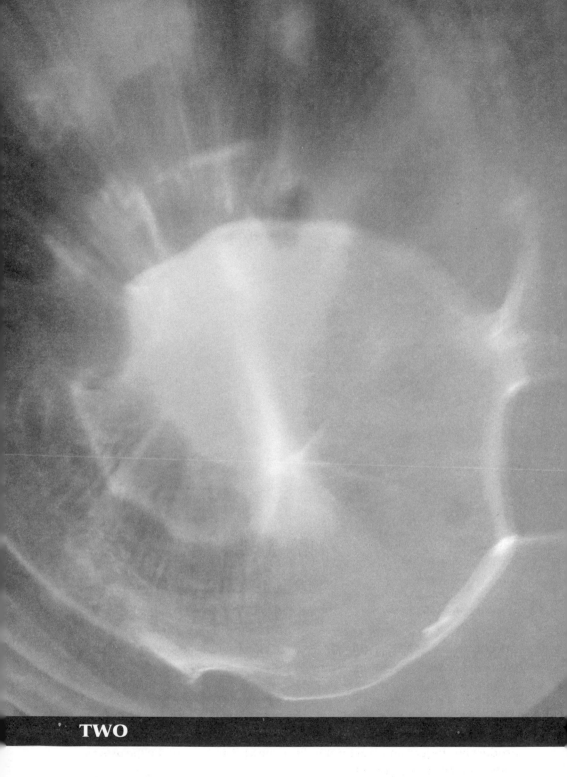

The Strategic Business Plan
– Tactical Section

TWO

The Strategic Business Plan
– Tactical Section

Chapter Objectives

Given the information in this chapter, you will be able to:

1. Describe the components of the tactical part of the SBP.

2. Interpret the guidelines by applying them to an actual company's SBP.

3. Develop your own SBP.

Overview

The tactical business plan, shown in the highlighted area of the Strategic Business Plan (Figure 2.1) is not a stand-alone plan. It is but a portion of the total SBP consisting of the top row of boxes and the lower row of boxes.

Where commonalties exist among products and markets, one tactical plan can work as long as you make the appropriate changes in such areas as the sales-force and the communications mix (advertising, sales promotion and publicity). Where you face substantial differences in the character of your product and markets, then develop separate tactical plans.

As a precautionary measure, however, avoid the temptation indulged in by some managers who attempt to develop a plan for a business, division, or product line by jumping in at the middle of the SBP and beginning the process with the tactical one-year plan.

There are no short-cuts. Reason: Input to the Tactical Business Plan flows from two directions: (1) from the strategic portion of the SBP (top row) containing the strategic direction, objectives, strategies and business portfolio; (2) from the situation analysis (bottom row), which progresses to opportunities, annual objectives, tactics and budgets. Also, the thought process that went into the strategic portion of the plan now flows down to feed the shorter-term, action-oriented annual plan.

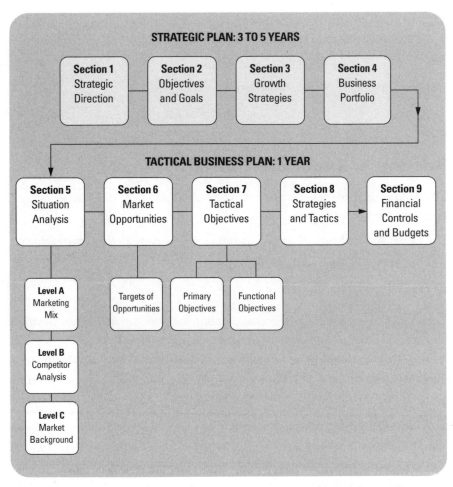

FIGURE 2.1: **STRATEGIC BUSINESS PLAN**

The tactical one-year business plan – Sections 5 through 9 – is presented in the same format as used in the strategic part of the SBP in Part 1. That is, planning guidelines are provided to explain the thought process. And applications will continue with the ZNI-Tech Company. For ease of explanation, however, only one product from that company's business portfolio, the hypodermic needle product line, will be used to illustrate the planning process.

As with the strategic section, use *Help Topics* in Part 5 to provide meaningful content to make your plan comprehensive and accurate. Also, you can refer to Part 3, *Marketing Problem Solver: The Strategic Business Plan in Action* for an extensive review of how actual companies apply the SBP to deal with real-world market conditions.

Let's begin with Section 5, Situation Analysis.

Section 5: Situation Analysis

The following three-level situation analysis describes in detail the past and current situation of your business:

Level A: The Marketing Mix (product, price, distribution, promotion).

Level B: Competitor Analysis.

Level C: Market Background.

Each level is a sub-section of the total situation analysis and defines the business in a detailed, factual and objective manner. Approach your situation analysis by answering a fundamental question, 'What are the key past and present events in the development of my business?'

Then compile historical data for a period of at least three years. Doing so provides an excellent perspective as you compare any significant events with the future trends you indicated for your market, industry, product line, or market segment as you defined them in your Strategic Direction (Part 1).

Planning Guidelines

Objectively describe the performance of your product or service by:

- Sales history, profitability, share of market and other required data. Where appropriate, you can display sales history with computer-generated graphics.

- Current market position in the industry related to market share, reputation, product life-cycle (introduction, growth, maturity, or decline), and competitive ranking.

- Future trends related to environment, industry, customer and competitive factors that may affect your product's position.

- Intended purpose of your product in terms of its applications or uniqueness.

- Features and benefits of your product as related to quality, performance, safety, convenience, or other factors important to customers.

- Other pertinent product information such as expected product improvements and additional product characteristics (size, model, price, packaging); recent features that enhance your product's position; competitive trends in features, benefits, technological changes; and changes that would add superior value to the product and provide a competitive advantage.

Application

Product – Hypodermic Needles (24-gauge)

SALES HISTORY

Year	200x	200x	200x
Net sales ($)	202,315	204,195	206,153
Units	754,405	769,614	768,397
Percent change from previous year	+6.8%	+1.8%	+1.9%
Market potential ($)	212,000	216,000	220,000
Market share (%)	88.6%	87.9%	87.6%

POSITION IN THE INDUSTRY

The 24-gauge needle, in the mature stage of its product life-cycle, is categorized as a market leader according to the above share of market figures. Market research positions ZNI as a technological innovator.

FUTURE TRENDS

- Our dominant position will continue to be challenged by low-priced brands from the Far East.

- Alternate injections systems such as the pen cartridge will compete with standard hypodermic needles.

- Growth of new distribution channels (medical insurance plans) will alter buying behavior, removing end-use customers from the purchase decision.

INTENDED PURPOSE OF OUR PRODUCT

Provide a reliable, safe, economical, and convenient delivery system of drugs to the body to maintain normal bodily functions, as well as provide systematic pre-emptive protection against disease.

FEATURES AND BENEFITS OF OUR PRODUCT

Needles and syringes satisfy design specifications of the medical establishment. Our syringes include permanently attached needles, storage capability for 25 needles, single-scale markings with large numbers and special protective caps to insure sterility. Our needles offer unmatched injection comfort.

OTHER

Our product rates as a high quality and reliable drug delivery device. Our packaging is convenient for use within all segments of the market, accompanied by easy-to-use instructions. A recognizable package displays ZNI's corporate logo conveying the image of high-quality health products.

Working Draft

Using the following outline begin gathering data that covers the following categories. You can then transfer this information to the planning forms in Part 6.

SALES HISTORY

Use or modify the table below or incorporate a format used in your organization.

Year	200x	200x	200x
Net sales ($)			
Units			
Percent change from previous year			
Market potential ($)			
Market share (%)			

Position in the industry:_____

_____

Intended purpose of product(s) or service(s):_____

_____

Features and benefits of product(s) or service(s):_____

_____

Level A: Marketing Mix – Pricing

Planning Guidelines

HISTORY OF PRICING

Examine the history of pricing policies for each market segment and/or distribution channel; consider their impact on your product's market position.

FUTURE PRICING TRENDS

Predict pricing trends as they pertain to product specification changes, (including formulation and design), financial constraints and expected market changes (trade/consumer attitudes and competitive responses to price changes).

Application

HISTORY OF PRICING POLICIES

Within the largest distribution channel (hospitals and clinics), ZNI's price leadership position is maintained. One competitor, Majestic, has traditionally followed our prices with aggressive promotional discounts. A second competitor, Apollo, has established the lower-priced branded segment with a list price 27% below ours. (Names of competitors are disguised.)

FUTURE PRICING TRENDS

For the next 12 months wholesale and retail prices are expected to remain at current levels. No major product innovations are anticipated during the planning period and no new competitive entries are predicted to significantly alter the pricing trend.

Working Draft

Examine your company's:

History of pricing policies _____

_____

Future pricing trends _____

_____

Planning Guidelines

CURRENT CHANNELS

Describe your current distribution channels. Identify the functions performed for each stage in the distribution system (distributor, dealer, direct) and indicate levels of performance (sales volume, profitability and percentage of business increases.)

Where appropriate, analyze your physical distribution system, such as warehouse locations, inventory systems, or just-in-time delivery procedures.

EFFECTIVENESS OF COVERAGE

Characterize the effectiveness of coverage of current channels from the programs and services provided.

Comment on effectiveness of distribution systems (distributors, dealers, direct). Specify the key activities performed at each point and indicate any areas that require corrective action. Also comment on the impact of future trends in distribution channels and methods.

SPECIAL FUNCTIONS

Indicate special functions performed by your company's sales-force for a particular distribution channel, and what effect they had on the targeted market segments. Also include your distributors' sales-forces, if applicable. Comment, too, on such approaches as 'push' strategy (through distributors) or 'pull' strategy (through consumers).

Finally, how effectively does your sales-force cover its assigned market area?

TARGET ACCOUNTS

List target customers and their level of performance related to quantity and dollars. Add comments related to special needs of any account.

FUTURE TRENDS

Indicate future trends in distribution methods and channels. Project what growth is expected in each major market segment. Also identify how this growth will affect your need for different distribution channels or methods of physical distribution.

Application

CURRENT CHANNEL

The largest distribution channel for our hypodermic needle products are hospitals and clinics, with 64.7% of unit sales volume distributed through these outlets. Drug stores and mass merchandisers account for the remaining category sales.

Within the hospital segment, hospitals with 500 beds or more represent 60.2% of our unit sales volume followed by 30.8% of units in hospitals with 300 to 499 beds.

EFFECTIVENESS OF COVERAGE

Our product has the broadest geographic distribution penetration throughout the U.S., as follows:

District		Market Penetration
North-east:	Boston	63%
	New York	58%
	Baltimore	52%
North-central:	Detroit	92%
	Chicago	89%
	St Paul	91%
Southern:	Miami	88%
	Atlanta	93%
	Houston	92%
West Coast:	Tacoma	73%
	San Francisco	69%
	San Diago	63%

SPECIAL FUNCTIONS

Special sales functions include meeting with hospital administrators, holding workshops for nurses, conducting technical seminars for physicians, and checking for out-of-stock situations. In addition, maintaining in-hospital distribution of educational literature establishes brand recognition where continuation of hypodermic needle usage is required at home.

TARGET ACCOUNTS

Target account coverage requires making joint sales calls with our dealers' sales-forces to maximize sales potential from each sales territory. Focusing on signing up hospitals to new three-year, price-protected sales contracts ensures continuity of supplier-customer relationships.

FUTURE TRENDS IN DISTRIBUTION METHODS

Product volume within hospitals and clinics will continue to grow. Smaller dealers will leave the market or be absorbed by the larger ones that provide just-in-time delivery through computerized inventory control systems. Where dealers in emerging market segments are not available, our company must distribute directly to serve the dealer function.

COMMENTARY

The above sampling of applications illustrates the type of information that goes into describing distribution. In your plan, you can add additional detail about types of products, services and specific sales activities. For example, you can make comparisons with your key competitors, provide insights on corrective actions to counter a threat, indicate how to displace a competitor, or identify how the Internet fits your market and product strategy.

Target accounts have not been shown in this example, since it would simply contain a listing of customers and is self-explanatory. For your working draft, as with other sections in this book, you may need to alter the format to fit your special requirements and specific industry terminology.

Working Draft

Analyze your distribution channels and methods by:

Current channel _____

_____

Effectiveness of coverage_____

_____

Special functions performed by the sales-force _____

_____

Target accounts by district, quantity and revenue _____

_____

Future trends in distribution methods _____

_____

Planning Guidelines

ANALYSIS

Analyze your advertising and sales promotion directed at each segment of the market or distribution channel, based on the following elements: advertising expenditures, creative strategy, media, trade promotions, consumer promotions and other forms of promotion unique to your industry.

COMPETITIVE TRENDS

Identify and evaluate competitive trends in the same categories as above. Your advertising agency (or advertising department) and the sales-force may prove helpful in providing this information.

STRATEGIES

Identify your company's past and current advertising and sales promotion strategies by product and market segment and describe trends in these areas.

OTHER SUPPORT STRATEGIES

Identify other support programs (publicity, educational, professional, trade shows, literature, films/videos, the Internet) that you have used, and evaluate their effectiveness. Describe what programs you should employ.

Application

ANALYSIS

- **Copy strategy**: ZNI's primary advertising is aimed at the hospital and clinic segments for 24-gauge hypodermic needles/syringes. Secondary levels of advertising focuses on the 32-gauge needle, SupraFine 111 and the 40-unit syringe/multiple dose therapy system.

  Advertising reminds customers of our full line of high quality products and product systems. Copy themes include clinical proof related to our unequaled injection comfort and superior quality to justify premium pricing.

- **Media**: Magazines are used to target consumers who use hypodermic injection for on-going therapy (pull strategy); professional journals reach the medical profession and the dealer (pull and push strategy.) Current consumer magazines that target consumers are limited in their ability to reach more than 15-20% of the potential market. Alternative media options such as the Internet, direct mail and broadcast are being explored.

- **Other**: Direct mail, posters, and in-pack circulars deliver continuity programs to our buyers and buying influences.

The following describe competitive trends for two major competitors: Apollo and Majestic.

COPY STRATEGY

Apollo's plans in this area:

- *Objective:* Encourage trial among purchasing agents.

- *Strategy:* Offer financial incentives on entire product line while reinforcing a high quality image.

- *Tactics:* Feature bonus packs on syringes. Offer free syringes and rebates with proof-of-purchase of competitive products.

Majestic's plans in this area:

- *Objective:* Encourage trial among physicians.

- *Strategy:* Attack all major competitors head-on with claims that Majestic needles/syringes are made to hurt less and that the product choice should be made only by the patient.

- *Tactics:* Feature an active, healthy looking individual that ties into the advertising theme.

MEDIA

Both competitors utilize print media and on-pack offers exclusively. Print media is limited to health-related publications to achieve high efficiency at the expense of limited reach.

OTHER

Rebates and targeted direct mail are the primary promotional strategies. However, Majestic is more aggressive than Apollo in the frequency of its rebate and discount program. Overall, both Apollo and Majestic have become more aggressive in promoting their product lines to both hospitals and dealers. This aggressiveness is evidenced in increased advertising expenditures over the past 24 months.

STRATEGIES

ZNI's past and current advertising and sales promotion strategies have focused on maintaining a national leadership position. Where regional market share is threatened, or where market intelligence calls for aggressive competitive action, fast promotional response is initiated against the target segment.

OTHER SUPPORT STRATEGIES

- Professional Programs: Continue to generate professional recommendations for our company's products in health-related market segments where treatment depends on hypodermic drug delivery products.

- Conventions and Trade Shows: Maintain a presence at key national and regional trade shows. Utilize new forms of video presentations to enhance the overall promotional strategy and support ZNI's market leadership position in quality and technological advancement.

COMMENTARY

The above sampling of applications shows how to write this portion of the situation analysis. Not all the information from the actual plan has been included, just enough to illustrate the planning guidelines. Your job is to add all pertinent information that provides a clear picture of your company's situation.

For instance, if you know actual advertising expenditures for your company and that of your competitors, display that comparative information and, if your advertising agency has useable advertising research, include relevant portions.

Also, you will find it beneficial to highlight any critical issues that emerge from your situation analysis. You can then deal with them in the opportunities and strategy/tactic sections of your SBP.

This concludes Level A of the Situation Analysis. After you prepare your working draft, begin Level B, Competitive Analysis.

Working Draft

Analyze the advertising and sales promotion directed at each segment of the market by:

Copy strategy:_____

_____

Media: _____

_____

Other: _____

_____

Identify and evaluate competitive trends in the same categories as you did for your analysis by:

Copy strategy:_____

_____

Media: _____

_____

Other: _____

_____

Planning Guidelines

MARKET SHARE

List all your competitors in descending size order along with their sales and market shares. Include your company's ranking within the listing. Show at least three competitors (more if the information is meaningful.)

COMPETITORS' STRENGTHS AND WEAKNESSES

Identify each competitor's strengths and weaknesses related to such factors as product quality, distribution, pricing, promotion, management leadership and financial condition. Also indicate any significant trends that would signal unsettling market situations, such as aggressiveness in growing market share or excessive discounting to maintain market position.

Attempt to make your competitive analysis as comprehensive as possible. The more competitive intelligence you gather, the more strategy options you have open to you. (To assist you in developing a quality analysis, go to the Developing Competitive Strategies Checklists in Part 4.)

PRODUCT COMPETITIVENESS

Identify competitive pricing strategies, price lines, and price discounts, if any. Identify competitors firmly entrenched in low-price segments of the market, those at the high-end of the market, or competitors that are low-cost producers.

PRODUCT FEATURES AND BENEFITS

Compare the specific product features and benefits with those of competitive products. In particular, focus on product quality, design factors and performance. Evaluate price/value relationships for each, discuss customer preferences (if available), and identify unique product innovations.

ADVERTISING EFFECTIVENESS

Identify competitive spending levels and their effectiveness, as measured by awareness levels, competitive copy test scores and reach/frequency levels (if available.) Such measurements are conducted through formal advertising research conducted by your advertising agency, independent marketing research firms or publications. Where no reliable quantitative research exists, use informal observation or rough measurements of advertising frequency and type.

EFFECTIVENESS OF DISTRIBUTION METHODS

Compare competitive distribution strengths and weaknesses. Address differences in market penetration, market coverage, delivery time and physical movement of the product by regions or territories. Where appropriate, identify major accounts where competitors' sales are weak or strong.

PACKAGING

Compare competitive products' package performance, innovation and preference. Also review size, shape, function, convenience of handling, ease of storage and shipping.

TRADE/CONSUMER ATTITUDES

Review both trade (distributor or dealer) and consumer attitudes toward product quality, customer/technical service, company image and company performance.

COMPETITIVE SHARE OF MARKET (SOM) TRENDS

While share of market was previously included as a way of determining overall performance, the intent here is to specify trends in market share gains by individual products, as well as by market segments. Further, you must identify where each competitor is making a major commitment and where it may be relinquishing control by product and segment.

SALES-FORCE EFFECTIVENESS AND MARKET COVERAGE

Review effectiveness as it relates to sales, service, frequency of contact, problem-solving capabilities by competitor and by market segment. Look to all sales-force performance within the distribution channel. For example, if you are a manufacturer, look at distributor coverage. Then examine distributors' coverage of their customers, which could be dealers, and finally end users.

Application

COMPETITORS' STRENGTHS AND WEAKNESSES

Name	Share of Market (SOM)	Strengths	Weaknesses	SOM Trends
ZNI	65%	Strong commitment to product improvements and product quality; broad distribution; low cost producer.	Weaker retail share compared to hospital share.	Flat growth.
Apollo	19%	Strong consumer promotion activities; higher retailer support relative to market share.	Limited resources devoted to key buying influences; higher cost-of-goods. No commitment to product improvement	Declining share.
Majestic	16%	Low selling price; overall high quality product; highly automated production capabilities.	Limited resources devoted to key buying influences; limited sales-force; no professional education program.	Slow build of share.

PRICING

Brand	Distributor Price ($)	Direct Price ($)
ZNI	8.86	13.98
Apollo	8.50	12.75
Majestic	6.75	10.60

PRODUCT FEATURES AND BENEFITS

Brand	Features	Benefits
ZNI	Self-contained design.	Convenient package.
	Clear, bold scale.	Easy to see for greater accuracy.
	Thin-line plunger tip.	Lines up precisely with scale markings for accurate reading – no waste.
Apollo	Sterile soft packs.	Easy to open package.
	No dead space.	More accurate dosage. Less waste.
	Permanently attached Needle.	Eliminates risk of needle separation.
Majestic	Smooth plunger action.	Precise control of dosage.
	Easy to read scale.	Greater accuracy.
	Individual safety seal packaging.	Ensures sterility until time of use.

This application contains only a sampling of the contents for this section. A full analysis would cover all the points specified in the planning guidelines. The comprehensiveness and quality of competitive information cannot be stressed enough. Your competitive strategy – the primary output of your SBP – and the desire to achieve competitive advantage rely heavily on this portion of the situation analysis. (Be sure to refer to Part 4 for the checklists supplementing this section.)

Now begin developing your working draft of a competitive analysis.

Working Draft

Analyze competitors' strengths and weaknesses by:

Product competitiveness _____

_____

Pricing _____

_____

Product features and benefits _____

_____

Advertising effectiveness _____

_____

Effectiveness of distribution methods _____

_____

Packaging _____

_____

Trade/consumer attitudes _____

_____

Competitive share of market trends _____

_____

Sales-force effectiveness _____

_____

Planning Guidelines

This last part of the situation analysis focuses on demographic and behavioral factors, which determine market size and customer preferences (both trade and consumer) in a changing competitive environment.

You can derive data from primary market research (market segmentation studies, awareness and usage studies) or data from secondary sources (trade and governmental reports). See extensive information provided on this subject in Part 5, *Help Topics*.

The information provided here is important because it serves as foundation material for developing Section 6 Opportunities, Section 7 Objectives, and Section 8 Strategies/Tactics. This information also highlights any gaps in knowledge about markets and customers and helps you determine types of marketing research needed to make more effective decisions.

The following categories are considered as part of the market background:

CUSTOMER PROFILE

Define the profile of present and potential end-use customers that you (or your distributors) serve. Your intent is to look further down the supply chain and view the end-use consumer. Examine the following factors:

The market segments distributors/dealers serve: Make sure you address this question from your distributors' point of view.

Distributors' overall sales: Concentrate on classifying the key customers that represent the majority of sales.

Other classifications: Profile your customers by such additional factors as type of products used, level of sophistication, price sensitivity and service. Also indicate any target accounts that you can reach directly, thereby bypassing the distributor.

Frequency and magnitude of products used: Define customer purchases by frequency, volume, and seasonality of purchase. Additional information might include customer inventory levels, retail stocking policies, volume discounts, or consumer buying behavior related to price, point of-purchase influences, or coupons.

Geographic aspects of products used: Define customer purchases regionally or territorially (both trade and consumer). Segment buyers by specific geographic area or by other factors relevant to your industry.

Market characteristics: Assess the demographic, psychographic (life-style), and other descriptive aspects of your customers, including age, income level and education. Examine level of product technology; purchase patterns and any distinctive individual or group behavioral styles; attitudes toward the company's products, services, quality and image.

Decision-maker: Define who makes the buying decisions and when and where they are made. Note the various individuals or departments that may influence the decision.

Customer motivations: Identify the key motivations that drive your customers to buy the product. Why do they select one manufacturer (or service provider) over another? Customers may buy your product because of quality, performance, image, technical/customer service, convenience, location, delivery, access to upper level management, friendship, or peer pressure.

Customer awareness: Define the level of consumer awareness of your products. To what extent do they:

- Recognize a need for your type of product?
- Identify your product, brand, or company as a possible supplier?
- Associate your product, brand, or company with desirable features?

Segment trends: Define the trends in the size and character of the various segments or niches. (A segment is a portion of an entire market; a niche is part of a segment.) A segment should be considered if it is accessible, measurable, potentially profitable and has long-term growth potential.

Segmenting a market also serves as an offensive strategy to identify emerging, neglected, or poorly served markets that can catapult you to further sales growth. You can also consider segments as a defensive strategy to prevent inroads of a potential competitor through an unattended market segment.

Other comments/critical issues: Add general comments that expand your knowledge of the market and customer base. Also identify any critical issues that have surfaced as a result of conducting the situation analysis – ones that should be singled out for special attention.

Application

There are an estimated 15.7 million hypodermic needles used daily in our served markets. The breakdown is as follows:

Classification	Distribution Units
Hospitals	Distributor and direct, 5.6M
Clinics	Distributor, 3.7M
Home	Distributor and retailer, 3.6M
Other	Distributor, 2.8M

Hospitals classified as 500 beds and over are increasingly looking for the newer systems of injection that eliminate the standard needle and syringe. Smaller hospitals and clinics are price sensitive and remain committed to the standard method of drug delivery. Home usage, primarily by diabetics, is increasing at the annual rate of 2.4% annually.

FREQUENCY AND MAGNITUDE OF PRODUCTS USED

Single-use needles and syringes comprise 89.5% of usage. Of the remaining 10.5%, usage consists of automatic infusion pumps, needle-less jet injectors, and reusable glass syringes.

Daily injection frequency in all markets remains a key factor in the consumption of single-use syringes. Presently the market is characterized as follows:

Numbers of injections per day	Percent of users
1	54%
2	44%
3 or more	2%

GEOGRAPHIC ASPECTS OF PRODUCTS USED

See competitive analysis for geographic breakdown.

CUSTOMER CHARACTERISTICS

Base	Usage of single-use needles and syringes in home market	
Sex	Male	44%
	Female	56%
	Median age at usage	42
	Median family income (000)	$18.7
	Median years of education	10.2
Employment	Employed	37%
	Unemployed	63%
Race	White	80%
	Mid-Eastern	15%
	Other	5%

DECISION-MAKER

At 65% of the hospitals, physicians make the brand selection in 58% of the purchasing decisions; 32% of the selections are made by purchasing agents; 10% by others, including nurses and administrators. Where drug delivery systems increase in complexity, it is anticipated that physicians will account for 75% of purchase decisions.

CUSTOMER MOTIVATION

Level of Satisfaction. (Results of ZNI's most recent independent survey of 1,200 physicians.)

	ZNI	Apollo	Majestic
Complete satisfaction	85%	84%	76%
Moderate satisfaction	14%	13%	9%
Not very satisfied	1%	2%	15%
Not at all satisfied	–	–	–

REASONS FOR PURCHASE

	ZNI	Apollo	Majestic
Price: Cheaper/lower price	36%	11%	43%
Availability: Bought what was available	12%	7%	21%
Product features: Likes brand Easier to use Comfort	9% 14% 34%	20% 4% 18%	5% 4% 17%
Recommendation: By physician	62%	13%	25%

CUSTOMER AWARENESS

A marketing research firm conducted an awareness study to measure need recognition for disposable needles/syringes, brand identification and seven feature/benefit categories. We used this study in conjunction with our advertising campaign to determine before and after awareness levels. We summarize the results below to show awareness at six-month intervals.

LEVEL OF AWARENESS

	July 200x	Jan. 200x	July 200x
ZNI	69%	71%	83%
Apollo	58%	59%	58%
Majestic	42%	45%	44%

SEGMENTATION TRENDS

With the trend toward smaller (1/2cc) syringes, but more frequent doses for most applications, the 1/2cc syringe will grow at the expense of the 1cc size. Introducing the 5/10cc syringe and the pen cartridge system will further segment the market resulting in a further reduction in the importance of the 1cc syringe.

OTHER GENERAL COMMENTS/CRITICAL ISSUES

- Can improving our product, segmenting the market, and providing greater consumer value maintain brand loyalty?
- How successful will pharmaceutical manufacturers be in expanding into the (drug delivery) device business?
- Will the entry of low-priced competitors encourage the emergence of private label brands?

The above presentation is a digest of ZNI's actual plan (only names and numbers have been disguised.) The statistics used in the plan originate from informal general observation to formal statistical data uncovered by primary research.

The key issue behind developing a market background is sensitizing yourself about markets, people and their behavior. Accept the notion that those buyers you dealt with three years ago had different needs from those you deal with today and will be different in wants, needs and behavior three year from now.

Therefore, emphasize the use of meaningful market research in a way that fills any gaps in information about changing patterns of behavior among your customers. If you use distributors, then learn about your distributors' customers – those end-users who actually consume your product.

Now complete the situation analysis by working on your rough draft of the market background.

Working Draft

(Note: The following list, as with others in the plan, is quite extensive. If you don't have all the information for a particular item do not stop. Push on. You can always add data as it becomes available.)

Develop a customer profile by:

The markets distributors/dealers serve _____

Distributors' overall sales_____

Other classifications_____

Frequency and magnitude of products used _____

Geographic aspects of products used _____

Customer characteristics _____

Decision-makers _____

Customer motivation_____

Customer awareness _____

Need recognition _____

Brand identification _____

Feature awareness _____

Segmentation trends _____

Other general comments/critical issues_____

Section 6: Market Opportunities

Planning Guidelines

In this section you'll examine market strengths, weaknesses and options. Opportunities will begin to emerge as you consider the variety of alternatives.

Try to avoid restricted thinking. Take your time and brainstorm. Dig for opportunities with other members of your planning team. If one doesn't exist, then put together a team representing different functional areas of the business (or persuade senior management to approve its formation).

Consider all possibilities for expanding existing market coverage and laying the groundwork for entering new markets. Also consider opportunities related to your competition. For instance, offensively, which of your competitors can be displaced from which market segments? Defensively, which competitors can be denied entry into your market?

As you go through this section, revisit your strategic portion of the SBP (top row of boxes in Figure 2.1). While that portion represents a 3 to 5-year period, work must begin at some point to activate the strategic direction, objectives, growth strategies and, in particular, the products and markets identified in the business portfolio section. Further, you should refer to the situation analysis in the last section, specifically the competitive analysis, for voids or weaknesses, which could represent opportunities.

Note the two-directional flow used to create opportunities: First, the future thinking that went into the strategic portion of the SBP now flows down to focus on one-year opportunities. Second, the situation analysis in Section 5 exposes the voids and weaknesses representing opportunities.

Now review the following screening process to identify your major opportunities and challenges. Once you identify and prioritize the opportunities, convert them into objectives and strategies, which are the topics of the next two sections of the SBP.

PRESENT MARKETS

Identify the best opportunities for expanding present markets through:

- Cultivating new business and new users.
- Displacing competition.
- Increasing product usage or programs by present customers.
- Redefining market segments.
- Reformulating or repackaging the product.
- Identifying new uses (applications) for the product.
- Repositioning the product to create a more favorable perception by consumers and develop a competitive advantage over rival products.
- Expanding into new or unserved market niches.

CUSTOMERS/BUYERS

Identify the best opportunities for expanding your customer base through:

- Improving or expanding distribution channels.
- Product pricing including discounts, rebates, volume purchases and allowances.
- Product promotion covering the Internet, advertising, sales promotion, publicity – including the promotional activities of the sales-force.
- Enhancing customer service, including technical support.
- Trade buying practices, identifying where the buying power is focused or has shifted (from manufacturer to distributor or to end-user).

GROWTH MARKETS

Identify the major product growth markets in key areas (geographic location) and specify which markets represent the greatest long-term potential.

PRODUCT AND SERVICE DEVELOPMENT AND INNOVATION

Identify the immediate and long range opportunities for product development and innovation through:

- Adding new products to the line.

- Diversifying into new or related products, product lines, and/or new items or features.

- Modifying and altering products.

- Improving packaging.

- Establishing new value-added or customer services.

TARGETS OF OPPORTUNITY

List any areas outside your current market segment or product line not included in the above categories that you would like to explore. Be innovative and entrepreneurial in your thinking. These areas are opportunistic, therefore, due to their innovative and risky characteristics, they are isolated from the other opportunities. Those you select for special attention are placed in a separate part of the objectives section of the SBP.

Application

PRESENT MARKETS

Intensify promotion of drug therapy management systems and educational programs among consumers, physicians and nurses. These systems and programs would displace Apollo and Majestic because of their poor perform-ance in such programs. This action – technologically improving our product's market position – will create new opportunities for increased usage.

CUSTOMERS/BUYERS

The mass merchandisers' importance within the consumer retail market will continue to grow at the expense of retail drugs. We will develop a new, dedicated sales team, hitting mass merchandisers during this planning period in order to attack Apollo and Majestic before they can mount a similar effort.

Growth in third party payer plans may change buying behavior by removing consumers from the purchase decision. Price may therefore become a key-purchasing variable for specific user groups. The pricing flexibility resulting from cost-cutting programs will position us to increase our customer base.

GROWTH MARKETS

As the overall market for drug delivery systems grows, specific geographic areas will be a function of population shifts. Disease control within target groups in urban areas, such as those segments related to AIDS control, represents a growing market. (See Section 4, Business Portfolio, for a comprehensive listing of existing products/new markets and new products/new markets.)

PRODUCT AND SERVICE DEVELOPMENT AND INNOVATION

Line extensions, modifications and new package designs will strengthen our dominant share position within the needle/syringe segment. Introducing the cartridge injection system will address specific groups needing multiple daily injections.

TARGETS OF OPPORTUNITY

Diversifying into drug monitoring systems represents a major opportunity. Expansion into these systems will provide synergies through marketing an entire line of products. Such an approach provides market leverage to enter Africa and Pacific Rim countries as a single source supplier.

Using the planning guidelines and the applications as reference, now prepare your working draft of opportunities.

Working Draft

List opportunities by:

Present markets_____

_____

Customers/buyers _____

_____

Growth markets _____

_____

Product and service development/innovation _____

_____

Targets of opportunity_____

_____

Section 7: Tactical Objectives

At this point, you have reported relevant factual data in Section 5, Situation Analysis and interpreted their potential in Section 6, Opportunities. You must now set the objectives you want to achieve during the current planning period – generally defined as a 12-month period.

Once again, you will find it useful to review Sections 5 and 6. Also, it will help to review the strategic portion of the plan (top row of boxes in Figure 2.1). It is in your best interest to be certain that actions related to your long-range strategic direction, objectives and strategies are incorporated in your tactical one-year objectives.

This section consists of three parts:

- **Assumptions**: Projections about future conditions and trends.

- **Primary Objectives**: Quantitative areas related to your responsibility, including targets of opportunity.

- **Functional Objectives**: Operational parts of the business.

- **Non-Product Objectives**

Assumptions

Planning Guidelines

For objectives to be realistic and achievable, you must first generate assumptions and projections about future conditions and trends. List only those major assumptions that will affect your business for the planning year as it relates to the following:

- Economic assumptions: Local market economics, industrial production, plant and equipment expenditures, consumer expenditures and changes in customer needs. Also document market size, growth rate, costs and trends in major market segments.

- Technological assumptions: Include depth of research and development efforts, likelihood of technological breakthroughs, availability of raw materials and plant capacity.

- Sociopolitical assumptions: Indicate prospective legislation, political tensions, tax outlook, population patterns, educational factors and changes in customer habits.

- Competitive assumptions: Identify activities of existing competitors, inroads of new competitors and changes in trade practices.

COMMENTARY

Make assumptions that relate to your business. It is not necessary to identify broad issues that fail to impact your business directly. For example, if the increase or decrease in national production has no effect, don't list it. If population shifts and geographic considerations are major factors influencing your business, list them.

Consider, too, other potential factors about your company or industry, such as labor strife or belt-tightening budgetary restraints that may affect your plans. Make your assumptions realistic, focused and practical.

Application

ECONOMIC ASSUMPTIONS

- The injecting population is projected to grow at 2.7% in the next 12 months.

- The entry of low-priced competitors will not encourage the emergence of private label brands.

- Third party payers will not significantly change current buying patterns by taking the purchase decision away from the consumer.

TECHNOLOGICAL ASSUMPTIONS

- Cartridge devices will compete primarily with single-use syringes.

- No significant cannibalization of sales from our product line resulting from internal pumps and oral agents is anticipated.

SOCIOPOLITICAL ASSUMPTIONS

- Twice-daily injection regimens will increase to 57% of the target population from 49%.

- Greater government intervention is expected in drug and drug-delivery systems related to such diseases as AIDS.

COMPETITIVE ASSUMPTIONS

- The basis of competition will continue to be product performance and differentiation.

- Competitive advantage will be achieved through extensive market segmentation by focusing goods and services on specific user groups.

Working Draft

As you think about assumptions, it is appropriate to ask senior executives about how they view the above categories. Also confer with technical and financial individuals in your firm. They should provide clues about significant internal and external assumptions that would impact your SBP.

Categorize your assumptions by:

Economic assumptions _____

_____

Technological assumptions _____

_____

Sociopolitical assumptions _____

_____

Competitive assumptions _____

_____

Planning Guidelines

Focus on the primary financial objectives that your organization requires. Also include targets of opportunity that you initially identified as innovative and entrepreneurial in Section 6.

Where there are multiple objectives you may find it helpful to rank them in priority order. Be sure to quantify expected results where possible. You can separate your objectives into the following categories:

- **Primary Objectives.** Current and projected sales, profits, market share and return on investment. (See Figure 2.2 or use a form provided by your organization.)

- **Targets of Opportunity Objectives.** Innovations in such areas as markets, product, price, promotion and distribution.

- **Functional Objectives.** Product and non-product objectives

Product Group Breakdown	Current				Projected			
	Sales	Units	Margins	Share of Market	Sales	Units	Margins	Share of Market
Product A								
Product B								
Product C								
Product D								
Other Financial Measures								

FIGURE 2.2. **PRIMARY OBJECTIVES**

Application

(Since the Situation Analysis provided financial information, additional numbers are unnecessary here. Instead, this section includes a suggested form, Figure 2.2, to define financial information that is usually reported in this portion of the SBP. Specific financial requirements usually originate from the on-going reporting systems within the organization.)

TARGETS OF OPPORTUNITY OBJECTIVES

Defend our needle/syringe leadership position by challenging the pen-cartridge system introduction, which looms as a competitive displacement threat.

Introduce new computerized customer tracking systems within the mass merchandiser class of trade.

Working Draft

Develop primary objectives (Use the form in Figure 2.2 or the format required by your organization.)

List targets of opportunity objectives_____

_____

Functional Objectives

Planning Guidelines

State the functional objectives relating to both product and non-product issues in the following categories:

PRODUCT OBJECTIVES:

- **Quality**. Achieve competitive advantage by exceeding industry standards in some or all segments of your market.

- **Development**. Deal with new technology through internal R&D, licensing, or joint ventures.

- **Modification**. Deliver major or minor product changes through reformulation or engineering.

- **Differentiation**. Enhance competitive position through function, design, or any other changes that can differentiate a product or service.

- **Diversification**. Transfer technology and use the actual product in new applications, or diversify into new geographic areas, such as to developing countries.

- **Deletion**. Remove a product from the line due to unsatisfactory performance. Or keep it in the line if the product serves some strategic purpose, such as presenting your company to the market as a full-line supplier.

- **Segmentation**. Create line extensions (adding product varieties) to reach new market niches or defend against an incoming competitor in an existing market segment.

- **Pricing**. Include list prices, volume discounts, and promotional rebates.

- **Promotion**. Develop sales, sales promotion, advertising and publicity to the trade and consumers.

- **Distribution channel**. Add new distributors to increase geographic coverage; develop programs or services to solidify relationships with the trade; remove distributors or dealers from the channel; or maintain direct contact with the end-user.

- **Physical distribution**. Utilize logistical factors from order entry to the physical movement of a product through the channel and eventual delivery to the end user.

- **Packaging.** Use functional design and/or decorative considerations for brand identification.

- **Service.** Broaden the range of services, from providing customer's access to key executives in your firm to providing on-site technical assistance.

- **Other.** Develop other categories as suggested in Targets of Opportunities.

Application

Product Objectives (sample listing)

- **Differentiation**. Continue to generate added value for ZNI's health care products by communicating product improvements to the target audience.

- **Segmentation**. Strengthen ZNI's leadership position within the needle/syringe segment by addressing the trend in therapy toward smaller and frequent injections.

- **Pricing**. Maintain the premium price position across all health care product lines.

- **Promotion**. Encourage continuity of purchase among current users. Attract new and infrequent users. Provide merchandising opportunities in support of trade programs. Broaden reach to poorly served market segments through the Internet.

- **Packaging**. Achieve a consistent look across the entire line to enhance brand name recognition.

Working Draft

Now prepare your rough draft. Keep in mind as you review the categories that competitive advantage, which incorporates long-term customer satisfaction, is the object of your efforts. Be selective and make value judgments about each objective in relation to the advantages you will gain.

As in most of the listings of this SBP, you may wish to edit the following list to incorporate your own trade terminology.

Quality _____

_____

Modification _____

_____

Differentiation _____

_____

Diversification _____

_____

Deletion _____

_____

Segmentation _____

_____

Pricing _____

_____

Promotion _____

_____

Distribution channel _____

_____

Physical distribution _____

_____

Packaging _____

_____

Service _____

_____

Other _____

_____

Planning Guidelines

Although most of the following activities eventually relate to the product or service, some are support functions, which you may or may not influence. How much clout you can exert depends on the functions represented on your planning team.

- **Targeted Accounts**. Indicate those customers with whom you can develop special relationships through customized products, distribution or warehousing, value-added services, or participation in quality improvement programs.

- **Manufacturing**. Identify special activities that would provide a competitive advantage, such as offering small production runs to accommodate the changing needs of customers and reduce inventory levels.

- **Marketing Research**. Cite any customer studies that identify key buying factors and include competitive intelligence.

- **Credit**. Include any programs that use credit and finance as a value-added component for a product offering, such as rendering financial advice or providing financial assistance to customers in certain situations.

- **Technical Sales Activities**. Include any support activities, such as 24-hour hot-line telephone assistance that offers on-site consultation to solve customers' problems.

- **R&D**. Indicate internal research and development projects as well as joint ventures that would complement the Strategic Direction identified in Section 1 of the SBP.

- **Training**. List training programs for internal use, as well as for distributor and end-user applications.

- **Human Resource Development**. Identify types of skills and levels of performance among individuals who would make the SBP operational.

- **Other**. Include those specialized activities that may be unique to your organization.

Application

This segment contains only a sampling of ZNI's actual SBP non-product objectives.

Manufacturing. Maintain low-cost producer status as product improvements are implemented.

Technical sales activities. Maintain the brand's sales focus by providing consumers with information and technical assistance to demonstrate our products' unequaled injection comfort. Project ZNI's dedication to meeting the needs of people dependent on drug delivery systems.

Training. Maintain full marketing support for professional educators.

Working Draft

Use the following categories to develop your non-product objectives

Targeted accounts: _____

_____

Manufacturing: _____

_____

Marketing research: _____

_____

Credit: _____

_____

Technical sales activities: _____

_____

R&D: _____

_____

Training: _____

_____

Human resource development: _____

_____

Other: _____

_____

Section 8: Strategies and Tactics

Strategies and tactics are actions to achieve objectives. Strategies fulfill longer-term objectives; tactics achieve shorter-term objectives.

In this section, strategies and tactics have to be identified and put into action to cover the 1-year timeframe. You must assign responsibilities, set schedules, establish budgets and determine checkpoints. Make sure that the planning team actively participates in this section. They are the ones who have to implement the strategies.

This section is the focal point of the SBP. All the previous work was done for one reason, and one reason only: to develop action-oriented strategies and tactics.

Strategies and Tactics

Planning Guidelines

Restate the functional product and non-product objectives from Section 7 and link them with a brief description of the course of action – strategies and tactics – you will use to reach each objective. Then put all actions together into a summary strategy.

One of the reasons for restating the objectives is to clarify the frequent misunderstanding between objectives and strategies. Objectives are what you want to accomplish; strategies are how (actions) to achieve objectives. If you state an objective and don't have a related strategy, you may not have an objective. The statement may be an action for some other objective.

Application

This segment contains only a sampling of strategies and tactics from ZNI's actual plan.

PRODUCT STRATEGIES/TACTICS

Differentiation objective

- Continue to generate added value for ZNI's health care products by communicating product improvements to the target audience.

Strategy/tactics

- Introduce SupraFine 111 needle to maintain superior product quality and performance versus competition as relates to injection comfort.
- Develop marketing plans for third quarter introduction.

  Responsibility: Marketing, Technical Support, Product Development.

Segmentation objective

- Strengthen our leadership position within the needle/syringe segment by addressing the trend towards smaller and frequent injections.

Strategy/tactics

- Introduce a 40-unit syringe to address the needs of target groups for multiple dose therapy.
- Integrate promotion activities on the entire product line to coincide with the new product introduction.
- Develop marketing plans for introduction during second quarter.

  Responsibility: Marketing, Technical Support, Logistics

Pricing objective

- Maintain price leadership across all health care product lines.

Strategy/tactics

- Hold manufacturers' list price at 200x levels.

  Responsibility: Marketing and Finance

Promotion objective

- Encourage continuity of purchase among current users. Attract new and infrequent users.

- Provide merchandising opportunities in support of trade programs.

Strategy/tactics

- Maximize effectiveness of consumer promotion events by coordinating them with trade programs and presenting them to the trade with sufficient lead-time to gain their support.

- Coordinate trade promotions with distribution allowances and extended dating programs.

- Utilize combinations of counter card rebate offers and in-pack programs to reach category and brand users.

- Submit promotion plans first quarter.

   Responsibility: Marketing and sales

Packaging objective

- Achieve a consistent look across the entire line to enhance brand name recognition.

Strategy/tactics

- Revise packaging to include new SupraFine 111 and product improvements.

- Determine key consumer benefits and revise packaging graphics to provide a consistent look across all sizes.

- Designs to be submitted during second quarter.

   Responsibility: Product development, marketing, and outside agencies

NON-PRODUCT STRATEGIES/TACTICS

Manufacturing objectives

- Maintain low-cost producer status as product improvements are implemented.

Strategy/tactics

- Continue to implement quality control (QC) program.
- Install new cost-reduction program.
- Develop a prototype for a disposable pen cartridge system with the assistance of product designers and marketing.
- Submit status and recommendation reports by second quarter.

   Responsibility: Manufacturing/Engineering

Technical sales activities objectives

- Maintain the brand's sales focus by providing consumers with information and technical assistance to demonstrate our products' unequaled injection comfort and project ZNI's dedication in meeting the needs of people dependent on drug delivery systems.

Strategy/tactics

- Achieve a level of 90% distribution of 'Getting Started' take-away kits.
- Develop video presentation with key medical professionals for use in hospitals and clinics.

   Responsibility: Marketing and sales.

Training objective

- Maintain educational support behind professional educators.

Strategy/tactics

- Continue technical education program for internal sales staff and distributors' sales staff to gain professional recommendations at time of diagnosis and maintain brand loyalty.
- Submit training plan by the third quarter.

   Responsibility: Human resources.

Planning Guidelines

Summarize the basic strategies for achieving your primary objectives. Include a discussion of alternative and contingency plans available if situations arise to prevent reaching your objectives. Relate these alternatives to the overall SBP.

Consider the following additional strategic issues:

- Alterations needed to the product or packaging.

- Changes in prices, discounts, or long-term contracts.

- Revamp of advertising strategy, related to the selection of features and benefits, or copy themes to special groups.

- Recast of media plan.

- Introduction of promotional strategies for private label, dealer and/or distributor, consumers and sales-force incentives.

Application

ZNI's industry leadership will be maintained by addressing our full range of drug delivery systems for health care. These include not only the marketing of delivery devices that are virtually painless, easy to read and convenient to use, but also programs and educational services to aid in the achievement of improved health care. The dominant strategies include the following:

- Segment the market through product differentiation and innovation.

- Maintain low cost producer status by achieving cost reductions of 32.5% by 200x.

- Develop a non-reusable syringe.

- Initiate anti-reuse campaign.

- Introduce the SupraFine 111 needle.

- Introduce a 40-unit syringe for multiple dose therapy. Superior quality and low cost producer status continue to be critical elements in strategies for success. If internal R&D and cost reduction programs do not meet projections, joint ventures will be pursued.

Working Draft

Now write a draft using the format shown above.

_____

_____

_____

Section 9: Financial Controls and Budgets

Planning Guidelines

Having completed the strategy phase of your SBP, you must decide how you will monitor its execution. Therefore, before implementing it, you have to develop procedures for both control (comparing actual and planned figures) and review (deciding whether planned figures should be adjusted or other corrective measures taken.)

This final section incorporates your operating budget. If your organization has standard reporting procedures, you should incorporate them within this section.

Included below are examples of additional reports or data sheets designed to monitor progress at key checkpoints of the plan and permit either major shifts in strategies or simple mid-course corrections:

- Forecast models.
- Sales by channel of distribution.
  - Inventory or out-of-stock reports.
  - Average selling price (including discounts, rebates, or allowances) by distribution channel and customer outlet.
- Profit and loss statements by product.
- Direct product budgets.
- R&D expenses.
- Administrative budget.
- Spending by quarter.

As an overall guideline – regardless of the forms you use – make certain that the system serves as a reliable feedback mechanism. Your interest is in maintaining explicit and timely control so you can react swiftly to impending problems. Further, it should serve as a procedure for reviewing schedules and strategies. Finally, the system could provide an upward flow of fresh market information that, in turn, could impact on broad policy revisions at the highest levels of the organization.

Application

Examples of ZNI's financial data were provided in other sections of the SBP.

Working Draft

Insert your company's forms or use the forms provided in the various sections of the SBP.

Summary

You now have the formal structure of the SBP. Once again a caution: Don't short-circuit the plan by skipping sections or altering the sequence in which the SBP is prepared. It is shown as a logical process leading you step-by-step from section to section, from the broad to the narrow, and from the strategic focus to the tactical implementation.

The intent is to free up your mind to think broadly about your product or service and convert your thinking into a total business perspective, followed by implementation. Further, the systematic process permits your next level of management – the level that approves and funds your plan – to observe the thought processes that went into the SBP.

The only other parts left in your SBP is an optional appendix and an executive summary. Your appendix should include the following items: copies of advertising campaigns for your product as well as those of your competitors, market research data, additional facts on competitors' leadership, market strategies and pricing schedules, and details about product features and benefits.

Functional Managers' Plans

Finally, the SBP serves as a core plan from which other functional managers create sub-plans. For example:

- The *sales manager* develops a sales plan by territory, indicating how sales people are deployed, trained and compensated. It specifies types of promotional support as well as targeting customers that require special attention.

- The *advertising manager* prepares copy strategy and media plans as well as designs sales promotion activities such as trade shows, direct mail campaigns, Internet campaigns, video presentations and educational workshops.

- The *financial manager* develops financial measures related to operating performance such as cash flow, return-on-investment and return-on-sales. Those measures monitor the financial health of the operating unit and aid in projecting financial needs to the organization.

- The *human resource* manager determines skills training, compensation programs, and new hiring needs to support the SBP.

- The *R&D and manufacturing managers* set in motion plans to support the strategies of the SBP as they relate to product innovations, packaging and manufacturing cost efficiencies.

The above functional managers, and others, are part of a cross-functional team charged with developing and implementing the SBP. Thus, the imperative is to initiate a team approach to develop the SBP, thereby coordinating the usually diverse functions into a cohesive, market-driven organizational force.

How do you seize the opportunity to convert the SBP into action? Go to Part 3 and see real company examples of how market-related problems are solved through the effective application of business-building strategies.

You will observe how some problems parallel those you may be facing. Then refer back to the section of the SBP where that type of difficulty is handled. You then have the opportunity to alter your working draft and begin in-putting the revised version into your final SBP.

Schedule for Strategic Business Planning

The purpose of a planning schedule is to demonstrate that effective planning is a participative process requiring input from all levels of management. While Figure 2.3, a calendar schedule, displays an optimum situation, the activities and units of responsibility may vary within each organization.

In practice, many organizations with formalized planning systems will take a six-month period to develop an operating plan. If a company is working on a calendar year, the process begins in July and is usually submitted to top management by November or early December.

Planning Activity	Unit Responsible	July	Aug.	Sept.	Oct.	Nov.	Dec.
1. Market research feeds data for situation analysis and generates competitive intelligence.	Marketing and sales	x	x				
2. Senior management and unit managers develop assumptions about future economic, competitive and market conditions.	Various levels of unit management, including input from field sales personnel		x	x			
3. Senior management reviews strategic direction and sets overall corporate objectives.	Senior management			x			

Planning Activity	Unit Responsible	July	Aug.	Sept.	Oct.	Nov.	Dec.
4. Executives from various functions, e.g., marketing, manufacturing, logistics, finance, etc. interpret corporate objectives with input from strategy team(s).	Various corporate functions				x		
5. Sales and expense forecasts are established	Finance with input from various unit managers				x	x	
6. Marketing and sales managers develop strategic business plans for their assigned product lines and markets. Manufacturing and logistics managers develop operational plans for producing and getting products into the pipeline.	All functional managers				x	x	
7. Mid-level managers design detailed action plans.	All units					x	
8. Senior management reviews and coordinates individual unit plans.	Senior management					x	x

Planning Activity	Unit Responsible	July	Aug.	Sept.	Oct.	Nov.	Dec.
9. District managers develop sales plans in consultation with sales people.	District managers, marketing and sales					X	X
10. Controller prepares operating budget.	Controller					X	X
Top management reviews and approves overall plan. Unit managers approve their respective plans.	Top management, unit, and functional managers						X

FIGURE 2.3: **SCHEDULE FOR STRATEGIC BUSINESS PLANNING**

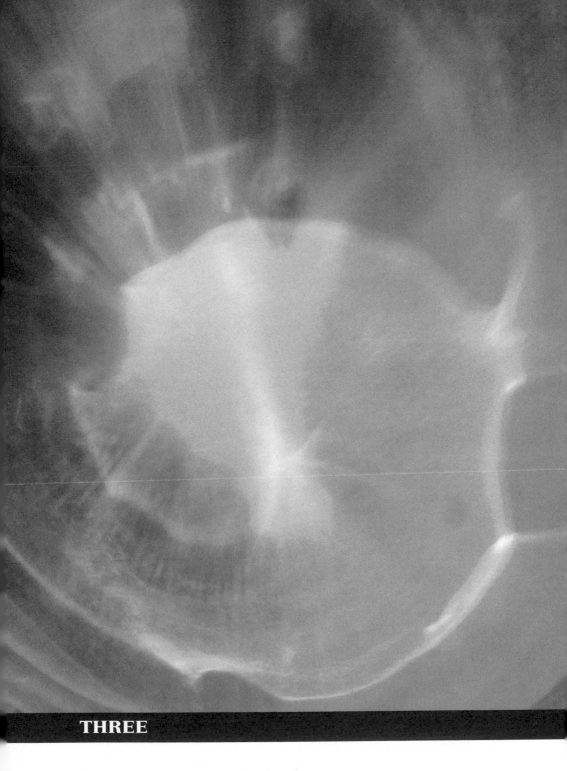

Business Problem Solver: The Strategic Business Plan in Action

THREE

Business Problem Solver: The Strategic Business Plan in Action

---

Chapter Objectives

Given the information in this chapter, you should be able to:

1. Use Strategic Business Planning techniques to solve competitive problems.

2. Strengthen your planning skills by applying the lessons of actual case histories to solving your competitive problems.

3. Link sections of the SBP to specific problems.

Overview

As emphasized in previous chapters, the primary outputs of strategic business planning are competitive strategies. Using actual case examples, this part illustrates how the planning process helps solve competitive problems – perhaps ones you currently face.

To strengthen your planning skills and enhance your ability to use the SBP process in practical applications, the following format is used.

1. A competitive problem is identified.

2. An actual case example is used to illustrate each problem.

3. Action strategies explain how the company solved the problem.

4. References indicate the SBP section where you would address such a problem.

The following case examples are discussed:

1. How do you sustain growth in a sluggish market? (Liz Claiborne)

2. With large organizations tending to dominate an industry, what strategies are possible? (Banking industry)

3. How can you use the SBP to identify long-term opportunities, yet manage day-to-day operations? (General Electric)

4. When developing a SBP, how can you use competitor analysis to justify the time and expense of gathering the information? (Nutrasweet)

5. How do you deal with offshore competitors selling into your market with prices 30% to 40% below yours? (Cummins Engines)

6. How do you cope with the possibility of your product becoming a dinosaur? (IBM)

7. How can you advance customer relationships to block the actions of enterprising competitors trying to make inroads against you? (Baldor Electric)

8. What defensive strategies are effective to protect market share? (SAS)

9. How can you maneuver into a market already occupied by an industry leader? (Canon, Sharp, Ricoh)

10. How can you justify the high up-front expenditures for new product development with the inevitable drop in prices as products move rapidly into the mature stage of their life-cycles? (Sony)

11. What strategies can help reverse a steep decline in a company's sales? (Siebel Systems)

12. How can a small company apply customer-driven techniques to grow against dominant competitors? (Southwest Airlines)

13. Is there a way to create a competitive advantage in a basic industry heavily dominated by large, low-cost competitors? (Hyundai Motor)

14. How do you make the culture of your organization the centerpiece of your strategy? (Graybar Electric)

15. How do you position your products effectively against a market leader? (Lowe's)

16. What strategies can outdistance competitors when entering a new market? (Ericsson)

17. What strategies can you use to regain lost market share? (John Deere)

1. Liz Claiborne

Problem: How do you sustain growth in a sluggish market?

Liz Claiborne Inc. is an apparel company that skillfully balances 26 brands that attract consumers spread over the demographic and psychographic (behavioral) spectrum, from teens to middle-aged women to bargain shoppers.

The company is the master of niche marketing and branding. Obsessively anchored to research trends and sales data, Claiborne's business practices have ingeniously assumed the status of a science in a business traditionally bent on fashion by inspiration, whim and by attempting to make trends rather than by following them.

Claiborne relies heavily on initiating numerous consumer studies and hiring color-and-trend-consulting firms. It even utilizes a small research firm staffed by psychologists who study women's shopping behavior going so far as to comb through their closets.

Armed with reams of data, Claiborne's 250 designers methodically interpret the market trends for their respective clothing labels, which include DKNY, Lucky Brand Dungarees, Shelli Segal, Kenneth Cole, Dana Buchman, Villager and Crazy Horse. Nine additional brands alone play off the Liz Claiborne name. Thus, the profile and buying behavior associated with each brand is carefully dedicated to the market niche in which each designer operates.

Does the system stifle creativity? Apparently not. In a stagnant market, where industry sales plummeted 7%, revenues at Claiborne jumped 11% in 2000 and in 2001 sales skyrocketed 66%. Dedicated market research continues to drive the business and permits Claiborne to prosper in a flat market that is as accessible to the giants as it is to numerous boutique firms.

Action Strategy

For Claiborne, the approach to sluggish sales is regionalization. Other titles given to the approach are segmentation, target marketing and niche marketing. Another aspect of regionalization is the use of *mass customization,* which combines mass marketing and computer integrated manufacturing to customize a product for various customer groupings.

For your purposes, recognize that segments are not static. You will find it useful to re-segment or regionalize your markets to latch on to new opportunities. For Claiborne, success is based on satisfying market segments by differentiating the product.

In short, segmenting markets is a creative process. It goes beyond the standard approaches of demographic, geographic and behavioral segmentation. The following list permits you to look at your market through a variety of lenses and re-segment for fresh opportunities.

To trigger your thinking look at some of the following approaches:

- Segment by common buying factors
    - Performance
    - Delivery
    - Price
    - Quality
    - Service (customer and/or technical)
- Segment by measurable characteristics
    - Customer size
    - Customer growth rate
    - Customer location(s)
- Segment by type of competitors and their respective strategies and strengths/weaknesses

- Segment by common sales and distribution channels

- Segment by business opportunities created through a technology breakthrough, new legislation, a competitor exiting the market, or blocking inroads of a new competitor, and similar situations.

Also, be aware of over-segmenting as well as under-segmenting your market. As a guideline use the following criteria to determine the viability of your segment:

- Is the segment of sufficient size and purchasing power to be profitable?

- Does the segment have growth potential?

- Is the segment of negligible interest to major competitors, especially if there is an aggressive leader in the total market?

- Does your organization (division, business unit) have the necessary skills and resources to serve the segment effectively?

- Do you have the ability to defend against an attacking major competitor?

- Can your group develop strategies to maintain a competitive advantage?

Additional in-depth coverage of segmentation is in Part 5, Help Topics.

SBP Reference:

Section 4 (Business Portfolio) and Section 6 (Market Opportunities).

2. Banking Industry

Problem: *With large organizations tending to dominate an industry, what strategies are possible?*

The banking industry has been consolidating for well over a decade into the hands of several megabanks, dominated by the likes of Citigroup, J. P. Morgan Chase and Wells Fargo. During the same period small banks fell by the wayside and remained in a somewhat dormant state during the high-profile maneuvering of the giants.

Then a fissure slowly appeared among the big banks into which a few surviving smaller banks forced a cavernous opening. The crack first became visible to executives at smaller banks as increased numbers of retail customers and commercial borrowers complained about long waiting periods for loan approvals, increasing account minimums, rising ATM fees and declining customer services.

Taking advantage of the opening, small banks charged forward offering scorned customers the royal treatment with an extensive variety of friendly efforts, from serving Starbucks coffee, free baby-sitting, investment advice, no minimum balances and customized account services, to super-fast approval of loan applications.

In effect the small banks played their winning hand by exposing the mega-banks' inability to respond appropriately with superior service; or to reach out to underserved niches within minority communities; or to open branches in areas abandoned by the big banks; or to cultivate loan terms backed by the personalized attention from senior-level bank executives.

Results: Deposits at small banks have grown by 5% a year since the mid-1990s, while growth at large banks has been flat, and profits have grown at 11.8 percent annually vs. 8.5 percent for the big players. Initially, the big banks did not generally respond appropriately during that period as they continued to pursue a very focused strategy: maximize profits through cost-cutting and similar financial-oriented measures.

Action Strategy

Attempting to tackle industry leaders is a formidable and risky task. It takes careful attention to determine the characteristics of the competitors you wish to take on before you commit resources. Consider the following types of competitor behavior:

Passive Competitor

Characterized as slow to react, this competitor believes it holds a solid position in the market and has earned customer loyalty. Or it may lack resources, have disorganized (or complacent) management and display an overall laid-back mentality. This type of competitor presents major opportunities for aggressive strategies. However, first find out the reasons for the passive behavior.

Discerning Competitor

Selective actions, such as attacking competitors' key accounts might provoke an aggressive competitive response from this type of competitor. Yet a price reduction or adding value to your product might not produce a counter move. Determine those selective actions that would produce a threatening competitive response. Detecting such behavior is vital to developing competitive strategies.

Aggressive Competitor

This type of competitor charges forward with quick and vigorous actions. In some instances the competitor sends out strong challenging signals simply on the news of your new product or service. The telltale signals indicate that any action you take will be hotly contested. In such a case, your response is to avoid a direct confrontation at all costs. Instead, focus on detecting weaknesses in your competitor's market coverage. Do so by examining the marketing mix (product, price, promotion and distribution) for opportunities to use your strengths against the competitor's weaknesses.

Unpredictable Competitor

This type of competitor is illusive without predictable behavior. The company's actions appear highly flexible and it shapes itself rapidly to market situations. This competitor might have a lean organization with few layers of management, which permits hands-on managers to exercise authority and responsibility right down to the field level. Careful monitoring through competitor intelligence by field sales and product managers is essential to prevent a surprise counter-attack to your strategies.

SBP Reference:

Section 3 (Growth Strategies) Section 5 (Situation Analysis).

3. General Electric

Problem: *How can you use the SBP to identify long-term opportunities, yet manage day-to-day operations?*

In one of GE's divisions, General Electric Aircraft Engines (GEAE), dramatic growth spiraled skyward as its executives' correctly read the marketplace and translated the signals into opportunities. Specifically, they spotted the explosive growth in regional jets – those with up to 100 seats and ranges of up to 1,500 miles – and set their sights on engines that would fit on narrow-body planes such as the Airbus A320 or Boeing Co.'s 737.

Then, they moved on geographical opportunities by targeting and winning the lucrative contract to supply China with aircraft engines for a planned-for fleet of 500 regional jets to be ready in time for the 2008 Beijing Olympics.

Backed by solid research and careful scrutiny of the marketplace, glowing opportunities emerged from the planning sessions to indicate that GEAE's future was tied to engines for short-haul jet aircraft.

For instance, air carriers wanted lower operating costs, particularly with the escalating price of fuel. Also, those airlines that survived bankruptcy planned to replace many big jets with the smaller, cheaper ones, and on short hops, consumers preferred them to propeller planes.

Further, in many countries regional jets in service was growing dramatically, while an increased number of big planes were going into mothballs. The small-plane market, in turn, was further segmented into a niche for even smaller jetliners of 70 to 90-seat capacity.

Thus, long-term planning with a future payout intersected with short-term opportunities and short-cycle revenue requirement.

Action Strategy

Like GEAE, you can utilize strategic business planning to grow present markets, spot growth markets, recognize new product innovations and stay alert to current opportunities. The following screening process will help you zero in on clear pathways for growth. Once identified and prioritized, then convert them into long-term and short-term objectives, strategies and tactics.

1. **Present Markets**. To identify the best opportunities for expanding present markets, you should:

   - Investigate emerging businesses or acquire new users for your product.

   - Determine how to displace competition – a particularly significant move in no-growth markets.

   - Increase product usage by your current customers and redefine market segments where there are changes in customers' buying patterns.

   - Work jointly with customers on innovative ideas to reformulate or repackage the product according to their specific needs.

   - Identify new uses (applications) for your product.

   - Reposition the product to create a more favorable perception over rival products.

   - Investigate where to expand into new or unserved market niches.

2. **Customers**. To identify the best opportunities for expanding your customer base, you should:

   - Improve or expand distribution channels.

   - Refine your product pricing policies to match market-share objectives.

   - Enrich your communications, including advertising, sales promotion, Internet, and publicity.

   - Deploy the sales-force to target new customers with high potential.

   - Enhance customer service, including technical service and complaint handling.

   - Identify changes in trade buying practices, where the buying power may have shifted from manufacturer to distributor or to end-user.

4. **Growth Markets**. To identify the major growth markets, you should:

    - Target key geographic locations, specifying which markets or user groups represent the greatest long-term potential.

5. **New Product Development**. To give priority to 'hot' candidates for new product and service development that will impact immediate and long-range opportunities, you should:

    - Focus on new products that can be differentiated and have the potential for an extended sales cycle.

    - Search for ways to diversify into new or related products, product lines and/or new items or features.

    - Examine techniques to modify products by customer groups, distribution outlets, or individual customer applications.

    - Work on improving packaging to conform to customers' specifications and to distinguish your product from its rivals.

    - Establish new value-added services.

6. **Targets of Opportunity**. To focus on areas outside your current market segment or product line not included in the other categories, you should:

    - Be innovative and entrepreneurial in your thinking. However, refer to your strategic direction (Section 1) as a guideline to how far your company can realistically diversify from its core business and still retain its vitality.

SBP Reference:

Section 1 (Strategic Direction), Section 6 (Opportunities) and Section 7 (Tactical Objectives).

4. Nutrasweet

Problem: When developing a SBP, how can you use competitor analysis to justify the time and expense of gathering the information?

Nutrasweet, a unit of Monsanto Co., found itself in a dilemma. Its sales reps had acquired reliable reports from customers that Johnson & Johnson was close to launching a rival sweetener and approval from a government agency was imminent. Acting on the information, managers at Nutrasweet proposed an elaborate and immediate defensive strategy backed-up with a lofty budget to protect market share and blunt the competitive product-launch effort.

In the meantime, Nutrasweet's competitive intelligence unit discreetly made inquiries among its contacts at the government agency. The scrutiny revealed that in fact agency approval was not imminent and launching an expensive defensive campaign would be a waste of money, time and manpower. Five years later, the product still hadn't received approval. A Nutrasweet senior executive estimated that its intelligence gathering was worth at least 25 million dollars a year in sales gained, or revenues not lost.

Action Strategy

Nutrasweet's ability to develop aggressive strategic business plans was based on satisfying customer needs. Parallel with that approach is the vitally important activity of conducting a thorough competitive analysis to provide a total view of the marketplace.

While there are numerous approaches to understanding competitors, the following criteria should be your primary consideration:

- Competitor's size. Categorized by market share, growth rate and profitability.

- Competitor's objectives. Related to quantitative (sales, profits, ROI, market share) and non-quantitative (technology innovation, market leadership, international, national or regional distribution) measures.

- Competitor's strategies. Analyzed by internal (speed of product development, manufacturing capabilities, marketing expertise) and external (distribution network, joint R&D relationships, market coverage and aggressiveness in defending or building share of market).

- Competitor's organization. Examined by structure, culture, systems and people.

- Competitor's cost structure. Examined by how efficiently it can compete and the ease or difficulty of exiting a business.

- Competitor's overall strengths and weaknesses. Identified by areas of vulnerability as well as areas of strength that can be bypassed or neutralized.

Note: If there is any one area of the SBP that deserves your major attention it is competitor analysis. By scrutinizing competitors' strengths, weaknesses, and intentions you can develop winning strategies and tactics.

SBP Reference:

Section 5 (Situation Analysis – Competitor Analysis Section). Also see the supplemental forms in Part 4 to conduct a more comprehensive competitor analysis.

5. Cummins Engines

Problem: *How do you deal with offshore competitors selling into your market with prices 30% to 40% below yours?*

Cummins Engines, the diesel engine manufacturer, fought aggressively against two formidable Japanese competitors: Komatsu and Nissan. The first indication of a problem came from Cummins' customers, Navistar and Freightliner. Both companies reported they were testing Japanese medium truck engines.

Knowing the Japanese strategy of using an indirect approach into a market, Cummins saw the medium engine entry as a strategic threat. The entry could lead to the next step of penetrating Cummins' dominant market share for heavy-duty diesel truck engines.

Cummins managers saw the strategy pattern evolve:

1. The Japanese competitors entered the market with prices 40% below prevailing levels to buy market share – fast.

2. They found a poorly served and emerging market segment in medium size engines.

3. They developed a quality product and were prepared to expand their product lines.

Faced with the problem, Cummins managers took the following actions:

*   Launched into the medium-size truck engine market with four new engine models. This timing, however, was coincidental. Cummins had been planning this market entry for five years through a joint venture with J.I. Case, a farm machinery producer that uses diesel engines.

*   Cummins immediately cut prices of the new engines to the Japanese level. As the then CEO Henry Schacht observed, "If you don't give the Japanese a major price advantage, they can't get in."

*   Cummins cut costs by one-third. This action was the toughest job in what was perceived as a bare bones, efficient manufacturing operation. Using more flexible machinery and cutting excess inventory from a 60-day supply to a four-day supply reduced overheads.

*   Cummins managers gained participation from suppliers on suggestions about cost cutting. The result: lowering of material costs by 18%. This impressive reduction was achieved by changing the traditional adversarial attitude toward suppliers to one of fostering cooperative relationships.

The strategy worked as an effective defense, particularly as it related to Cummins' concerns about retaining its leading market share in the heavy-duty diesel business.

Action Strategy

A number of strategy lessons came out of the Cummins case:

First, there are options open to you against a price attack, but the action must begin with a mental attitude of 'fighting back' and not giving up market share without a battle.

Second, blunting a competitor's price attack by lowering one's own price is conditional on a set of factors related to your organization versus those of key competitors. Meaning: It is necessary in your competitive analysis to compare cost structures based on the following considerations:

- Assess the nature of the project then calculate a breakdown of direct labor and overhead costs.

- Use relative costs of raw material and components to determine which item should be made or outsourced.

- Calculate the investment in inventory, plant and equipment.

- Determine if there are any unique manufacturing or marketing innovations that could affect costs.

- Look at sales costs as they relate to number of plants, warehousing locations and other distribution procedures.

Although the above factors relate primarily to a manufacturing situation, the approach is applicable to non-manufacturing and service organizations. It is applicable to any organization that expends resources to operate a business.

Examining such factors needs the active participation of financial, manufacturing (or the equivalent function of a service provider), sales and all appropriate functional managers. Therefore, it is extremely valuable to form a strategy team of managers from the various functions who can assist in the evaluation. The aim is to develop strategies to meet the threat; in this case, countering a price attack.

SBP Reference:

Section 5 (Situation Analysis), with particular attention aimed at determining the delivery, manufacturing cost and product availability of competition; Section 6 (Opportunities).

6. IBM

Problem: How do you cope with the possibility of your product becoming a dinosaur?

Prior to its turnaround in the 1980s, IBM projected a ponderous dinosaur image of an old economy, brick-and-mortar company. Then, under the brilliant leadership of CEO Louis V. Gerstner Jr., IBM recast its culture and redefined itself as a key player in the Internet business.

By 1999, Gerstner was able to glory in the announcement that IBM generated more e-business revenues and more profits than all of the top Internet companies combined – including Yahoo!, America Online, Amazon.com, eBay and E*Trade. About 75% of IBM's e-business revenue resulted from sales of Net technology, software and services – and not from mainframe computers, which once dominated its sales.

With a revamped strategic direction, IBM shifted internal functions to latch on to an emerging trend of providing solutions to customers' problems through a vast array of services.

Gerstner realized as early as 1994 that mainframes and other tech products were becoming commodities and that the real movement was away from the creation of technology to the application of technology. He redeployed 25% of IBM's research and development budget into Net projects. He also ordered that every IBM product must be Internet-ready.

Thus, IBM was among the first to recognize the explosive growth in services. As a result, Gerstner established an Internet Global Services Division within IBM. Its mandate: Help companies design operations to take advantage of technology and the Internet, install and maintain complex software and hardware systems, and operate computer systems for large corporate customers.

Important as technology was in reinventing IBM, still another necessity required Gerstner's attention. He had to create a new IBM culture – an Internet culture. At the onset, that meant attracting and retaining Web-savvy employees. Gerstner began with an experimental, highly unstructured, 'anything goes' Web-design office in Atlanta. That unorthodox approach led to setting up shop in 'cool' areas of the U. S., such as Los Angeles and close to the MTV and Sony studios.

His goals: To help contribute to shaping the new corporate doctrine and also attract a breed of individuals who could work comfortably and creatively with a new set of values, procedures, mindsets, and ideas that were 180-degrees opposite from the old-line IBM culture that existed in prior decades.

The intended outcome: Infuse IBM's employees with the inventive approaches that would result in a string of breakthrough products and services for the successive waves of changes underway for the Internet – and for a changing global economy.

Action Strategy

One striking lesson comes out of IBM's turnaround: Don't rollover prematurely and claim that a business is totally outdated. Forging alternative objectives, such as joining new product development with technology, a company can regain lost market share.

Making a changeover is one thing, creating a new perception or a new position that will stick in customers' minds is quite another challenge. If you face a situation of transforming your product's image into a new market position, follow these guidelines:

- Be certain your position is distinctive and doesn't create confusion or misinterpretation, so that a competitor is mistakenly identified with your position.

- Select a position that conforms to your firm's unique core competencies, so that competitors cannot easily duplicate the differentiating factors for which you can claim superiority.

- Communicate your position in precise terms through product application, sales promotion and advertising. For example, determine what makes up your position. Do you position your product with a single benefit, such as lowest cost? Do you use a double-benefit position of lowest cost and best technical support? Or do you select a multi-benefit position of lowest cost, best technical support and state-of-the-art technology?

These benefit positions, in turn, lay the foundation for developing the tactical programs that you incorporate into a marketing mix, consisting of product, price, promotion and distribution.

SBP Reference:

Section 1 (Strategic Direction), Section 2 (Objectives), Section 3 (Growth Strategies) and Section 4 (Business Portfolio).

7. Baldor Electric Co.

Problem: *How can you advance customer relationships to block the actions of enterprising competitors trying to make inroads against you?*

Baldor considers customer relationship management and the total orientation toward satisfying unfilled wants and needs as more than just a management buzzword. In the mid-1990s, the company was dwarfed by two stalwart rivals, Reliance Electric and General Electric, competitors in electric motors that power pumps, fans, conveyor belts and the variety of automated components used in modern factories.

"If you have good relationships, you can weather the bad times," declared Baldor CEO Roland Boreham Jr. Relationships, according to Boreham, extend beyond customers and include workers at Baldor, where there has not been a single layoff since 1962. Even during the recession of 1991, workers were busy increasing inventory and expanding the product line in·readiness for the eventual upswing in business. Since 1991, sales have skyrocketed by 46%.

Customer Relationships

Focusing on fulfilling customers' wants and needs at Baldor means providing customers with the motors they need, on time and according to their speci-fications. The company accomplishes this by building up ready-to-go inventory early in the production cycle, permitting it to fill an order overnight for the numerous motors it stocks – ranging in size from 1/50 h.p. to 700 h.p. It assem-bles all other sizes on short-order from a database that includes over 20,000 different specifications.

The core ingredients behind Baldor's ability to sustain sound customer relationships are:

- First, a bulk of its inventory is stored in 31 warehouses strategically located around the country in close proximity to customers' locations.

- Second, each warehousing facility is owned and operated by an independent Baldor sales representative who is in continuous contact with other reps around the country.

- Third, each facility is linked by computer, so that constant availability is online to respond to a customer's urgent request for a motor to prevent a potential manufacturing interruption.

Result: Unsurpassed customer relationships for reliability, responsiveness and flexibility where almost any size motor ships on virtually an overnight schedule – and exceeds the capabilities of most of its formidable competitors.

Action Strategy

With the customer as the centerpiece behind Baldor's success, examine the following eight steps of a customer satisfaction program for your own operation:

1. **Define customer requirements and expectations**. Begin by establishing continuous dialogue with customers to define their current and future expectations. Gather information by personal customer contact – usually obtained by the sales-force. Then match customer expectations against promises made in the sales presentation. The feedback often falls into such basic areas as orders being shipped complete and on-time and complaints handled rapidly and to the customer's satisfaction.

2. **Maintain a system of customer relationship management**. On-going customer contact is a key component of the program. It means assigning permanent customer contact people, such as customer service, sales and technical service to selected customers. Each contact person is then empowered to initiate actions to resolve customers' problems.

   Other features of customer relations include toll-free telephone lines and online 'expert systems' that connect customers to information on inventory, production and technical problem-solving assistance. **Overall goal**: Achieve a preferred supplier status with 100% conformance to expectations.

3. **Adhere to customer service standards**. All quality plans, product performance and customer relationships are driven by customers' standards. Most often those standards are measured by the time it takes to handle complaints, the number of on-time shipments compared to previous time periods, and the amount of invoicing errors, freight claims and product returns. Once indexed, the information is forwarded to a steering committee made up of various functional managers for evaluation and action.

4. **Make the commitment to customers a company ritual**. A commitment means guarantees that include: stock orders shipped the same day they're received, technical service teams sent to customers' locations when needed, specialized training provided to customers' employees, products that conform to data supplied by customers, and a 24-hour 'hot-line' for support services.

5. **Resolve complaints to achieve quality-improvement results**. Empower customer-contact personnel to resolve customer problems on the spot. In particular, sales reps should follow up complaints and make a formal report to a Customer Satisfaction Committee.

6. **Determine what constitutes customer satisfaction**. Develop an index to measure customer satisfaction. With customer feedback as the input, assemble information from various sources, such as: direct customer contact, customer audits, independent surveys, and quality assurance cards with shipments, suggestions, inquiries and complaints.

7. **Customer satisfaction results**. Circulate the results so that functional managers can design customer satisfaction objectives for the following year.

8. **Compare customer satisfaction levels**. Contrast your results with those of competitors and with industry standards through formal and informal benchmarking. Then share the results with distributors to help them improve their customer satisfaction ratings.

SBP Reference:

Section 2 (Objectives) and Section 6 (Market Opportunities).

8. SAS

Problem: What defensive strategies are effective to protect market share?

SAP, Europe's largest software company, had been falling desperately behind U.S. rivals in the fast-growing business-to-business (B2B) marketplaces on the Web. To ease the painful effects of a direct confrontation with competitors, SAP bought 3% of U.S.-based Commerce One, an outstanding Net software company that was also a competitor. The collaboration gave SAP's sales reps immediate access to Commerce One's suite of e-market software for its European customers.

The move during 2000 couldn't have been timelier. Europe's market was growing at triple-digit speed. Unless SAP moved rapidly, the revolution in business practice would pass it by. There was even danger of losing its hard-won standing as the world leader in enterprise resource systems – software that runs the internal operations of a company, from finance to managing inventories. At the time, SAP's core markets were showing signs of penetration by such swift-moving companies as Ariba Inc., Siebel Systems Inc. and i2 Technologies Inc. Even archrival Oracle Corp. was growing faster in SAP's hub markets.

With the Commerce One link-up, SAP halted the revenue drain and interrupted the brain drain of key sales and technical personnel who were looking for growth opportunities in other organizations. As important, SAP stopped the additional pouring out of resources in battling its former competitor – and now partner – Commerce One.

As anticipated, however, merging the two diverse organizations didn't come without some internal fighting. There was visible resistance from both sides in trying to blend the cultures of a swift-moving Silicon Valley start-up with a slower moving and more conservative European organization.

The initial problem emerged when many of Commerce One's business-related decisions needed the prompt approval of SAP management. Instead, it received an unhurried response from its bureaucratic headquarters in distant Walldorf, Germany.

At the other end, SAP's German engineers also faced a cultural upheaval. They watched their methodical approach in perfecting a product become unhinged as some customers defected and made deals with start-up firms, based on the mere promise of dazzling new technology.

All told, even with those numerous cultural and procedural issues at stake, enticing a competitor to join in a cooperative and market-building undertaking is a far superior strategy to slugging it out in open market conflict – barring, of course, any monopolistic and collusion issues that could jeopardize the arrangement.

Action Strategy

Overall, it's often cheaper to protect existing market share in which you already have an investment and a stake in its growth, than to gain new market share. Specifically, consider using these guidelines:

1. Where a competitor attempts to clone your product innovation to gain market entry or reduce your market penetration, blunt its efforts by rapidly matching the innovation. Doing so deprives the competitor of any promotional impact of its product advantage.

    The result you are looking for is to cut off the competitors' successful entry into your market. SAS pulled off that strategy by acquiring an interest in Commerce One.

2. Believe in the maxim, 'The best defense is a good offense'. In the context of competitive strategy, that means employ continuous innovation and continuous improvement. Your aim is to protect your market share by becoming as invincible as possible.

3. Search for possibilities within the marketing mix. For example, SAS's active defense included acquiring much-needed e-business software to maintain its competitive position in its core European markets.

SBP Reference:

Section 3 (Growth Strategies), Section 4 (Business Portfolio), Section 6 (Market Opportunities) and Section 7 (Tactical Objectives).

9. Canon, Sharp, Ricoh

Problem: How can you maneuver into a market already occupied by an industry leader?

Canon, Sharp and Ricoh provide a dramatic illustration of a classic maneuver into a market dominated by an industry leader. In the mid-1970's, Xerox enjoyed 88% share of the copier market, mostly in large and mid-sized copiers. By the mid-1980's, Xerox forfeited to competitors more than half of the primary markets for plain copiers, even though it had virtually created the plain copier machine with its classic 914 model. What happened to cause the disastrous plunge?

The three Japanese companies, hoping to expand in to North America during the mid-1970's, looked to the vast office products field and, in particular, to the still emerging copier market. Scanning the market they saw a sizable segment that was virtually unattended by Xerox: small-size copiers for use in small-size companies.

Research indicated that clerks in tens of thousands of companies were making copies at coin-operated machines in local stationery shops. At that time, those business owners never thought they could afford to own a copier.

Noting the opportunity, the Japanese companies implemented a differentiated market-entry strategy into the exposed segment of the small business market. Meanwhile, Xerox continued to face in one direction by supplying large copiers to medium and large organizations. Initially, they paid little attention to the adventurous competitors coming from across the Pacific.

If the Japanese companies had tried to force their way into the North American market with large machines, they would have been blocked by Xerox's dominant market presence. They would have expended huge amounts of time and money, exhausted their resources for future progress, and might well have failed completely. Instead, they used the following entry strategies:

- **Product**: The Japanese companies introduced a small tabletop copier that used plain paper, no chemicals and performed only the basic copying function. It could not copy two sides, staple, punch three holes, or collate. It simply made a copy. That was exactly what the small business owners wanted at that time.

- **Price**: They entered with low prices to penetrate the small-business market and gain market share rapidly. They reasoned that profits would come later as market share increased.

- **Promotion**: They selected relevant media to target the small business audience.

- **Distribution**: The Japanese manufacturers could not match Xerox's huge direct sales-force. Instead, using indirect distribution, they engaged office supply dealers as middlemen to gain immediate access to the vacant small business market.

Action Strategy

Few strategies are more difficult to execute than maneuver. First, it requires defining the most roundabout route to the customer, rather than suffer the consequences of a direct confrontation against a stronger market leader. The Japanese companies maneuvered by entering with a table-top copier at an affordable price to an unserved market segment.

Finally, before you undertake a maneuver strategy, be aware of these guidelines for success:

- **Know your market**. Pinpoint the critical strategic points for market entry. Initially look at geographic location, availability of distributors and buying motives of the targeted buyers. What entry point would give you the best possibility to maneuver?

- **Assess competitors' intentions and strategies**. Evaluate how energetically competitors will challenge your intrusion into their market domain. Are they willing to forfeit a piece of the business to you as long as you don't become too aggressive?

- **Determine the level of technology required**. While technology adeptness often wins many of today's markets, there are still numerous low-tech niche opportunities open to a smaller company. Where does your company fit on the technology issue?

- **Evaluate your internal capabilities and competencies**. One of the cornerstones to maneuvering in today's market is the ability to turn out a quality product equal to, or better than, competitors. For the Japanese companies, it was to introduce a product that Xerox did not have in its line at the time of entry. What are your company's outstanding competencies?

- **Maintain discipline and vision**. Attempting to maneuver among market leaders takes confidence, courage and know-how in developing a winning strategy. How would you assess your company's willingness to challenge a market leader?

- **Secure financial resources**. Upper-level management support is necessary to obtain the finances to sustain an ongoing activity. If competitors detect any weakness, they can easily play the waiting game for the financially unsteady organization to cave in. What type of support can you count on?

- **Develop a launch plan to market the product**. Shape a marketing mix that incorporates a quality *product*, appropriate *distribution*, adequate *promotion* and a market-oriented *price* to attract buyers. Which part of the mix would represent your driving force?

- **Maintain a discerning awareness of how customers will respond to your product offering**. Use market research to gain insight about what motivates various groups to buy your product. What immediate action can you undertake to target a niche and avoid a head-on confrontation with a market leader?

SBP Reference:

Section 3 (Growth Strategies), Section 6 (Market Opportunities), Section 7 (Tactical Objectives) and Section 8 (Strategies and Tactics).

10. Sony

Problem: How can you justify the high up-front expenditures for new product development with the inevitable drop in prices as products move rapidly into the mature stage of their life-cycles?

Sony Corp. enjoys the reputation of owning one of the world's 10 most powerful consumer brands. From camcorders, digital cameras, video games and computers that cover the spectrum of music, movies and the Net, it clearly holds the high ground with an incredible array of products, with more than 100 million devices produced a year.

Holding that highly valued position, however, is quite another issue. During 2002, lurking in the shadows were a host of signs, signals and movements that threatened to topple Sony from its lofty position. For one, an aggressive incursion began in earnest during 2000 as Korean and Chinese rivals churned out ever-cheaper alternatives to Sony DVD players, TVs and digital cameras.

For another: While Sony mastered key technologies, from the manufacture of DVD players to digital storage, to the miniaturization needed for its palm-size Net camcorder, to seamless data transmission between devices, to digital television, there hasn't been a truly breakthrough product introduced in over two decades.

On the more positive side, however, Sony wisely recognized that hanging on to the high ground is always tenuous. Essential to its overall future prosperity and profitability is the protection of its renowned brand name. By harnessing a monumental effort, the company earnestly pushed to transform itself into a broadband-entertainment company.

Sony's plan: Shift its weight from making low-margin 'boxes' to selling movies, music, games and Internet services. Central to that effort is the fusion of its digital devices along with content, all transmitted within a network of high-speed connections, both wired and wireless.

Action Strategy

The strategies related to new product development, as well as to the life-cycles of existing products, vary with external market and internal organizational situations.

Here are guidelines for you to consider:

1. Before you deal with new product development, assess the state of your long-term business strategy. How does it relate to the strategic direction you set for your company or business unit? If you recast your direction, then your strategies will change. As with products, strategies also have life-cycles. In time they will be mismatched with your mission and objectives, thereby losing their potency and will eventually decline in usefulness.

   Further, watch the competitive activity within your industry. This was the key to Sony moving toward a redefinition of its strategic direction, which subsequently dictated the course of its new product development activity.

2. The conventional wisdom about preventing products from reaching a mature or commodity stage in the life-cycle bears rethinking, particularly if your organization has little R&D funds. Evidence suggests that there is room in the market for standard, reliable, no-frills products. However, you may want to tweak the strategy by enhancing your products with a competitive advantage, such as technical backup, rapid delivery, or extra guarantees.

   The effort may reward you with an optimum market position, somewhere between an enhanced commodity and a differentiated product. Above all, however, the big prize goes to managers who discover new applications for their products.

3. Finally, use the cross-functional team to focus on your total product portfolio. Where team members methodically think of customers' needs and match them with the strategic direction of the organization or business unit, the outcome can prove enormously effective in prioritizing new product strategies and expenditures.

SBP Reference:

Section 4 (Business Portfolio), Section 6 (Market Opportunities).

11. Siebel Systems

Problem: What strategies can help reverse a steep decline in a company's sales?

Siebel Systems, the sales-automation software company, made magnificent progress from 1993 through 2000 by doubling sales and profits for each of those years. The company achieved a commanding 70% share in its core market and optimistic plans called for continuing the same double-digit growth.

Then the alarm sounded. In February 2001, before the opening signs of recession, CEO Thomas M. Siebel looked with shock at his company's internal situation. The backlog of pending sales had declined sharply from just days before and, for the first time, the figures showed that hundreds of potential deals, ranging in value from a few thousand dollars to several million each, suddenly stalled.

Sales reports began to include the stinging phrases: 'budget eliminated', 'all IT spending frozen', or 'decision deferred to following quarter'.

With his own forecasting software quantifying the signals that foretold bad times lay ahead, Siebel moved at turbo speed to re-deploy his resources. He ordered his senior executives to alter the just-completed strategic plans and move to recession mode.

Executives, managers and sales reps hit the road with urgent orders to lock-in as many pending deals as quickly as possible. They did so before lagging competitors could take notice and move to counter the action.

Siebel was clearly ahead of the curve. Even economists took nine months to confirm that a recession had settled on the economy.

To hunker down for the rough times and take all possible moves to preserve the company's viability, Siebel furloughed 800 employees, eliminated three money-losing business units, and slashed budgets for travel, marketing and hiring, including cutting 20% of executives' pay.

Once the signs of an improved economy appeared, Siebel was in trim shape and ready to return to its growth plan. By December 2001, Siebel reps began knocking on customers' doors with resounding success in closing deals. They were again in prime position to leapfrog the competition.

Action Strategy

In coping with the threat of declining sales, pay particular attention to those market segments that would be most receptive to your offerings. Doing so will help you deploy your resources efficiently, conserve costs and maximize your impact on the points of greatest return.

Selecting segments depends on a group of variables, including knowledge of your customers' needs and competitors' capabilities. Grasping the significance of each will add greater precision to selecting viable segments.

Customer Needs and Behavior

By maintaining an on-going customer analysis that accurately defines the needs and wants of customer groups and individuals, you satisfy a primary ingredient of successful segmentation. Specifically, analyzing needs and behavior requires you to:

- **Categorize segments**. Begin by adding structure to your view of the market. Doing so allows you to properly allocate marketing and sales resources for the greatest impact. For example, categorize your segments by geographic location, demographics, product attributes, market size, common buying factors, shared distribution channels, and any other factors that are unique to your industry.

- **Determine purchase patterns**. Next, analyze purchasing variables so you can develop customized packages of benefits that will increase your chances of success by segment and key customers.

  For example, divide customer purchase patterns into two categories: regular use and infrequent special application of your product. Review how customers perceive your product benefits in terms of price/value, convenience, or prestige factors. Analyze and rank customer loyalty as nonexistent, medium, or strong. Examine customer awareness and readiness to buy your product as unaware, informed, interested, or intending to buy. And evaluate your buyers' existing (and evolving) needs related to product quality, delivery, guarantees, technical serv Ices, or promotional support.

Competitor Capabilities

While customer analysis lets you examine how to attract and satisfy customers, competitor analysis gives you a picture of your competitors' capabilities by segment. For example, view competitors from the following perspective:

1. How they segment their markets.

2. How customers select rival products.

3. What purchasing patterns their behavior exhibits.

4. How competitors develop their strategies and how likely they are to dislodge you from a particular segment.

You can utilize this information in several ways:

First, should you want to avoid a direct confrontation with competitors, you have the option of positioning your product line in a market niche unattended by rivals. Second, you can isolate areas where your competitors' are weak, such as in product, price, promotion, or distribution. Third, you can draft effective market strategies by pinpointing vacant segments and identifying your competitors' vulnerabilities.

SBP Reference:

Section 2 (Objectives), Section 6 (Market Opportunities) and Section 7 (Tactical Objectives).

12. Southwest Airlines

Problem: How can a small company apply customer-driven techniques to grow against dominant competitors?

Southwest Airlines, a regional carrier, has been dealing successfully with airline passengers who are increasingly disenchanted with long departure and arrival delays and congested airports. With most major airlines plagued with skyrocketing fuel costs, labor problems and charges of predatory pricing, Southwest Airlines stands apart from the turmoil.

The carrier has learned to overcome competitive obstacles and solve customers' travel dilemmas through the effective application of indirect strategies. Instead of a frontal assault on its formidable competitors, Southwest has managed to avoid most of the problems associated with its competitors.

With major airlines locked into mainstream airports where most of the snarls occur, Southwest flies in and out of smaller regional airports. It also maintains a lower cost by selling about one-third of its tickets online (a higher percentage than any other airline) and by hedging fuel costs during 2000 and 2001. All together, Southwest's strategies result in low cost, low fares, high growth and outstanding profits.

What Southwest has done so successfully is to implement a solid three-point winning strategy: First, it avoided a costly confrontation with bigger and financially stronger competitors. Second, it established internal procedures that lead to cost savings. Third, it resolved the travel dilemmas of harassed passengers.

Action Strategy

First, applying customer-driven techniques to head-off competition begins with a mindset in yourself and those with whom you work that keeps your customers' needs in the forefront of service. Second, and critical part, is to install a systematic approach that permits you to learn about your customers' business.

Here's one system that works:

Explore customers' needs and problems in two broad categories that would appeal to their self-interests: *revenue-expansion* and *cost-reduction* opportunities. This approach will chalk up positive results for your customers and aid you in dealing with dominant competitors.

To conduct the analysis, ask the following questions.

Revenue Expansion Opportunities:

- What approaches would reduce customer returns and complaints?
- What processes would speed up production and delivery to benefit your customer?
- How can you improve a customer's market position and image?
- How would adding a name brand impact your customers' revenues?

- What product or service benefits would enhance your customers' operation?

- How can you create differentiation that gives your customers' a competitive advantage?

- How would improving re-ordering procedures impact revenues?

Cost Reduction Opportunities:

- What procedures would cut customers' purchase costs?

- What processes would cut customers' production costs?

- What systems would cut customers' production downtime?

- What approaches would cut customers' delivery costs?

- What methods would cut customers' administrative overhead?

- What strategies would maximize customers' working capital?

Several of those areas reach beyond the scope of a particular manager. Therefore, involve various functional managers to interpret findings and translate them into customer-oriented business solutions.

Finally, implementing the process is a sticky problem. Especially so when it involves various individuals into actively thinking about such areas as customers' needs, market growth and competitive advantage. There is no easy solution.

For starters, however, enlist the assistance of the senior executives in your group or company. Have them brief the involved personnel on the benefits of paying attention to market-driven issues for the welfare of the company as well as their personal career growth – and even survival. If that doesn't do the trick, you might recommend that an orientation seminar be used to help instill the appropriate attitudes.

SBP Reference:

Section 6 (Market Opportunities), Section 7 (Tactical Objectives) and Section 8 (Strategies and Tactics).

13. Hyundai Motor Co.

Problem: Is there a way to create a competitive advantage in a basic industry heavily dominated by large, low-cost competitors?

Hyundai Motor Co. found itself in a dilemma. In 1999, its lines of cars were cheap knockoffs of Japanese cars. The future looked bleak as it served a fluid market where competitors were striving for quality, consumers were demanding performance and the company was losing money and market share. Brand loyalty was virtually non-existent, especially in the transitory and lackluster market segment it served.

During that same timeframe, a new CEO, Chung Mong Koo, son of the company's founder, took charge. The immediate range of decisions dealt with righting the past wrongs that were getting in the way of catering to what the market demanded and what rivals were offering; namely, quality and performance.

Chung didn't wait long to tour the manufacturing plants and to his dismay looked under the hoods at cars coming off the assembly line with loose wires, tangled hoses and bolts painted four different colors. With unabashed anger, he demanded immediate action to fix the problems and ordered that no car would role off the line until the faults were resolved. So that there would be no misunderstanding, Chung made certain to communicate clearly to the rank and file that they would use Toyota's level of quality as the company's benchmark.

In the first 10 months of the declarations for change, Hyundai's worldwide sales increased by a healthy 8% over the previous year. In North America alone, sales skyrocketed by 42%.

Staying on a roll, Chung established a quality-control unit. Still using the Japanese cars as its standard for quality, performance and features, the unit bought several models of Toyotas and Hondas. Engineers tore them apart to analyze them and devise innovative approaches to meet and, where possible, beat their rivals.

Still looking to the future, Chung sold 10% of Hyundai Motor to Daimler-Chrysler with the aim of building a strategic alliance and gaining access to its state-of-the-art technology.

Action Strategy

Hyundai created a clear-cut competitive advantage. Listed below are broad-based strategy guidelines:

PRICE ADVANTAGE

Through off-shore sourcing, internal belt-tightening, or installing new equipment and systems, find ways to offer users a product comparable to your competitors at a lower price. Organizations in every sector of the economy are desperately searching for ways to lower costs.

NO-FRILLS PRODUCT

Provide a segment of the market with a product that has fewer features or minimal services. Such a product could use a different package or another name to eliminate confusion and minimize cannibalizing sales from a main-line product.

UP-SCALE PRODUCT

Launch a higher-quality product that may include improved warranties, after-sales support, installation, or improved packaging. However, be sure that your company's image can support a move up-scale and that you have selected the appropriate segment that is willing to pay the higher price.

PRODUCT EXPANSION

Introduce a large number of product versions, thereby offering buyers more choices. This expansion strategy lends itself to more applications, sizes, shapes, models and features. It also blocks any open market niches through which a competitor can enter.

PRODUCT INNOVATION

Use product or service innovation as an offensive strategy with which to attack a competitor's position. Muster extensive competitor analysis to determine areas of strengths and weaknesses from which the innovation can be initiated.

IMPROVED SERVICES

Services can include customer service and technical service. Technical advice, hot-line service, repair service, or availability of spare parts are all examples of such service. This strategy also includes value-added approaches, such as: providing financial packages for customers, establishing quality control systems, installing computerized inventory control systems, or providing computer-based expert systems for resolving problems.

DISTRIBUTION INNOVATION

Examine creative new approaches to managing channels of distribution, or improving on your position in the supply chain. This strategy is especially appropriate when some competitors alter their distribution strategies, such as changing from pushing their products through distributors to pulling through products by creating end-user demand. Also, there is an opportunity to strengthen relationships with distributors who may give you extra support because of disagreements with their former suppliers.

COST-IMPROVEMENT

Initiate ways to achieve lower manufacturing costs. The technologies abound and are increasingly becoming more affordable for even the smallest company. Many systems are now used on desktop computers as compared with its original applications with large mainframe computers.

MARKET IDENTIFICATION

Continue to monitor changing customer behavior and unfilled needs and wants. Establish end-user and distributor councils to identify emerging, neglected, or poorly served niches that represent opportunities for new products and services.

SBP Reference:

Section 3 (Growth Strategies), Section 6 (Opportunities), Section 7 (Tactical Objectives) and Section 8 (Strategies and Tactics).

14. Graybar Electric

Problem: How do you make the culture of your organization the centerpiece of your strategy?

Graybar Electric Co., a distributor of communications and electrical gear, has survived through numerous business cycles since its founding in 1869. Throughout the decades, the company for the most part kept up with the various business and technology cycles.

Other times it trailed its competitors. Such was the case in 1997 with the explosive rise of the Internet followed by the increasing demand for related technology. With persistent calls for speed from suppliers and customers, the problem – and subsequently the opportunity – for Graybar was to meet the demand by delivering its products to customers quickly and efficiently.

On-time delivery was, in fact, the deep-rooted problem that caused the company to lose ground to competitors. With its network of 231 local distribution centers, each run as an independent entity, Graybar could take as long as a week to fill an order. Worse yet, deliveries arrived at a customer's location from as many as eight different branches with eight different invoices to pay.

The solution was clear to Graybar's leaders: Centralize supplies of certain products so orders could be filled quickly and from one facility. Also, build new warehouses to supplement the existing network of distribution centers.

The problem for senior management: How to implement the solution without undermining the basic culture at the employee-owned company that worked so well, for so long. In particular, the dilemma of how to deal with those local managers who traditionally exercised almost complete authority over their regional warehouse operations?

It was a daunting task to change a tradition-bound company with its steadfast culture. Only by gingerly introducing modifications could senior management expect to affect changes and reinvent the mindsets of individuals, many of whom spent virtually their entire careers at Graybar. That said, rather than take away local independence or close any branches, the new warehouses were designed to coexist with local facilities.

With sensitivity to the ongoing systems and the existing work patterns of managers and other key personnel, a new corporate culture slowly and steadily evolved. The 'old time' managers accepted the changes as essential to Graybar's success in the Internet age.

Results: With the new logistical framework in place, customers exuded surprise and pleasure as most orders began arriving overnight. Even better, the consolidated orders came from a single warehouse with only one invoice to pay. Once the solution for creating an opportunity was clearly identified, it was the attention to and sensitivity for Graybar's innate culture that made the opportunities a reality.

Action Strategy

You can use the culture of your organization to best advantage if you can sensitize your awareness of the history of the organization as well as the backgrounds of the key individuals who are responsible for making things happen. Then, you can more easily mobilize the attention of individuals to focus on those strategies that would directly impact customers' needs.

For instance, to develop a successful competing brand, be certain you apply a differentiation strategy to distinguish your product from the standard offerings in the market.

Follow these guidelines to involve key personnel:

- **Features and benefits**. Focus on those characteristics that complement the product's basic function. Start with your core product. Then envision adding unique features and services; ideally, ones based on users' expectations. (Graybar refocused attention on Internet-related products and technology.)

- **Performance**. This factor relates to the level at which the product operates – including quality. (For Graybar, performance translated to speed of delivery.)

- **Acceptance**. This characteristic measures how close the product comes to established standards or specifications.

- **Endurance**. This factor relates to the product's expected operating life.

- **Dependability**. This attribute measures the probability of the product breaking or malfunctioning within a specified period.

- **Appearance**. This factor covers numerous considerations ranging from image, function, look, or feel. Different from performance, appearance integrates the product with all its differentiating components, including packaging.

- **Design**. While design encompasses the product's appearance, endurance and dependability, there is particular emphasis placed on ease of use and appropriateness to the function for which it was designed.

SBP Reference:

Section 6 (Business Portfolio), Section 7 (Tactical Objectives) and Section 8 (Strategies and Tactics).

15. Lowe's

Problem: *How do you position your products effectively against a market leader?*

Lowe's is a mass merchandiser of basic products such as bolts, ceiling fans, clothes washers and dryers, as well as a wide assortment of appliances. For years the firm, although growing and prosperous, was lagging behind market leader Home Depot.

Beginning in earnest during 2000, Lowe's charged forward with a forceful strategy that placed its rival on the defensive. Although selling similar merchandise at competitive prices, Lowe's decided on target marketing as the focal point of its approach. The strategy: Attract women who, in turn, will lure their husbands into the stores. In contrast, Home Depot gears its efforts to the male shopper.

The strategy, supported by Lowe's research, reveals that women initiate 80% of all home-improvement purchase decisions, especially the big-ticket items such as kitchen cabinets, flooring and bathrooms. "We focused on a customer that nobody else in home improvement is focused on," declared CEO Robert Tillman.

To make the strategy come alive and appeal to women, Lowe's stores are bright and airy, with uncluttered aisles and supermarket-like signs that list what is in each aisle. Some areas have particular allure, such as the window-décor aisle with displays of valances, tiers and cotton drapes, all of which the customer can take home immediately. In contrast, similar purchases have a wait of six weeks for delivery from its competitor.

The strategy of focusing on women and pushing into big-city markets has turned Lowe's into one of the fastest growing, most profitable operations in its industry. The genesis of the strategy began during a period of identity crisis in the early 1990s.

A plan evolved after conducting a mammoth six-month effort involving extensive surveys among 8,000 customers as they exited selected Lowe's stores. The feedback was bitter with criticism ranging from slow service, narrow aisles, dark floors, dull assortments and high prices.

The remedies proceeded during the 1990s with extensive experimenting of displays, colors, lighting and overall eye-appeal until the optimum mix of elements came together. For instance, to set the tone of a customer orientation, Lowe's goes so far as to install call buttons in most aisles to bring the salesperson to the customer, rather than the exhaustive effort of hunting for sales help.

Also, for convenience, hardware is located at the entrance so that shoppers who only need wing nuts can grab a handful and go. This breaks with the general retail rule, which calls for placing everyday staples in parts of the store to force customers to walk past other merchandise.

Action Strategy

If you want to position your product effectively against market leaders, consider some of the following action strategies suggested by the Lowe's example:

1. Select a competitive advantage that larger competitors cannot perform efficiently.

   Action: Employ market research, such as customer buying practices, to identify possibilities for differentiation.

2. Commit to quality and service as an organizational priority.

   Action: Initiate programs that encourage individuals at various functions to strive for quality. These are not one-time motivational talks, but continuous training.

3. Focus on specialty products, where possible, that command premium prices; leave the commodity price segment to others.

   Action: Practice segmenting your market for specific product applications. Get closer to your customers and their problems.

4. Establish long-term alliances with customers to grow with them and to build technology and product relationships.

   Action: Encourage trust with customers or suppliers so that sensitive information can be shared for mutual interests.

5. Maintain a market-driven orientation throughout the organization – within all functions – to maintain a competitive advantage.

   Action: Organize strategy teams made up of functional managers. Then, use the teams' strategic business plans as lines of communications to respond rapidly to market opportunities.

6. Seek global opportunities that complement long-term objectives.

   Action: Through joint ventures, licensing, or exporting develop a global presence – if consistent with your corporate strategic direction.

7. Partner salespeople with customers to provide product solutions to customers' problems.

   Action: Go beyond traditional forms of sales training. Instead, teach salespeople how to think like strategists so they can help their customers achieve a competitive advantage.

8. Identify market niches that are emerging, neglected, or poorly served.

   Action: Re-assess how you segment your markets. Search for additional approaches beyond the usual criteria of customer size, frequency of purchase, geographic location. Look for potential niches related to just-in-time delivery, performance, application, quality, or technical assistance.

SBP Reference:

Section 2 (Objectives), Section 3 (Growth Strategy), Section 4 (Business Portfolio), Section 6 (Opportunities) and Section 8 (Strategies and Tactics).

16. Ericsson

Problem: What strategies can outdistance competitors when entering a new market?

Ericsson, the Swedish phone giant, operates in existing and growth markets within a maelstrom of intense competition and swift movements in technology. Inside that two-tier framework, managers faced tough decisions about defending their hard-won positions in established segments against aggressive competitors, while obtaining a foothold in new segments.

For Ericsson, there remained a nagging problem: Even with a substantial share of wireless and fixed-line networks by 2001, it lagged in a key telecom growth market: mobile handsets. That void provided hard-driving competitors with an opening to gain solid positions.

For example, Finland's Nokia consolidated its hold on the mobile-handset business, with a 23% market share vs. Ericsson's third-place 15%. Such power-houses as Cisco Systems, Lucent Technologies and Nortel seized the lead in the Internet telephony field.

The situation: Telephone handsets, once a big earner, were barely profitable because of pricing pressure, aging products and bulky designs.

Ericsson's Strategy

To fight back, the Stockholm-based company advanced using the following steps:

- Recognizing a prime opportunity, Ericsson employed its vast technical expertise to concentrate heavily on the growing application for mobile phones to transmit reams of information Also, the company expanded the segment for mobile phones by intensifying its efforts to offer wireless Internet access.

- As the wireless networks multiplied, Ericsson managers concentrated on the stunning forecast of one billion mobile subscribers worldwide by 2004, along with 30% to 40% using mobile systems to access the

Internet. With those healthy projections, a massive market for equipment upgrades looked particularly attractive, and Ericsson positioned itself to grab a significant piece of that lucrative market segment, and outdistance competitors – at least, until the next technology breakthroughs emerge.

Action Strategy

Two primary lessons emerge from the Ericsson case: First, focusing on updated products, technologies and trends should be given maximum attention to meet customers' needs and maintain a lead over competition. Second, concentrate on gaining a comprehensive view of the marketplace.

Use the following guidelines to provide such a perspective:

1. **Suppliers**. If a few dominant suppliers maintain control over the flow of materials that result in the control of prices, then a powerful influence is exerted on all the other forces within the industry. Accordingly, review supplier practices for clues to future patterns of supplier behavior, which in turn will shape your strategies.

2. **Existing competitors**. Examine the intensity of competitive actions. For instance, decide which competitors seem likely to retaliate against movements in price. Review the amount of advertising and identify the themes of the competitors' advertisements. Determine if environmental, technological or other issues are changing the character of the market.

3. **Emerging competitors**. In conducting a market analysis, there is a tendency to focus only on existing players. The wrenching lesson from organizations that blindly entered markets and failed, is that they did not analyze emerging competitors with the same intensity they applied to existing ones. This issue is particularly pertinent with the proliferation of new and powerful competitors resulting from joint ventures, mergers, and acquisitions.

4. **Alternative product offerings**. As with analyzing emerging competitors, give similar emphasis to alternative products or services. In this type of analysis it is valuable to employ the skills and knowledge of R&D and manufacturing. Also tap the expertise of outside industry experts who are more likely to be aware of substitute products.

Finally, keep the customer as the primary focal point around which you make your assessments and you'll reduce the risk of entering a new market.

SBP Reference:

Section 4 (Business Portfolio), Section 5 (Situation Analysis,) and Section 6 (Market Opportunities).

17. John Deere

Problem: What strategies can you use to regain lost market share?

John Deere, producers of farm equipment, taps the expertise of its managerial and hourly work-force to implement its customer loyalty strategies. Deere's resourcefulness in capitalizing on its employees' skills has contributed to regaining lost market share, increasing net income and gaining sizable jumps in sales.

To execute Deere's strategy, teams of assembly-line workers fanned out and talked to dealers and farmers about Deere equipment. They traveled singly or in small groups and pitched their sales stories to farmers at regional trade exhibits. Workers in various job functions routinely made unscheduled visits to local farmers to discuss their problems and needs.

In most places the 'new' reps are accepted as friendly, non-threatening individuals who had no ulterior motive other than to present an honest, grass-roots account of what goes into making a quality Deere product. At the time of initiating the strategy, enlisting the work force for marketing duties was triggered by the weakening of demand for farm equipment during a recession period, as well as by the aggressive actions of competition – in particular from Deere's chief rival, Caterpillar Inc.

Underlying the work-force strategy is Deere's view of customer loyalty· All employees are valuable resources to serve the needs of customers. Further, many of the workers supporting the effort had over 15 years experience with the company. They were trained in advanced manufacturing methods, total quality programs and teamwork. According to Deere's management, harnessing that expertise demonstrates to customers that as makers of the products, they are the best company spokespeople.

Noteworthy benefits of Deere's strategy:

- **Early identification of customers' problems**. Equipment performance or maintenance problems are quickly identified, with some handled on the spot by Deere workers. Others are addressed back at the plant by cross-functional teams.

- **Early detection of competition and the identification of new benefits for customers**. As the Deere workers hustle it in the sales territories, they experience real-world training that sensitize them to the issues of product quality, technical assistance, on-time delivery, cost reduction, customer relationships – and the potential threats of competition.

- **Mobilization of the work-force to support the customer-loyalty effort**. This fits the broad strategy of marketing the whole company – the sum of its competencies, products, services and value systems – in a form that makes customers want to do business with Deere.

- **A subtle, yet powerful image of management-labor harmony**. The implication of this strategy is that with unity of effort comes continuous product improvement and speedy resolution of customers' problems.

- **Strengthening of relationships**. Customers develop a stronger loyalty for the company through their meetings with workers from functions other than sales and marketing. This coming together has the positive result of breaking down sales resistance.

Action Strategy

Tied to regaining lost market share and maintaining customer loyalty are the pragmatic financial numbers that result from customer retention.

It can cost up to 10 times as much to attract a new customer as to retain a current one. Consequently, sales models that focus on attracting as many new customers as possible – at the expense of properly servicing existing ones – are obsolete.

You will gain far more in the lifetime value of keeping a customer, unless you can find a way to decrease selling expenditures, reduce the number of sales calls, or increase lifetime value. Therefore, retaining the loyalty of a customer is far more cost effective, since the acquisition costs are sharply reduced or eliminated altogether.

SBP Reference:

Section 7 (Tactical Objectives), Section 8 (Strategies and Tactics) and Section 9 (Financial Controls and Budgets).

Summary

The intent of this chapter is to show you how real companies, of all sizes, and in diverse industries, solved difficult business problems. Some of those problems flowed out of deteriorating internal organizational conditions; others arose from an uncompromising competitive environment.

It is conceivable that you, too, could be facing some or all of those tough situations. Therefore, the sole purpose of highlighting the assorted case problems is to demonstrate that developing and implementing *action strategies and tactics* are the dominant ingredients in overcoming numerous internal and external obstacles.

The overriding lesson: Rely on your Strategic Business Plan to churn out action strategies and tactics to guide your actions through the maze of organizational and market conditions.

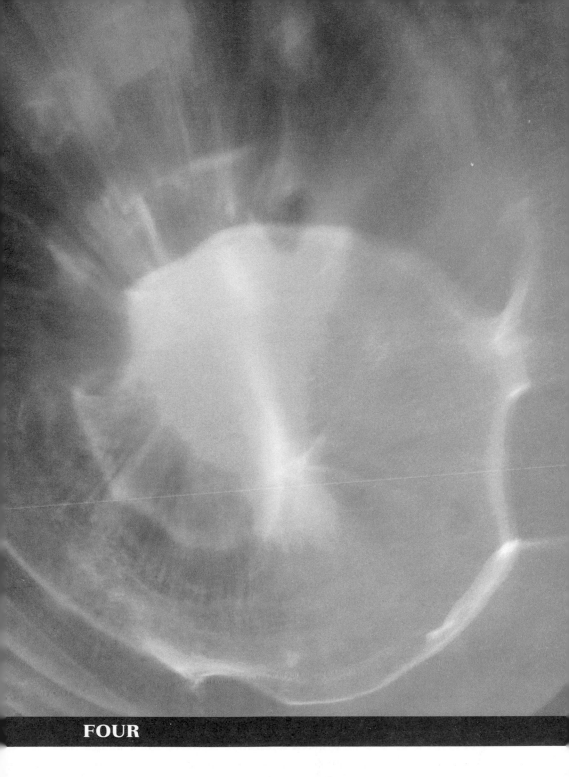

Checklists for Developing
Competitive Strategies

Checklists for Developing Competitive Strategies

Overview

There are two parts to developing competitive strategies that, when utilized, would improve the reliability of your SBP:

Part 1: Competitive Advantage Analysis

The first part consists of a comprehensive checklist to analyze the strengths and weaknesses of your company versus those of your competitors in the key areas of product, price, distribution and promotion. While the factors for rating strengths and weaknesses are applicable to most companies and product lines, you may find it useful to edit the list with factors and vocabulary pertinent to your business and industry.

The intent of the analysis is to (a) determine where there are opportunities to attack the weaknesses of competitors, and (b) expose potential weaknesses through which competitors can devise strategies against you.

Part 2: Competitive Strategies Analysis

The second part consists of a more expansive group of checklists to help you determine competitors' strategies. Accordingly, the analyses warrant more interpretation, judgment and insight than Part 1. Here, you dig behind the mere facts and determine the patterns of competitors' behavior.

For instance, look at such patterns as when and how your competitors enter a market, their introductory pricing strategies, type of promotional support to the sales-force, overall distribution strategies, or after-sales support service.

You may never be able to predict with complete accuracy the behavior of competing managers. But there is a good chance of predicting general forms of competitors' reactions. You can thereby anticipate actions, avoid surprise and develop contingency plans.

It is still a time-honored maxim that surprise is a major success factor in implementing strategies and tactics. Consequently, to the extent that you can, make every effort to avoid competitors' surprising you. On the other hand, make every attempt to create surprise when attacking competitors.

How to Conduct the Analysis

As recommended throughout this book, the ideal approach to developing a quality SBP is to use a team effort.

For best results have each team member privately conduct the analysis by using the 1 to 10 rating scale for each item on the checklist. Then reconvene the team and review each individual's comparative ratings, along with the supporting information behind the ratings.

Where there are extreme differences in the results, ask the members to go through a second round of ratings, this time armed with the information discussed at the first meeting. Once again reconvene the group and aim for consensus. Continue the procedure until a reliable result is produced.

Where possible, attempt to validate the results through formal market research. Above all, remember the purpose of the analysis is to:

- Add more precision to your SBP.
- Devise competitive strategies and tactics that will permit you to sustain a competitive advantage.

Checklists for Developing Competitive Analysis

Part 1: Competitive Advantage Analysis

1-10 rating, 10 = best

A. Product/Service	Your Firm's Product/Service	Competitor A	Competitor B	Competitor C	List Advantages and Define Strategies
Quality					
Features					
Options					
Style					
Brand Name					
Packaging					
Sizes					
Services					
Warranties					
Returns					
Versatility					
Uniqueness					
Utility					
Reliability					
Durability					
Patent Protection					
Guarantees					

B. Price	Your Firm's Product/Service	Competitor A	Competitor B	Competitor C	List Advantages and Define Strategies
List Price					
Discounts					
Allowances					
Payment Period					
Credit Terms					
Financing					

C. Promotion	Your Firm's Product/Service	Competitor A	Competitor B	Competitor C	List Advantages and Define Strategies
Advertising:					
Consumer					
Trade					
Personal Selling:					
Incentives					
Sales Aids					
Samples					
Training					
Sales Promotions:					
Demonstrations					

C. Promotion *continued*	Your Firm's Product/Service	Competitor A	Competitor B	Competitor C	List Advantages and Define Strategies
Contests					
Premiums					
Coupons					
Telemarketing					
Internet					
Publicity					
Other					
TOTAL SCORE					

Part 2: Competitive Advantage Analysis: Market

1-10 rating by market or product. 10 = best

A. Market Dimension (List product/market segments)	Your Firm's Product/Service	Competitor A	Competitor B	Competitor C	Total Current Sales ($)	Total Potential Sales ($)
Segment 1						
Segment 2						
Segment 3						
TOTAL						

B. Market Entry

How do competitors usually enter a market? Is there a market leader among the competitors? Who are the followers? Identify by:

		Your Firm's Product/Service	Competitor A	Competitor B	Competitor C
First-in Strategy	Product:				
	Price:				
	Distribution:				
	Promotion:				
Follow-the-Leader Strategy	Product:				
	Price:				
	Distribution:				
	Promotion:				
Last-in Strategy	Product:				
	Price:				
	Distribution:				
	Promotion:				

C. Market Commitment

How much commitment do competitors give to a specific market in terms of people, dollars, research, and products?

	Your Firm's Product/Service	Competitor A	Competitor B	Competitor C

D. Market Demand

How flexible are competitors in changing strategies for different market situations?

	Your Firm's Product/Service	Competitor A	Competitor B	Competitor C
Prune markets when demand slackens				
Concentrate on key markets when demand increases				
Harvest profits when sales plateau				

E. Market Diversification

How have competitors responded to diversification opportunities?

	Your Firm's Product/Service	Competitor A	Competitor B	Competitor C
Allocated additional resources to new segments				
Added another stage of distribution				

Competitive Advantage Analysis: Product

A. Positioning

How efficient are competitors in monitoring customer perceptions and identifying customer niches? Related to:

	Your Firm's Product/Service	Competitor A	Competitor B	Competitor C
Positioning a single brand				
Positioning a multiple brand				
Repositioning older products				

B. Product Life-Cycle

How efficient are competitors in extending the life-cycle of their products? Related to:

	Your Firm's Product/Service	Competitor A	Competitor B	Competitor C
Promoting more frequent usage				
Finding new users				
Finding more uses for products				

C. Product Competition

To what extent do competitors attempt to gain a larger share of a market? By introducing:

	Your Firm's Product/Service	Competitor A	Competitor B	Competitor C
New packaging				
Competing brand				
Private label				
Generic product				

D. Product Mix Where do competitors stand as related to width and depth of product lines?	Your Firm's Product/Service	Competitor A	Competitor B	Competitor C
Single product				
Multiple products				
Product systems				

E. Product Application How much manufacturing and application flexibility do competitors display as related to:	Your Firm's Product/Service	Competitor A	Competitor B	Competitor C
Standard products				
Private label products				
Standard product, modified				

F. New Products What has been the pattern of competitors related to the following areas of new product development?	Your Firm's Product/Service	Competitor A	Competitor B	Competitor C
Innovation				
Modification				
Line extension				
Diversification				
Re-merchandising or reformulating existing products				
Market extending existing products				

G. Product Audit How flexible have competitors been in managing their product lines as demonstrated by:	Your Firm's Product/Service	Competitor A	Competitor B	Competitor C
Line reduction				
Line elimination				

Competitive Advantage Analysis: Price

A. New Products What has been the pattern of competitors in pricing new products? Do they tend to use:	Your Firm's Product/Service	Competitor A	Competitor B	Competitor C
Skim (high) pricing				
Penetration (low) pricing				
Follow-the-leader pricing				
Cost-plus pricing				

B. Established Products

What has been the pattern of competitors in pricing established products? Do they tend to use:

	Your Firm's Product/Service	Competitor A	Competitor B	Competitor C
Slide-down (gradual reduction) pricing				
Segment pricing				
Flexible pricing				
Preemptive pricing (Reacting first to anticipated action from competitors)				
Loss-leader pricing				

Competitive Advantage Analysis: Promotion

A. Advertising

To what extent do competitors use advertising to do the following:

	Your Firm's Product/Service	Competitor A	Competitor B	Competitor C
Support personal selling				
Inform target audience about availability of product				
Persuade prospects to buy directly from advertising				
Integrate the Internet as part of the overall advertising effort				

B. Sales-force

What is the profile of competitors' sales-forces related to:

	Your Firm's Product/Service	Competitor A	Competitor B	Competitor C
Sales-force size				
Sales-force territorial design				
Compensation systems				
Training				
Technical or service backup				

C. Sales Promotion

How well do competitors integrate sales promotion with their advertising and sales-force strategies? Is sales promotion used to:

	Your Firm's Product/Service	Competitor A	Competitor B	Competitor C
Encourage more product usage				
Induce distributor and dealer involvement				
Stimulate greater sales-force efforts				

Competitive Advantage Analysis: Distribution

A. Channel Structure What has been the distribution strategy of competitors in reaching customer markets?	Your Firm's Product/Service	Competitor A	Competitor B	Competitor C
Direct distribution to the end user				
Indirect distribution through intermediaries (distributors, dealers)				
Direct sale to end users				
Impact of e-commerce on distribution strategy				

The Business Audit

An immensely valuable evaluation tool, the Business Audit, is found on the following pages. Consisting of 100 questions, it is an accurate diagnostic tool to determine the condition of your internal and external capabilities.

Taking the time to conduct the audit reduces some of the risk of planning, strategizing and implementing the SBP. For instance, you have the opportunity to anticipate the weaknesses and strengths from both your side and that of your competitors, and make hard decisions based on analysis and fact – not speculation.

What also follows is that the boldness or timidity of your plans will be determined by your ability to execute balanced strategies, as defined by the internal capabilities of your organization, and as matched to the market environment of your customers and competitors.

As with any physical examination or a financial audit, the aim of the business audit is to highlight a set of symptoms for further evaluation. Then, with the detailed output, you can take corrective actions or modify plans to meet those circumstances. Thus, the business audit permits you to conduct a structured analysis of internal and external considerations divided into three areas:

1. Your firm's competitive environment.

2. Management procedures and policies.

3. Tactical aspects of your product, price, promotion and distribution.

Your can conduct the analysis by using the same team approach described in Developing Competitive Analysis. Where possible, however, it is more beneficial to gain an objective outside opinion from an individual or group that can add a broader perspective to evaluating your organization's competencies.

Part I: Reviewing the Firm's Market Environment

CONSUMERS (END USERS)

1. Who are our ultimate buyers?

2. Who or what influences them in their buying decisions?

3. What are our consumers' demographic and psychographic (behavioral) profiles?

4. When, where and how do they shop for and consume our product?

5. What need(s) can our product or service satisfy?

6. How well does it satisfy?

7. How can we segment our target market?

8. How do prospective buyers perceive our product in their minds?

9. What are the economic conditions and expectations of our target market?

10. Are our consumers' attitudes, values, or habits changing

CUSTOMERS (INTERMEDIARIES)

11. Who are our direct customers? Are they intermediate buyers, such as wholesalers, distributors, or retailers?

12. Who or what influences them in their buying decisions?

13. Where are our customers located?

14. What other products do they carry?

15. What is their size and what percentage of our total revenue does each group represent?

16. How well do they serve our target market?

17. How well do we serve their needs?

18. How much support do they give our product?

19. What factors made us select them and them select us?

20. How can we motivate them to work harder for us?

21. Do we need them?

22. Do they need us?

23. Do we use multiple channels, including e-commerce?

24. Would we be better off setting up our own distribution system?

25. Should we go direct?

COMPETITORS

26. Who are our competitors?

27. Where are they located?

28. How big are they overall and, specifically, in our product areas?

29. What is their product mix?

30. Is their participation in this field growing or declining?

31. Which competitors may be leaving the field?

32. What new domestic competitors may be entering the market?

33. What new international competitors may be on the horizon?

34. Which competitive strategies and tactics appear particularly successful or unsuccessful?

35. What new direction is the competition pursuing?

OTHER RELEVANT ENVIRONMENTAL COMPONENTS

36. What are the legal constraints affecting our marketing effort?

37. To what extent do government regulations restrict our flexibility in making market-related decisions?

38. What requirements do we have to meet?

39. What political or legal developments are looming that will improve or worsen our situation?

40. What threats or opportunities do advances in technology hold for our company?

41. How well do we keep up with technology in day-to-day operations?

42. What broad cultural shifts are occurring in segments of our market that may impact our business?

43. What consequences will demographic and geographic shifts have for our business?

44. Are any changes in resource availability foreseeable?

45. How do we propose to cope with environmental or social issues that can impact our business?

Part II:
Reviewing Management Procedures and Policies

ANALYSIS

46. Do we have an established market research function or use outside resources?

47. Do we conduct regular, systematic market analyses?

48. Do we subscribe to any regular market data service?

49. Do we test and retest carefully before we introduce a new product?

50. Are all our major market-related decisions based on solidly researched facts?

PLANNING

51. How carefully do we examine and how aggressively do we cope with problems, difficulties, challenges and threats to our business?

52. How do we identify and capitalize on opportunities in out marketplace?

53. What procedure do we use to determine gaps in customers' needs?

54. Do we develop clearly stated and prioritized short-term and long-term objectives?

55. Do our long-term and short-term objectives complement our strategic direction?

56. Are our objectives achievable and measurable?

57. Do we have a formalized procedure to develop a Strategic Business Plan?

58. Do we utilize objectives to assess performance and make appropriate mid-course corrections?

59. What are our core strategies and tactics for achieving our business objectives?

60. Are we employing a push-pull strategy in dealing with our customers and consumers?

61. How aggressively are we considering diversification?

62. How effectively are we segmenting our target market?

63. Are we committing sufficient resources to accomplish our objectives?

64. Are our resources optimally allocated to the major elements of our marketing mix?

65. How well do we tie in our SBP with the other functional plans of our organization?

IMPLEMENTATION AND CONTROL

66. Is our SBP (or any of the functions plans) realistically followed or just filed away?

67. Do we continuously monitor our environment to determine the adequacy of our plan?

68. Do we use control mechanisms, such as generally available software and analytics to monitor performance?

69. Do we compare planned and actual figures periodically and take appropriate measures if they differ significantly?

70. Do we systematically study the contribution and effectiveness of various functions and activities?

ORGANIZATION

71. Does our firm have a high-level function to analyze, plan and oversee the implementation of our strategic efforts?

72. How capable and dedicated are our personnel?

73. Is there a need for more internal skills and leadership training?

74. Are our managerial responsibilities structured to best serve the needs of different products, target markets and sales territories?

75. Does our entire organization embrace and practice the market-driven concept?

Part III: Reviewing Strategy Factors

PRODUCT POLICY

76. What is the makeup of our product mix and how effective are our new product development plans?

77. Does it have optimal breadth and depth to maintain customer loyalty and prevent unwelcome entry by aggressive competitors?

78. Should any of our products be phased out?

79. Do we carefully evaluate any negative ripple effects on the remaining product mix before we make a decision to phase out a product?

80. Have we considered modification, repositioning, and/or extension of sagging products?

81. What immediate additions, if any, should be made to our product mix to maintain a competitive advantage?

82. Which products are we best equipped to make ourselves and which items should we outsource and resell under our own name?

83. Do we routinely check product safety and product liability?

84. Do we have a formalized and tested product recall procedure?

85. Is any recall imminent?

PRICING

86. To what degree are our prices based on cost, demand and/or competitive considerations?

87. How would our customers react to higher or lower prices?

88. Do we use temporary price promotions and, if so, how effective are they?

89. Do we suggest resale prices?

90. How do our wholesale or retail margins and discounts compare with those of the competition?

PROMOTION

91. Do we state our advertising objectives clearly?

92. Do we spend enough, too much, or too little on advertising'?

93. Are our ad themes and copy effective?

94. Is our media mix optimal?

95. Do we make aggressive use of sales promotion techniques and the Internet?

PERSONAL SELLING AND DISTRIBUTION

96. Is our sales-force large enough to accomplish our strategic and tactical objectives?

97. Is it optimally organized according to geographic, market, or product criteria?

98. Is it adequately trained and motivated, and characterized by high morale, ability and effectiveness?

99. Have we optimized our distribution setup, or are there opportunities for further streamlining?

100. Does our customer service meet customer requirements?

FIGURE 4.1: BUSINESS AUDIT

As a final note: Conditions within your company are likely to change. That is unquestionably true of today's volatile markets. Therefore, to make clear-cut decisions (or recommend changes to the next level of management), it is indispensable to skillful management to give your operation a once-a-year checkup. You will find the above business audit, as well as the other check-lists in this chapter, highly useful to assist in clarifying your thinking and permitting you to grasp the sum and substance of your firm in its operating environment.

Once again, you can customize the items and questions in the checklists to conform to your company's and market's needs.

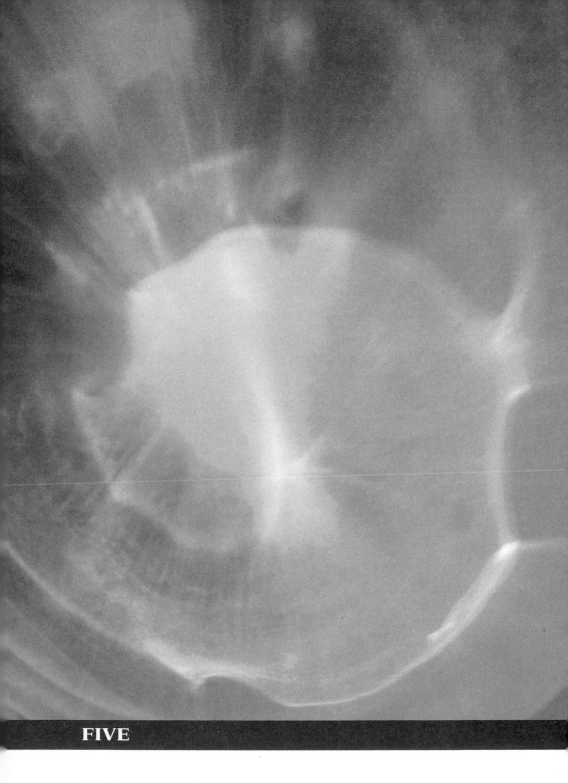

Help Topics

Help Topics

Chapter Objectives

Given the information in this chapter, you should be able to:

1. Refer to Help Topics as a general resource and add broader perspective to your thinking and planning.

2. Apply the in-depth information and techniques to various sections of your Strategic Business Plan.

3. Make liberal use of the information to add greater precision to the plan, thereby improving your chances for senior management's approval – or for funding by an outside lender.

Overview

Help Topics is divided into 12 parts. Each part begins with a table of contents and references to specific sections of the SBP.

Suggestion: Select carefully from the numerous checklists and guidelines provided throughout the following parts. Certainly, you want accuracy and precision in developing a credible SBP. However, don't get caught up with a case of 'paralysis by analysis', so that little gets done in finalizing your plan. Therefore, use your best judgment about what are the most essential pieces of information you need to develop a reliable SBP.

Help Topics Contents

Help Topics	Applies to SBP in	Page
PART 11	Sections 1 through 4	
11.1 Creating a global perspective		347
11.2 Achieving a global perspective		348
11.3 Entry strategies for international markets		349
Exporting		
Licensing		
Joint venture		
Wholly owned subsidiaries		
Management contract		
PART 12	Sections 1 through 9	
12.1 Thinking like a strategist		356
12.2 Roles and responsibilities of strategy teams		357
12.3 Identifying business-building opportunities		359

FIVE: PART 1
Competitive Strategy

1.1 Why should you be concerned with competitive strategy?

First, strategy has been the key planning challenge since the 1980s, and it will continue to dominate the thinking and actions of executives into the 21st century. Second, it remains the primary focus of your Strategic Business Plan. Third, competitive strategies are the measurable output of your SBP through which actions are taken to achieve your objectives.

Competitive strategy encompasses such diverse issues as the:

- Competitive capabilities of both your company and your competitors.
- Changing demographics.
- Shifting customers' buying patterns.
- Globalization of companies, markets and products.
- Saturated markets.
- Price wars initiated by hostile competitors.
- Rapid technological change.
- Shortened product life-cycles.

Your ability to develop competitive strategies and implement them through a well-developed plan is, and will remain, the hallmark of a good manager and critical to the survival and growth of a company. To acquire that unique skill, you need to understand what strategy is and how to incorporate it into your SBP.

Put into practical terms, the following strategy applications are directed within a two-pronged effort: First, to sustain an advantage over competitors; second, to satisfy customers' needs and establish a strong relationship for a prolonged period.

Strategy applications include:

- Seeking competitive advantage.
- Establishing long-term customer relationships.
- Incorporating business intelligence into decision-making.
- Determining optimum product positioning to satisfy customer needs and deter competitive threats.
- Identifying areas for market expansion and penetration.
- Developing an ongoing stream of products and services.

1.2 Strategy Defined for Your SBP

As you develop your SBP, keep in mind the broader definition of strategy: Strategy is the art of coordinating the means (money, human resources and materials) to achieve the ends (profit, customer satisfaction and company growth) as defined by company policy and objectives.

Strategy is further defined at three levels:

1. **Higher-level corporate strategy** directs your company's capabilities toward fulfilling your firm's strategic direction without exhausting its material and human resources. Specifically, that means shaping strategies with the long-term view of sustaining your company's potential for ongoing market development with profitable growth.

2. **Mid-level strategy** operates at the division, business unit, department, or product-line level. While contributing to the overall company's mission, it is more precise than corporate strategy. It covers a period of 3 to 5 years (SBP Sections 1 through to 4) and focuses on quantitative and non-quantitative objectives.

Here, the intent is to provide for continued growth by (a) penetrating existing markets with existing products, (b) expanding into new markets with existing products, (c) developing new products for existing markets, and (d) developing new products for new markets. (These items form the structure of SBP Section 4.)

3. **Lower-level strategy or tactics** requires a shorter timeframe (usually one year) and correlates most often with the annual tactical plan (SBP Sections 5 through to 9.) Tactics are actions designed to achieve short-term objectives and link up to longer-term objectives and strategies.

These precise actions cover such definable issues as: pricing and discounts, advertising media and copy approaches, sales-force deployment, technical support, distributor selection and training, product packaging and service, and the selection of target segments for a product launch.

1.3 Implementing Strategy

Ultimately, the effectiveness of your SBP boils down to the skill, motivation and boldness of your actions opposed to those of competing managers. Yet, with the immense quantities of computerized reports available, many managers rely exclusively on quantified data to implement strategic and tactical plans.

Mistakenly, they often consider the market as a set of impartial factors that can be predicted, analyzed and managed through a variety of logic-based techniques. While correct calculations and well-coordinated objectives are absolutely indispensable for devising strategies, they are not sufficient for handling unpredictable business conditions and erratic buying behavior.

Thus, the practice of conducting business operations emerges as a battle of mind against mind, manager against competing manager, and strategy against competitor's strategy. It is essentially a conflict of human wills. Therefore, strategies must meet and counter unpredictable human responses.

Impact of Human Will

To understand how strategy correlates with the human will, consider what happens when an existing firm enters a new market. At once the newcomer is likely to encounter resistance from existing companies already dominating the market.

Therefore, the prime purpose of strategy is to *lessen resistance*. Meaning: the goal of strategy is not head-to-head conflict with entrenched competitors. The effect of which would drain an entering company's resources and increase resistance. Rather, the aim of strategy is to initially *surprise, upset* and *confuse* the competition of your intentions. In turn, those actions are followed by a rapid concentration of your resources at points of opportunity; such as markets that are emerging, neglected, or poorly served.

Surprise takes place at two levels – physical and psychological:

1. At the **physical** level, it entails a series of moves to upset and confuse the competitor's plans through a sudden attack on a market segment. For instance, a move might impair a company's ability to supply outlets or make deliveries on time by dislocating its distribution and organization. That move depends on calculations of market conditions, competitor's resistance, timing, geography, distribution and transportation. Thus, you can see the importance of inputting such calculations into your SBP.

2. At the **psychological** level, surprise and confusion are the effects any disruptive physical move has on the mind of the competing manager. It relies on surprise to distract and upset the competing manager into making sudden and faulty decisions. When the competing manager feels trapped and unable to counter your moves quickly enough, he or she may hastily form mistakes in judgment, and thus play the market into your hands. Therefore, surprise depends on a calculation of the conditions that are likely to affect the will and mindset of the competition.

To create surprise and confusion, the physical and psychological elements must join together for strategy to work. The intent is to (1) distract the competing manager from interfering with your own efforts, (2) disperse his attention among many unprofitable avenues, and (3) dislocate him from his grip on the market. Over-extended and limited in his options, the opposing manager will be less able to oppose your moves.

Distracting Competition

To distract your competition, you may have to deploy your efforts temporarily in order to appear being spread out. Once you have weakened your competition, however, you must *concentrate* your strength at the point of greatest market potential. The familiar terms given to such concentration are *segmentation*, *niches*, or *target markets*.

The best way to achieve this concentration is to develop *alternative objectives* (SBP Sections 2 and 7). If the competing manager is certain of your aim, he has the best chance of blunting your efforts. By taking a line that threatens him with alternative objectives, you distract his attention, divide his efforts, and place him on the 'horns of a dilemma'. By leaving yourself a number of options, you ensure the achievement of at least one objective, perhaps more. Therefore, your SBP must be flexible enough to respond to changing circumstances.

In sum, your aim is not to battle the competition directly, but rather to use strategy to surprise, unbalance and weaken the competitor, while concentrating your company's strength on market opportunities. It all boils down to manager versus manager, one person competing against another.

As you consider your strategy, be aware of the following guidelines for success, most of which apply to SBP Sections 1 through 4.

- **Know your market**. Pinpoint the critical strategic points for market entry. Initially look at geographic location, availability of distributors and buying motives of the targeted buyers. Which point of entry would give you the best possibility to maneuver?

- **Assess competitors' intentions and strategies**. Evaluate how energetically competitors will challenge your intrusion into their market domain. Are they willing to forfeit a piece of the business to you as long as you don't become too aggressive?

- **Determine the level of technology required**. While technology adeptness often wins many of today's markets, there are still numerous low-tech niche opportunities open to a smaller company. Where does your company fit on the technology issue?

- **Evaluate your internal capabilities and competencies**. One of the cornerstones to maneuvering in today's market is the ability to turn out a quality product equal to, or better than, competitors. What are your company's outstanding competencies?

- **Maintain discipline and vision**. Attempting to maneuver among market leaders takes confidence, courage and know-how to develop a winning strategy. How would you assess your company's willingness to challenge a market leader?

- **Secure financial resources**. Upper-level management support is necessary to obtain the finances to sustain an ongoing activity. If competitors detect any weakness, they can easily play the waiting game for the financially unsteady organization to cave in. What type of support can you count on?

- **Develop a launch plan within your SBP to market the product**. Shape a marketing mix in the tactical section (Sections 7 and 8) that incorporates a quality *product*, appropriate *distribution*, adequate *promotion* and a market-oriented *price* to attract buyers. Which part of the mix would represent your driving force?

- **Maintain a sensitive awareness of how customers will respond to your product offering**. Use market research to gain insight about what motivates various groups to buy your product. What immediate action can you undertake to target a niche and avoid a head-on confrontation with a market leader?

1.4 Strategy Principles

As you immerse yourself in the practices of developing winning strategies, five principles emerge as the underpinnings for developing competitive strategies, and apply to SBP Section 3 and 8.

The principles include *speed, indirect approach, concentration, alternative objectives* and *unbalancing competition*. A thorough understanding of these pragmatic standards is critical for you to implement business-building strategies.

Speed

Speed is essential to most operations of the enterprise. There are few cases of overlong, dragged-out market-driven campaigns that have been successful. The draining of resources without achieving planning objectives has ruined more companies than almost any other factor.

Extended deliberation, procrastination, cumbersome committees, and unwieldy organizational hierarchies from home office to field sales are all detriments to success. Drawn out efforts divert interest, diminish enthusiasm and depress morale. Individuals become bored and their skills lose sharpness. The gaps of time created through lack of action give competitors a greater chance to react and blunt your efforts.

In today's hotly contested markets, a manager must evaluate, maneuver and concentrate marketing forces quickly to gain the most profit and least cost, and in the shortest span of time. The proverb 'Opportunities are fleeting' or 'The window of opportunity is open' has an intensified truth in today's markets. Speed is essential to overtake the lead and exploit any advantages gained.

Organizing for Speed and Quick Reaction

Two factors make it possible for you to react with speed. First, new technologies in product development, communications and computerization afford you the opportunity to react quickly and decisively, in a ratio of a short span of time to a large amount of space. The second factor for maximum speed – the essential ingredient – is an efficient organization.

In a small organization the founder or president is at the helm. He or she is in a unique position to control both policy-making and execution. Because decisions do not have to be channeled through others, they are unlikely to be misinterpreted, delayed, or contested. For the most part, they can be implemented with consistency and speed.

While there exists a preponderance of small businesses, the composition of many have swung to the multi-product firms with an array of services. In turn, this movement is creating the new breed of diversified firms created by leveraged buyouts, consolidations, joint ventures and special purpose alliances.

With these developments are problems of organization. New people, new products, new positions and new levels of authority blending into one organization may well result in a cumbersome, inflexible operation.

Individuals in the field often feel that there are obstructions in the decision-making process that prevents moving into new markets. Missed opportunities are common, and 'go' decisions get stuck for reasons other than the competition. Even first-line managers think that there are too many people at the staff level or in service departments and not enough on the job with revenue-producing responsibilities.

The large office staffs and the shortage of efficient managers are sources of constant complaint. As a result, an increasing number of companies have followed the trend of downsizing and reengineering to reduce their staffs to efficient 'lean and mean' levels.

Your own experience may well support the obvious conclusion that an organization with many levels in its decision-making process cannot operate with speed. This situation exists because each link in a chain of command carries four drawbacks:

1. Loss of time in getting information back.

2. Loss of time in sending orders forward.

3. Reduction of the top executive's full knowledge of the situation.

4. Reduction of the top executive's personal influence on managers.

Therefore, to make your efforts effective, and if in your power to influence, reduce the chain of command. The fewer the intermediate levels, the more dynamic operations tend to become. The result is improved effectiveness for the total business effort – and increased flexibility.

A more flexible organization can achieve greater market penetration because it has the capacity to adjust to varying circumstances, follow alternative objectives and concentrate at the decisive point. You can enhance organizational flexibility by using a cross-functional strategy team made up of junior and middle managers representing different functional areas of the organization.

To increase the speed of your operations and improve your flexibility, do the following:

1. Reduce the chain of command in your company and increase the pace of communications from the field to the home office.

2. Utilize junior managers for ideas, flexibility and initiatives for identifying and taking advantage of new opportunities.

3. Use your team to tap any cultural diversity that exists in your firm, thereby benefiting from multiple perspectives.

Indirect Approach

The object of the indirect approach is to circumvent the strong points of resistance and concentrate in the markets of opportunity with a competitive advantage built around product, price, promotion and distribution.

Using the indirect approach to your advantage means positioning a product or service based on a two-pronged effort: *customer relationships* and *competitive position*.

CUSTOMER RELATIONSHIPS

As basic as it sounds, bonding with customers remains the controlling factor in positioning. Managers must infuse all company personnel, from salespeople to packers and shippers, with an attitude that strengthens customer relationships.

In particular, where face-to-face contact permits interaction with customers, delve into the processes customers use to conduct business. What are their priority needs? What special problems do they face to remain competitive? Ultimately, the point is to resolve customers' problems with innovative products and services. When you do so, include the resulting products and services in the Business Portfolio (Section 4).

Therefore, as part of the bonding process, get out in the field and talk directly to customers on a regular basis. Such visits include marketing and sales personnel, as well as to senior management and technical individuals.

For instance, companies such as Deere & Co., makers of farm machinery, routinely send out manufacturing and technical personnel to call on customers and track down information about product performance and technical problems. (See details of Deere case in Chapter 3, Business Problem Solver.) Customers often view such contact by non-marketing individuals whose interests center on resolving operational problems as helpful, unobtrusive and non-threatening.

To properly interpret and quantify the intelligence you have gathered from these face-to-face visits, it is wise to verify the findings through formal market research. This process benefits you with benchmarks to measure product performance, customer service, distribution efficiency, pricing strategy and promotion effectiveness. All of which can help to monitor the progress of your SBP.

COMPETITIVE POSITION

Once you activate the customer bonding and the market intelligence procedures, you can use the new benchmarks to determine how your market position compares with that of competitors. The key issues here are the *perceptions* embedded in the customers' minds about your company and its products and how they stack up against those of your competitors.

APPLICATION

To use an indirect approach, do the following:

1. Search for emerging, neglected, or poorly served market segments through competitive analysis and then fill those gaps with products. (SBP Section 4.)

2. Identify a competitive advantage centered on price, product, promotion, or distribution. (SBP Sections 3 and 8.)

3. Use movement, surprise, speed and alternative objectives to surprise, confuse and upset your competitor. (SBP Section 2.)

4. Once you have gained a point of entry, move toward market expansion. (SBP Sections 2, 3, and 4.)

Concentration

Concentration has two uses in business terms.

First, it means directing your resources toward a market or group and fulfilling its specific needs and wants. In modern business practices, concentration is used in target marketing, segmentation and niche selling.

Second, as applied to strategy, concentration means focusing your strengths against the weaknesses of your competitor.

How do you determine the weaknesses of the competitor? You use *competitive analysis* in your strategy development to detect the strength-weakness relationship. Internal analysis – used at both the strategic and tactical level of your SBP – allows you to identify your unique competencies or natural strengths. External analysis allows you to identify your competitor's weaknesses.

APPLICATION

To concentrate in a market, do the following:

1. Use competitive analysis to identify your competitors' weaknesses and your company's strengths.

2. Concentrate on an unserved, poorly served, or emerging segment of the market that you have determined represents growth and, in turn, could help launch you into additional market segments.

3. Introduce a product (or product modification) not already developed by existing competitors in the overall product category.

4. Develop multilevel distribution by private labeling of your product for existing suppliers, concurrent with establishing your own brand. Therefore, if one strategy falters the alternative strategy wins.

5. Follow up by expanding into additional market segments with the appropriate products so you can envelop the entire market category.

Alternate Objectives

There are four central reasons for developing alternative, or multiple objectives in SBP Sections 2 and 7:

1. On a corporate scale, most businesses have to fulfill a variety of long-term and short-term objectives and require various approaches for their attainment. Therefore, a wide range of objectives are needed with a variety of timeframes.

2. As already discussed, the strategy principle of concentration is implemented successfully only by applying alternative objectives.

3. Alternative objectives permit enough flexibility to exploit opportunities as they arise. By designing a number of objectives, you hold options for achieving one objective should others fail.

4. Most important, alternative objectives keep your competitors from detecting your real intentions. By displaying a number of possible threats, you force a competing manager to spread his resources and attention to match your action.

While you have dispersed intentionally in order to gain control, you cause him to disperse erratically, inconveniently and without full knowledge of the situation. Thus, you cause the opposing manager to lose control. You can then concentrate rapidly on the objective that offers the best potential for success.

As noted earlier, since the major incalculable is the human will (the mind of one manager against the mind of a competing manager), the intent of alternative objectives is to unbalance the opposing manager into making mistakes through inaction, distraction, wrong decisions, false moves, or misinterpretation of your real intent. You thereby expose a weakness that you can exploit through concentration of effort. This unbalancing or distraction is achieved through movement and surprise.

APPLICATION

To use alternative objectives, do the following:

1. Consider such areas as customer service, improved delivery time, extended warranties, sales terms, after-sales support, packaging and management training as sources of alternative objectives.

2. Identify alternative niches in the initial stages of attack to cause distraction among your competitors.

3. Exploit your competitors' confusion by concentrating your efforts on the weak spots that represent opportunities.

Unbalancing Competition

While the overriding outputs of your SBP are strategies, its indisputable bottom-line goals translate to outperforming competition, satisfying evolving customers' needs and wants, and sustaining the profitable long-term growth of markets. In that demanding context, how do you unbalance and thereby out-perform competition?

First, victory in many competitive situations is not necessarily due to the brilliance of the attacker, but to the mistakes of the opposing manager. If brilliance plays a roll at all, it is in the manager's deliberate efforts to develop situations that confuse and unbalance the competition. Moreover unbalancing fulfills strategy's ultimate purpose: the reduction of resistance.

One major approach to outperforming competition is to try an unbalancing action. For example, announce a new product that could make the competing manager's product line obsolete. Even a press release about a yet-to-be released product line can 'make them sweat' and create panic – and mistakes.

Most often, this unbalancing is developed in the tactical sections of your SBP and through the day-to-day activities that range from the threat of legal action to the effects of mergers and acquisitions.

APPLICATION

To unbalance competition, do the following:

- Identify the areas in which the competition is not able (or willing) to respond to your actions. (Use the competitor analysis checklists in Part 4 for this purpose.)

- Make a conscious effort to create an unbalancing effect through surprise announcements. For example, tout your new computerized ordering procedures, just-in-time delivery, or technical on-site assistance. The unbalancing effect will have the greatest impact to the extent that you are able to maintain secrecy until the last possible moment.

- Utilize new technology to unbalance competitors and make them scramble to catch up. Investigate the various technologies, such as the software related to supply chain management that would affect speed of delivery from manufacturer to customer, interactive video systems and the Internet to enhance your promotion and distribution strategies.

Strategy Lessons

From these strategy principles, five major lessons stand out:

1. While the applications of strategies and tactics are physical acts, a mental process directs them. The better thought-out your strategy, the more easily you will gain the upper hand, and the less it will cost.

2. The tougher you make your competitive practices, the more your rivals will consolidate against you. Result: You will harden the resistance you are trying to overcome. Even if you succeed in winning the market, you will have fewer resources with which to profit from the victory.

3. The more intent you are in securing a market entirely of your own choosing and terms, the stiffer the obstacles you will raise in your path and the more cause competitors will have to reverse what you have achieved.

4. When you are trying to dislodge your competitor from a strong market position that will be costly to abandon, leave that competitor a quick way to retreat from the market.

5. If you face a situation of transforming your product's image into a new market position, follow these guidelines:

   • Be certain your position is *distinctive* and doesn't create confusion or misinterpretation, so that a competitor is mistakenly identified with your position.

   • Select a position that conforms to your firm's unique, core competencies, so that competitors cannot easily duplicate the differentiating factors for which you can claim *superiority*.

   • Communicate your position in precise terms through product application, sales promotion and advertising. For example, determine what constitutes your position. Do you position your product with a single benefit, such as lowest cost; do you use a double-benefit position of lowest cost and best technical support; or do you select a multi-benefit position of lowest cost, best technical support and state-of-the-art technology?

These benefit positions lay the foundation for developing the tactical sections of your SBP that incorporates the marketing mix. (Sections 7 and 8.)

FIVE: PART 2
Looking at Your Market

2.1 Why Look at Your Market?

The purpose of looking at your market is to uncover opportunities and threats that result in alternative strategies and, ultimately, to competitive advantage. The most comprehensive approach to looking at your market is to concentrate on four market spheres: analyzing customer groups, identifying competitor behavior, viewing the industry and scanning the environment.

2.2 Analyzing Customer Groups

As a business model, a customer-driven firm consists of interacting business activities designed to plan, price, promote and distribute want-satisfying products and services to organizational and household users at a profit.

From this functional definition you can see that the customer is the center of a business's attention – and your entire SBP. To produce want-satisfying products and services, you must know what your customers want, where they can find what they want, and how to communicate to them that you are able to meet their needs and solve their problems.

In both the strategic and tactical sections of the SBP, use the following guidelines as you look at your market:

- **Define your customers by demographic and psychographic (behavioral) characteristics**. Observe changes in the character of your markets. For instance, look for any unmet customer needs that would enable you to respond rapidly in the form of products, services, methods of delivery, credit terms, or technical assistance. Talk with customers to detect their most troublesome problems and frustrations. Meet with sales people and draw them out on ways in which to innovate.

- **Examine customer usage patterns or frequency of purchase**. Watch for alternative and substitute products that could represent an opportunity to replace competitive products. Also observe deviations in regional and seasonal purchase patterns. Check for changes from past purchasing and usage practices that could translate into opportunities.

- **Survey selling practices**. Innovations often occur in selling. Stay tuned-in to current trends in promotional allowances, selling tactics, trade discounts, rebates, point-of-purchase opportunities, or seasonal/holiday requirements. Here, again, stay close to sales people for such information. Encourage them to input all behavioral information about perceptions dealing with your product, delivery, company image, complaint handling, and any other factors that influence a sale and contribute to a long-term relationship.

- **Survey channels of distribution**. Examine your distribution methods and look for opportunities to customize services consistent with the characteristics of the segment. Pay attention to warehousing (if applicable) and what could be fertile possibilities to innovate, such as electronic ordering and computerized inventory control systems. Look, too, at the direct marketing channels pioneered by such companies as Dell Computer and Gateway 2000 and experiment with innovative approaches to integrate the Internet into your distribution channel.

- **Look at product possibilities**. Search for innovations with product line extensions to maintain an ongoing presence in your existing markets or to gain a foothold in an emerging segment. Harnessing new technology might broaden your customer base and leverage your company's expertise.

- **Explore opportunities to cut costs for you and your customers**. Investigate such areas as strengthening quality assurance and introducing new warranties related to product performance and reliability. Also look for possibilities to replace products or systems, improve internal and external operating procedures, and discover new product applications.

To fully benefit from your look at the market, you should familiarize yourself with these components: market and product segments, and customer needs and wants.

Market and Product Segments

Segmentation means splitting the overall market into smaller sub-markets or segments that have more in common with one another than with the total market. Sub-dividing the market helps you to identify and satisfy the specific needs of individuals within your chosen segments and thereby strengthen your market position. Segmentation also allows you to concentrate your strength against the weakness of your competitor and improve your competitive ranking.

Examples abound of companies concentrating on segments: White Rock Corp. products concentrate on smaller segments or niches that have little interest to Coca-Cola or Pepsi Cola; Godiva Chocolates aims at an affluent 'me' generation; Women's Health Centers in various regional locations serve female patients only; Honda Motor Co., Ltd. originally focused on selling high-quality, small motorcycles to an entirely new type of customer, the suburban middle-class male.

Thus, selecting segments depends on a group of variables, including knowledge of *customer needs* and *competitor capabilities*. Grasping the significance of each will add greater precision to selecting viable segments, especially so as you develop your Business Portfolio, Section 4.

CUSTOMER NEEDS AND BEHAVIOR

If you maintain an on-going customer analysis that accurately defines the needs and wants of customer groups and individuals, you satisfy a primary ingredient of successful segmentation. Specifically, analyzing customer needs requires you to:

- **Categorize segments**. Begin by adding structure to your view of the market. This approach allows you to properly allocate financial and sales resources for the greatest impact. For example, categorize your segments by one or more of the following: geographic location, demographics, product attributes, market size, common buying factors, shared distribution channels and any other categories that are unique to your industry.

- **Determine purchase patterns**. Next, analyze purchasing variables so you can develop customized packages of benefits that will increase your chances of success – by segment and key customers. For example, divide customer purchase patterns into two categories: regular use and infrequent special application of your product.

Review how customers perceive your product benefits in terms of *price/value, convenience*, or *prestige* factors. Rank customer loyalty as *non-existent, medium,* or *strong*.

Also examine customer awareness and readiness to buy your product as *unaware, informed, interested,* or *intending to buy*. Finally, evaluate your buyers' by *product quality, delivery, guarantees, technical services,* or *promotional support*.

Choosing Market Segments

With your SBP projecting a market-driven focus, segmentation ranks as an essential part of your analysis. And concentration in one or more segments is the essence of a competitive strategy. Therefore, in doing your own customer analysis in both the strategic and tactical sections of your SBP, you should know which criteria to use in choosing market segments, what factors to use in identifying a market segment, and how to develop a segmentation analysis.

Therefore, segmentation is particularly applicable in developing your portfolio in Section 4 of the plan. Use the following criteria to guide your thinking in selecting market segments:

- **Measurable**. Can you quantify the segment? For example, you should be able to assign a number to how many factories, how many farm acres, or how many people are within the market segment.

- **Accessible**. Do you have access to the market through a dedicated sales-force, distributors, transportation, or warehousing?

- **Substantial**. Is the segment of sufficient size to warrant attention as a segment? Further, is the segment declining, maturing, or growing?

- **Profitable**. Does concentrating on the segment provide sufficient profitability to make it worthwhile? Use your organization's standard measurements for profitability, such as return on investment, gross margin, or profits.

- **Compatible with Competition**. To what extent do your major competitors have an interest in the segment? Is it of active interest or of negligible concern to your competitors?

- **Effectiveness**. Does your organization have sufficient skills and resources to serve the segment effectively?

- **Defendable**. Does your firm have the capabilities to defend itself against the attack of a major competitor?

Answering those questions will help you select a market segment with good potential for concentrating your resources and with sufficient information for customer analysis. Once you have chosen a market segment, then use these criteria to test its viability.

But how do you select a segment? You can identify market segments by dividing a market into groups of customers with common characteristics.

Categories for Segmenting Markets

The four most common ways to segment a market is by demographic, geographic, psychographic (behavioral) and product attributes. Each of these factors, particularly when used in combination with the others, represent an opportunity or identifies a need that can be satisfied with a product. Table 2.1 defines each of the categories.

GEOGRAPHIC

Region, City, Population density, Climate

DEMOGRAPHIC

Age, Family size, Gender, Income, Occupation, Education, Religion, Race, Nationality, Social class

PSYCHOGRAPHIC

Lifestyles, Personality

PRODUCT ATTRIBUTES

Benefits preferred, Buying-readiness status, Usage rate, Loyalty ranking, Attitudes toward product or service

TABLE 2.1: **CATEGORIES FOR SEGMENTING MARKETS**

Let's examine these segmentation categories in greater detail:

GEOGRAPHIC SEGMENTATION

Geographic segmentation is relatively easy to perform because the individual segments can be clearly delineated on a map. It is a sensible strategy to employ when there are distinct differences in climatic conditions or cultural patterns.

Internationally, blocks or clusters of countries can be approached in a similar fashion, particularly if they share the same language and cultural heritage. For instance, in most of Latin America the same advertising media are often appropriate for several countries. While there are numerous cultural differences in many of those countries – as well as in other parts of the world – there are common problems that share several common features, known as *cultural universals*. These include economic systems, marriage and family systems, educational systems, social control systems, and supernatural belief systems.

Domestically, you can segment by region, city size, population density, or by other geopolitical criteria. However, such segmentation is effective only if it reflects differences in need and motivation patterns. Many firms, for example, adjust their advertising efforts to as small an area as a town or city.

DEMOGRAPHIC SEGMENTATION

Along with geographic information, demographic variables are among the longest-used segmentation factors. They owe their popularity to two facts: (1) they are easier to observe and/or measure than most other characteristics and (2) their breakdown is often closely linked to differences in behavioral patterns. Demographic factors include age, sex, family size, stage in the family life-cycle, income, occupation, education, religion, race, nationality and social class.

PSYCHOGRAPHIC SEGMENTATION

This form of segmentation results from the application of psychographic variables, such as life-style, personality, spending behavior and market sensitivity. Banks, car manufacturers and liquor producers, to name a few, employ the advantages of psychographic segmentation. It is a branch of market segmentation that continues to evolve as companies get involved with increasingly sophisticated customer relationship management (CRM) software.

2.3 Determining Patterns of Customer Behavior

A central component of market segmentation deals with patterns of customer behavior. In turn, to connect behavior with practical application raises these questions:

- How is a customer likely to think, behave and make decisions regarding your products and services?

- How can you use that information to reach and attract potential customers?

- What impact does behavior analysis have on customer analysis and, therefore, on the selection of strategies?

It takes diligent research to understand customer behavior and translate the findings into market entry and product development strategies for SBP Section 3, Growth Strategies and Section 8, Strategies and Tactics.

Here are planning guidelines to follow that are particularly applicable to those sections:

- Locate the optimum product/market entry point through a systematic probe of customers' behavior and competitors' positions.

- Maintain growth with a continuous flow of new products, applications and value-added services.

- Quantify existing products by sales, profits, market share, position in the market and any other pertinent criteria that permit you to appraise market performance.

- List new markets in which your existing products can be sold.

- Identify new products that can be sold to existing customers. New products include any new systems you have licensed or private-labeled, as well as modified products with wrap-around services that customers perceive as new.

- List new products for new markets. While this is the riskiest of the steps, it allows you to test emerging segments that have opened up through expanding applications of technology, government regulations, or unique requirements tied to customers' behavior.

UNDERSTANDING THE BEHAVIORAL CYCLE

The problem for the manager is that consumers act rarely, if ever, from a single motive. Rather, multiple and even conflicting motives govern most behavioral acts. For instance, the purchase of a car may be influenced by the motives of prestige, comfort, safety and economy. It is unlikely that all these motives will point to the same choice.

Therefore, consumers have to assign priorities to their motives and decide which ones are more important. Your efforts should be directed to determining your customers' motives and priorities, and then triggering them with your advertising, packaging, and other elements of the marketing mix.

CONSUMER BEHAVIOR

How a consumer behaves toward a product is an attempt to decrease or eliminate tension. As such, a response may take three major directions: The consumer (1) decides to purchase and use your product, (2) determines that he or she needs more information and so begins a search effort, or (3) decides to drop the whole matter and take no action.

Once a purchase has been made, the consumer compares expectations and fulfillment in a process called *feedback*. The outcome of this comparison affects future behavior. A single positive experience produces satisfaction that leads to reinforcement. In turn, continued reinforcement results in the formation of a habit, which is an ideal situation because it means repeat purchase of your product and results in brand loyalty. A negative experience, on the other hand, may wind up in the consumer changing brands, avoiding an entire product category, or creating a negative morale situation.

USING THE BEHAVIOR MODEL

Table 2.2 is helpful in developing the tactical portion of your SBP. It reviews the different factors related to behavior and tells you how to influence consumers in each of these areas. For example, regarding motives, the chart counsels you to investigate how consumers choose the brand they will use, and then to use this information in designing your product and promotion.

FACTOR	WHAT YOU SHOULD DO TO INFLUENCE CONSUMERS
Stimuli	In a competitive environment, test how much attention your stimuli create (e.g., product design, advertising, packaging).
Sensations	Unless you can create sensory impressions, no action is likely to follow. Stimuli must stand out from their environment to be distinguishable.
Needs and predispositions	Look at your product design and/or advertising as you consider the most pressing current need(s) or most positive predispositions.
Perceptions	Ask consumers what your advertising and packaging tell them about your product.
Personality	Consumers try to match personality profiles of the products they buy with their own. Make sure that yours has a clear-cut profile. It cannot be all things to all people.
Social factors	Be aware of current social issues in your advertising.
Image	Unless you can create a positive image for your product, consumers are unlikely to buy. Ask them how they view your product and adjust its image, if necessary.
Information search	Provide informative and persuasive booklets, free for the asking.
Motive	Investigate what ultimately makes consumers choose one product over another. Build this argument into your product and advertising.

FACTOR	WHAT YOU SHOULD DO TO INFLUENCE CONSUMERS
decision-making	Make the decision atmosphere easy and pleasant. For instance, offer financing or other special incentives for making a decision before the specified date.
Behavior	At this point, your product's package is probably the most powerful influence on consumer behavior – the 'silent salesperson' on the store shelf. Make sure that it encourages purchase and consumption.
Goal orientation	Explain how your product gives desired results.
Feedback	Find out who is repurchasing or abandoning your product and why.

TABLE 2.2: **APPLYING THE BEHAVIORAL MODEL**

2.4 Examining Unfilled Wants and Needs

The third component of looking at your market is determining the unfilled wants and needs of various customer segments. This area also impacts SBP Section 2 Objectives, Section 3 Growth Strategy, and Section 4 Business Portfolio. The analysis, however, goes beyond simply identifying these wants. It specifies ways to fulfill them by examining how consumers adopt a new product and how you can communicate your offerings to them.

With the customer as the centerpiece behind market success, consider using the following eight steps of a customer satisfaction program for your own operation:

1. DEFINE CUSTOMER REQUIREMENTS AND EXPECTATIONS

Begin by establishing continuous dialogue through personal customer contact to define their current and future expectations. Then match customer expectations against promises made in the sales presentation. The feedback often falls into such basic areas as orders being shipped complete and on time, and complaints being handled rapidly and to the customer's satisfaction.

2. MAINTAIN A SYSTEM OF CUSTOMER RELATIONSHIP MANAGEMENT

On-going customer contact is a key component of the program. It means assigning permanent customer contact people, such as customer service, sales and technical service to selected customers. Each contact person is then empowered to initiate actions to resolve customers' problems.

Other features of customer relations include toll-free telephone lines and on-line 'expert systems' that connect customers to information on inventory, production, and technical problem-solving assistance. Your overall goal: Achieve a preferred supplier status with 100% conformance to expectations.

3. ADHERE TO CUSTOMER SERVICE STANDARDS

All quality plans, product performance and customer relationships are driven by customers' standards. Most often those standards are measured by the time it takes to handle complaints, the number of on-time shipments compared to previous time periods, and the amount of invoicing errors, freight claims and product returns. Once indexed, the information is forwarded to a steering committee made up of various functional managers for evaluation and action.

4. MAKE THE COMMITMENT TO CUSTOMERS A COMPANY RITUAL

A commitment means guarantees that include: stock orders shipped the same day received, technical service teams sent to customers' locations when needed, specialized training provided to customers' employees, products that conform to data supplied by customers, and a 24-hour 'hot-line' for support services.

5. RESOLVE COMPLAINTS TO ACHIEVE QUALITY-IMPROVEMENT RESULTS

Empower customer-contact personnel to resolve customer problems on the spot. In particular, sales reps should follow-up complaints and make a formal report to a Customer Satisfaction Committee.

6. DETERMINE WHAT CONSTITUTES CUSTOMER SATISFACTION

Develop an index to measure customer satisfaction. With customer feedback as the input, assemble information from various sources, such as: direct customer contact, customer audits, independent surveys, quality assurance cards with shipments, suggestions, inquiries and complaints.

7. CUSTOMER SATISFACTION RESULTS

Circulate the results so that functional managers can design customer satisfaction objectives for the following year.

8. COMPARE CUSTOMER SATISFACTION LEVELS

Contrast your results with those of competitors and with industry standards through formal and informal benchmarking. Then share the results with distributors to help them improve their customer satisfaction ratings.

How Customers Adopt a New Product

Identifying and fulfilling needs and wants with products and services is particularly appropriate in developing SBP Sections 7 and 8.

Table 2.3 offers a fertile list of factors to define areas for differentiation and innovation that you can apply to fulfilling your customers' wants and needs. Once defined and solutions provided, the new innovation must be *communicated* to and *adopted* by the customer.

PRODUCT	PRICE	DISTRIBUTION CHANNELS	PROMOTION
Quality	List price	Direct sales	Advertising
Features	Discounts	force	Customer
Options	Allowances	Manufacturers'	Trade
Style	Payment period	reps	Personal
Brand name	Credit terms	Distributors	selling
Packaging	Financing	Jobbers	Incentives
Sizes		Dealers	Sales aids
Services		Market	Samples
Warranties		coverage	Training
Returns		Warehouse	Sales
Versatility		locations	promotion
Uniqueness		Inventory	Demonstrations
Utility		control systems	Contests
Reliability		Physical	Premiums
Durability		transport	Coupons
Patent			Manuals
protection			Telemarketing
Guarantees			Internet
			Publicity

TABLE 2.3: **SOURCE OF IDEAS FOR DIFFERENTIATION AND INNOVATION**

DIFFUSION AND ADOPTION

When a new product is introduced to the marketplace, two interrelated processes are brought into play: *diffusion* and *adoption*.

Diffusion is the spread of a new idea from your company to its ultimate users or adopters. Adoption, on the other hand, is the decision-making process that prospective users go through after they learn about an innovation. In the final stage of the adoption process the consumer decides whether or not to purchase your new product on a regular basis.

DIFFUSION: COMMUNICATION OF INNOVATION

You initiate diffusion by spreading the word about your new product. But it is only partially under your control because a great deal of it occurs in face-to-face encounters and exchanges between customers, over which you have no direct influence. Thus, it is important to give them every reason to think and speak favorably about your innovation. In this context, it is particularly crucial to understand the nature of innovation and communication.

An *innovation* is an idea perceived as new by customers. This fact has far-reaching implications. First of all, *ideas*, not products, are spread in the diffusion process. Only if you can convince customers to accept the new idea underlying your product will they consider the product itself.

Further, if customers view your new product as being the same as all the others, they will not consider it worth trying. Again, it makes very little difference whether or not your product represents a substantial departure from other products on the market. The only thing that counts is what customers *think* your product is.

What customers perceive is, to a large degree, the outcome of what and how you *communicate* to them. When introducing a new product or service, you must expose your target market to messages that are both informative and persuasive.

ADOPTION: A MULTISTAGE DECISION-MAKING PROCESS

Diffusion of your new idea is a prerequisite for adoption. Only after a customer has learned about the existence, availability and desirability of your innovation can he or she decide about its adoption.

Information and persuasion are passed on from your firm via the mass media and opinion leaders to individual consumers who, in turn, go through several phases of decision-making, as indicated below. Besides that mainstream of information and influence through which consumers first become aware of and interested in your innovation, other sources of communication come into play at different stages of the adoption process.

Therefore, although the diffusion process reaches into every stage of the adoption process by means of communication flow, adoption is essentially an individual matter. In the end, it is the consumer alone who must make the decision after giving due consideration to outside factors.

A consumer adopting your innovation passes through five distinct phases: awareness, interest, evaluation, trial and adoption.

1. **Awareness**. At the awareness stage, product information flows to the customer with no initiative on his part. He receives it passively but experiences little emotional response. His information at this point is incomplete in that he may not be sufficiently informed about your innovation's availability, price and features.

2. **Interest**. As the information received in the awareness stage is absorbed, a customer may say to himself, "That sounds good. Let me find out more about it." Thus, the interest stage is initiated. It represents a 180-degree turnaround from the nonchalance of the awareness phase. The customer is now turned on, at least sufficiently to investigate the matter further. He conducts an active search for more information.

3. **Evaluation**. Having collected as much additional information as possible, the customer examines the evidence and ponders whether or not to try the product. In the evaluation stage, after weighing the pros and cons of a purchase, the prospect solicits the advice of relevant individuals who are trusted personal sources.

4. **Trial**. During the trial stage, a prospect will test your new product, often by purchasing it on a small scale. Since this usually forces consumers to enter a store, it is the salesperson who potentially

becomes the most powerful source of information, sometimes influential even to the point of altering the prospect's original purchasing intention. While many items can be sampled in small quantities, difficulties arise in the case of durable goods that require trial under conditions of normal use, which is all but impossible unless the product is rented or purchased.

5. **Adoption**. When the prospect completes a personal trial of your innovation, he will determine whether or not it has proved to be useful and desirable in a particular situation. If the decision is positive, the customer will adopt – that is, decide to continue using your product. Besides the trial experience, your company and product image as well as his or her social environment will influence this final decision.

Of course, your target market can reject your innovation at any stage. A customer can eliminate your product idea even at the awareness stage as being of no interest. This rejection may well be due to a misunderstanding, if your advertising message was not strong enough.

During the course of his information gathering, the prospect can decide your product is inappropriate or unaffordable. An evaluation of benefits and drawbacks may cause the prospect to reject it as unsatisfactory after the trial period.

APPLICATION

The picture of a customer's reaction to the introduction of your new product is now complete. You can see that potential buyers react differently, though somewhat predictably, in accordance with their psychological and cultural makeup, financial situation and interactive patterns. The spread of new ideas via various communications channels is closely related to individual adoption decisions.

The following guidelines will help you internalize the essential concepts:

1. Conducting a customer analysis will indicate how you can manipulate the information input at each stage of the adoption process. It also shows how you can differentiate between adopter categories, and finally, and most importantly, how the acceptance of your innovation can be speeded up.

2. If your product is truly news, you may even want to think about a press conference with appropriate fringe benefits for the attendees. To trigger adoption in medical circles, for instance, pharmaceuticals

manufacturers frequently encourage an outstanding authority in a particular field (often from a university) to conduct research with a new drug and report his or her findings in a prestigious professional journal. Such a procedure is akin to an independent personal endorsement.

3. While you cannot directly control independent personal sources, you can attempt to either simulate or stimulate personal influence. One approach is to use a highly credible celebrity in your advertising as a substitute for the influence of friends. Stimulating personal influence is the approach that suggests, 'Ask somebody who knows' – namely, a user of your product.

4. Winning over your dealers' sales personnel is a further crucial step in your game plan. You can motivate them to sell your product more aggressively if you conduct a contest, or even pay them a commission. Improving your prospect's own experience with your innovation can provide the ultimate push.

5. It would give a great boost to the adoption of your product if you could identify and persuade likely opinion leaders. Because opinion leadership and mobility are correlated, some firms avail themselves of lists of credit card holders, for example, who have used their cards for travel purposes within the past twelve months, and communicate with them via direct mail.

2.5 Identifying Competitor Behavior

While customer behavior lets you examine how to attract and satisfy customers, competitor behavior gives you a picture of your competitors' positions in the market. Such a view becomes the focus of the entire SBP process. You can use information of that kind to concentrate on competitors' weak spots or differentiate your product line, with the overall aim of creating your own competitive advantage.

You can view competitor analysis from a variety of perspectives: Analyze competitors by (1) how customers select a particular product or choose a company from which they purchase; (2) how competitors segment their market; (3) how customers display their various behavioral purchase patterns; and (4) how competitors develop their strategies against you.

In short, competitor analysis can be categorized by *customer selection, competitor segmentation, behavioral purchase patterns* and *competitor strategies*.

CUSTOMER SELECTION

When you branch into new markets and products, competitors are, in effect, pre-selected for you. By observing purchasing activities of customers, you can identify your competitors and then group them so that you can examine competitors by such factors as product quality, versatility, accuracy, reliability, speed of access to information, cost and types of additional services offered.

Further, there are direct and indirect competitors. Looking to other industries, for example, bankers find their traditional depositor customers are placing their savings in a variety of channels that are now competitors to banks. Some insurance policies have an investment component that serves as a savings vehicle. Brokerage houses, mutual funds consisting of stocks and bonds, and government securities are also competitors of banks.

In other fields, Pepsi and Coke battle between themselves as well as with non-cola drinks. Airlines also have indirect competitors when their customers select teleconferencing and the Internet to transmit detailed information as alternatives to expensive and time-consuming travel. The filtering-down process continues when airport limousines, hotels and restaurants feel the effect of such indirect competition.

COMPETITOR SEGMENTATION

Market segmentation has already been discussed in connection with customer analysis. Now we can examine it from another vantage point: how competitors might segment their markets. Your interest is in knowing the various possibilities through which an existing or new competitor can attack you. In addition, such an examination provides insights from which you can develop a counterstrategy.

You should be aware that in addition to competitors segmenting to protect their own positions against inroads of rivals, they could use a set of common buying factors to attack you. Used singly or in any combination, these factors include:

- Performance, quality, service, delivery and price.
- Measurable characteristics, such as customer size, growth rate and location.

- Common sales and distribution channels.

- Applications of new technology.

BEHAVIORAL PURCHASE PATTERNS

Why do prospects buy from your competitor rather than from you? What are the behavioral patterns most noticeable in customer behavior? What are the trends as they relate to such factors as product, price, promotion, distribution, research and development, service and courtesy of salespeople?

It is to your best advantage, as it relates to competitors, to categorize these trend areas so you can consciously look to the behavioral patterns that cause a prospect to purchase from your competitor rather than from you, or vice versa.

See Part 4 for a Competitive Advantage Checklist to provide a side-by-side analysis of the key factors that affect purchase considerations.

Competitor Strategies

Of the four components of competitor analysis, you should single out competitors' strategies for major emphasis. Other parts of the analysis are subordinate to those strategies your competitors will use against you.

Strategy means mobilizing every human and functional part of a company, then focusing those resources to achieve corporate, divisional, or product-line planning objectives. Therefore, to identify competitor behavior you have to analyze the total competitor organization and compare it with your own.

In realistic terms, however, the extent of the analysis may be the responsibility of a vice-president of marketing, product manager, marketing manager, or sales manager, and focus only on selected competitors within a target segment. The aim of the analysis is to answer the following questions:

- What are the competitors' market objectives as to size, growth, profitability and market share?

- What are the competitors' current strategies?

- How are they performing?

- What are their strengths and weaknesses?

- What actions can be expected from existing and emerging competitors in the future?

Developing a strengths/weaknesses checklist is one format for analysis. (See Part 4.) A second approach is to determine how competitors fit into strategic groups.

2.6 Viewing the Industry

The next part of looking at your market is an industry analysis. It is most applicable as you focus on your firm's strategic direction in SBP Section 1.

An industry is the sum of many parts: sources of supply, existing competitors, emerging competitors, alternative product and service offerings, and various levels of customers from intermediate types such as original equipment manufacturers (OEM) to after-market end users. Within these powerful factors are ranges of influences that also affect an industry.

Conducting an Industry Analysis

A key element in taking a strategic focus to your SBP is recognizing the interacting forces that characterize an industry. It proceeds from the broad *level one* analysis of suppliers, existing competitors, emerging competitors, alternative product offerings, and customers to a finite *level two* listing that can be used as a checklist.

LEVEL ONE ANALYSIS

Suppliers: If a few suppliers in an industry control the flow of materials that result in the control of prices, then a powerful influence is exerted on all the other forces within the industry. Therefore, a review of supplier practices at key stages of the distribution chain will provide you with a clue to future patterns of supplier behavior. In turn, that will push you to develop alternative strategies in SBP Section 3.

Existing Competitors: How do you rate the intensity of competitive actions? Examine the pattern of price wars. Which competitors seem to retaliate first against movements in prices? Review the amount of advertising and identify its themes. Is there a tendency to 'knock the competition' or is a more professional approach used? Is there a warlike environment that is changing the character of the industry?

You can also characterize existing competitors within an industry by answering the following questions:

- How would you rank the commitment of most competitors to the industry? Is there a major, average, or minor commitment?

- How diverse are competitors in shaping their objectives and strategies? Are there some entrepreneurial firms using innovations to increase market share? Are others ready to hold their markets at all costs?

- What are the nature of the products in the industry? Have they reached a commodity status, or is there a tendency toward product differentiation?

- Is the industry plagued with overcapacity or undercapacity? What effect would each condition have on the strategies of competitors?

Emerging Competitors: The entry of new competitors over the last 25 years in many industries – such as steel, automobiles, consumer appliances, textiles, footwear and high technology – has had a jarring effect on the established companies. Some companies have succumbed to the ravages of aggressive competitors. Others have risen to the threat by reinventing their companies through reengineering, downsizing, and imbuing personnel with the spirit to fight back with new skills to develop competitive strategies.

In viewing your industry there may be a tendency to focus only on existing players. The wrenching lesson is that you must identify and analyze emerging competitors with the same intensity of detail as you apply to existing ones. The job is more difficult when applied to emerging competitors because patterns of behavior are not always visible.

Alternative Product Offerings: Using the lessons from competitor analysis, you should give similar emphasis to alternative products or services. It is appropriate in this type of analysis to employ the knowledge of R&D and manufacturing personnel in your organization who are more likely to know about alternate products.

Outside industry specialists from academia, research organizations and other industry consultants are also useful sources of information. The auto industry provides a familiar example of how aluminum is replacing steel and how plastics and other space age materials are increasingly providing an alternative to aluminum.

Customer: Customers are classified at all stages of the buying cycle: from end-use consumers to industrial and commercial buyers as well as to intermediaries such as distributors, wholesalers and retailers. Each stage represents a force within an industry that warrants investigation.

Answering the following questions will provide you with insights about the influences or power of customers:

- Do customers tend to dictate buying terms because of large volume or concentrated purchases?

- Are customers knowledgeable about costs of raw materials and manufacturing, and do they use such information as bargaining power?

- Is there a threat of key customers using backward integration to take over the suppliers' functions?

- Is there sufficient product differentiation or can customers simply switch from one supplier (domestic or foreign) to another?

LEVEL TWO ANALYSIS

Industry analysis continues with Level Two. This aspect of the analysis contains a more detailed breakdown that you can use as a checklist:

- **Current demand for product**: Indicate, in quantitative terms, the demand or usage of your product in sales, units, number of users, share of market, or whatever measurement provides a reliable indication of demand.

- **Future potential for product**: Use a timeframe of 3 to 5 years (the same period covering the strategic sections of your SBP) to forecast the potential for your product and try to use the same unit of measurement as that used for determining current demand.

- **Industry life-cycle**: Identify, even in broad terms, the stage the industry is at in its life-cycle – for example, introduction, growth, maturity, or decline.

- **Emerging technology**: Identify specific technology that is currently available or may be in use even on an experimental basis with competitors. Determine where the technology is coming from and who holds patents or copyrights.

- **Changing customer profiles**: Use segmentation techniques (identified earlier in this Part) to track any emerging changes in demographics, geographics, or psychographics.

- **Frequency of new product introductions**: Monitor the introduction of new products to establish if there is an industry pattern that can serve as a standard for your own level of product development.

- **Level of government regulation**: Determine if government regulation is increasing or declining and assess the impact on your industry.

- **Distribution networks**: Indicate if there are any innovations in the use of distributor channels. For example, is there emphasis on pushing the product through distributors, or pulling the product through the channel by influencing the end user, or perhaps eliminating distributors entirely. Also determine if there is evidence of forward integration in which producers are acquiring distributors.

- **Entry and exit barriers**: Assess the ease or difficulty of entering and exiting an industry. Entry barriers include amount of capital investment needed, extent of economies of scale, access to distribution channels and opportunities for product differentiation. Exit barriers include types and value of fixed assets, length of time needed in market through labor contracts, leases, services and parts provided to customers, and government regulations.

- **Marketing innovation**: Determine if there are innovations involving areas such as electronic ordering systems, computer-driven diagnostic systems, interactive product demonstrations, new promotional incentives, Internet advertising (e-commerce) and sales-force utilization.

- **Cost structures**: Evaluate the impact of economies of scale on costs and profits as they relate to manufacturing, purchasing, R&D, marketing and distribution. Determine specifically the impact on costs of the current movement to automation and its potential impact on your industry.

Summarizing: Industry analysis helps you define many factors in your industry, such as customer profiles, existing and emerging competitors, products and technology.

By giving you a picture of the overall industry from all these vantage points, the analysis lets you look at trends so you can stake out opportunities for growth. Such an analysis benefits you in preparing SBP Sections 1, 4 and 6.

2.7 Scanning the Environment

The final part of looking at your market concerns the environment and its impact on business opportunities. Scanning the environment permits you to look outward within a framework of adding credibility to your SBP Section 1 (Strategic Direction).

Also, the value of looking at environmental influences opens fresh possibilities as you focus on new markets and products in SBP Section 4 (Business Portfolio). The following is a sampling from principle categories:

Conducting an Environmental Analysis

DEMOGRAPHICS

What potential do the following circumstances hold for your SBP?

1. World population is expected to grow from its present level of approximately 6.2 billion. Although much of the population growth will occur within poor countries, there will be potential markets for foods, medicines, machines, clothing, agricultural products and various low-technology products.

2. In some Western countries, environmental issues contribute to the slowdown in the birth rate and the movement to smaller families, as is the increasing number of women working outside the home and improved methods of birth control. Possible areas of growth include convenience items, new types of foods, quantity and styles of clothes, and number of automobiles per family.

ECONOMICS

What potential do the following circumstances hold for your SBP?

1. With the continuing intensity of competition from the Pacific Rim, in particular from the dynamic expansion in China, there is tremendous pressure on firms to stay competitive. Although some countries have experienced a revitalization of manufacturing during the 1990s, many firms still import finished products. Notwithstanding, there is an ongoing trend to reengineer, downsize, and use technology to identify areas of growth through efficiency and innovation. In turn, these trends reflect in new lean and energetic organizations.

2. The various economic cycles have an impact on consumer spending patterns. During downturns in the economy the basics of food, housing and clothing require a good part of household income. During rising economic periods, such products as transportation, medical care and recreation take on an increasing proportion of expenditures. It is especially important to utilize economic forecasting if your business is income-sensitive. With sufficient forewarning, you can take the steps necessary to exploit the economic cycle or to guard against its negative effect on your operation.

NATURAL RESOURCES

What potential do the following circumstances hold for your SBP?

1. Surveys indicate that diminishing supplies of various minerals could pose a serious problem for some industrialized countries; and that the quantities of platinum, gold, zinc and lead are not sufficient to meet demands.

   By the year 2050, several more minerals may be exhausted if the current rate of consumption continues. Diminishing supplies of other resources, such as wood and water, are continuing to pose problems in many areas of the world. While firms that use these resources face cost increases and potential shortages, for other firms there is the exciting prospect of discovering new sources of materials or alternative synthetic products for natural resources.

2. The availability and cost of energy continue to be major factors for the future economic growth around the world. In the meantime, an intensive search continues for alternative forms of energy, with investigations taking place to harness solar, nuclear, wind and other forms of energy. Some firms are searching for ways to make practical products using alternative forms of energy. Among automotive companies, such are the efforts of General Motors, Ford, Toyota and Honda, intensive research is well on the way to market vehicles using hydrogen as fuel.

TECHNOLOGY

What potential do the following circumstances hold for your SBP?

1. The often-quoted statistic that 90% of all the scientists who ever lived are alive today sums up the accelerating pace of technological change. Only in the past few years has technology resulted in a tremendous number of new high-tech products, with audio and video links from workplace to home to other distant locations. New technological advances are changing the way workers are handling their jobs.

2. The United States still leads the world in research and development expenditures, with Japan a close second, and other countries along the Pacific Rim making enormous strides. The United States is reported to have 12,000 academic, government and industrial laboratories. Research continues in such areas as cancer cures, chemical control of mental illness, household robots, new types of nutritional foods, clones and other types of spectacular products. Organizations are forming joint ventures to bolster their research and development capability.

LEGISLATION

What potential do the following circumstances hold for your SBP?

1. Businesses are in various stages of regulation and deregulation. Some of the businesses that have entered into the deregulation phase are airlines, banks, utilities and insurance companies. Yet these, too, are constantly being watched for possible infractions of the law. In general, legislation has a number of purposes: first, to protect companies from one another with respect to competition; second, to protect consumers from unfair business practices; and third, to protect the larger interest of society against unscrupulous business behavior.

2. Within the political and legal environment, the number of public interest groups is increasing. These groups lobby government officials and put pressure on managers to pay more attention to minority rights, senior citizen rights, women's rights and consumer rights in general. They also deal with such areas as cleaning up the environment and protecting natural resources.

CULTURAL VALUES

What potential do the following circumstances hold for your SBP?

1. Cultural values come and go. The three basic components of culture (things, ideas and behavior patterns) undergo additions, deletions, or modifications. Some components die out, new ones are accepted, and existing ones change in some observable way.

2. Society holds a variety of values. Some are classified as primary beliefs and values and tend to be long lasting. These values relate to work, marriage, charity and honesty. They are usually passed on from parents to children and are reinforced within the institutions of schools, houses of worship, businesses and government.

Summarizing: In conducting your environmental analysis, focus on six categories of environmental factors: demographics, economics, natural resources, technology, legislation and cultural values. These guidelines should help you focus on the major environmental events that might affect the overall direction of your SBP.

Looking at Your Company

3.1 Why Look at Your Company?

Developing an insightful SBP is one thing; implementing it is quite another consideration. Looking at the innards of your company enables you to examine its capabilities, as well as your ability to implement the SBP. As you analyze your company's strengths and weaknesses, also match your strong points against those weak spots of competitors, so that you can mount an effective competitive attack.

With this type of precision analysis you can determine what state of readiness your operation is in to win against competition. To get a complete picture of your organization, evaluate it along the following lines:

- **Performance** relates to organizational structure, people, culture, systems, resource utilization, innovation and productivity. It examines the ability to react to aggressive competition, to defend existing markets and to attack new markets.

- **Strategic priorities** concern the long-term effects on strategic direction, commitment to quality, customer orientation and human resource development.

- **Cost analysis** relates to achieving competitive advantage.

- **Portfolio** reviews markets and the strengths of business units in each market.

- **Financial resources** looks at the availability of cash within different competitive scenarios.

- **Strength/weakness** surveys areas of distinctive competencies and types of unique assets.

Let's examine these six factors in greater detail.

3.2 Your Company's Performance

Looking at your company begins with a thorough examination of the organizational structure of your company, division, business unit, or department. It is within that unique structure that business life exists and where the relationships with those of the same level, with superiors, or subordinates interact.

It is also within the organizational unit that the SBP, consisting of product, promotion, pricing and distribution strategies emerge. It is where leadership is exercised, which influences the individual attitudes and collective morale of individuals within the group.

Various schools of thought extol the merits of either a highly structured or loosely run operation. With either form, organizational structure and culture do exist. You need to shape your own company or business unit and then evaluate its effectiveness in supporting your SBP, along with its long-term objectives and strategies.

Organizing a Market-Driven Organization

Organization involves the structuring of various elements to achieve a smooth interplay between people (positions) and the work they perform (activities). These are the two basic elements that you can structure within a company.

Organization by positions is called *structural organization* (or chain of command), while organization by activities is labeled *process organization*. Structural organization identifies the authority and responsibilities associated with each job. Since this job-related package normally changes very little over time, it can be considered static. When converted into a diagram, it takes the form of an organization chart.

In contrast, the main objectives of a process organization are to streamline the accomplishment of specific tasks and to facilitate control over the progress of a project. Thus, it should be clear that the nature of a process organization is dynamic – that is, task-related – and therefore subject to review and possible change.

BASIC ORGANIZATIONAL ALTERNATIVES

The product-market mix of your firm, as well as the competitive situation in the marketplace, may have changed dramatically over the years. Whatever the present structure, it probably warrants review for its resourcefulness, flexibility, efficiency – and ability to compete in a global environment. Only an organization that is fully in tune with the market will realize its potential.

In trying to evolve the optimum organizational setup to achieve competitive advantages, you should examine the four major alternatives open to most firms: *functional organization, geographic organization, product organization and market organization.*

Functional Organization: A functional organization works best for small to medium-size companies. It assigns responsibilities and creates positions to conform to the various functions to be performed, resulting in a horizontal division of labor, which in turn results in specialization.

The basic strength of this approach lies in assigning the ultimate responsibility for a function, such as marketing, with a single individual. Functional organization is the only setup in which there is no duplication or paralleling of functions. Within a functional framework, the responsibility of each manager thus extends to the entire product and market mix.

As a firm grows, however, this kind of functional setup can become unwieldy and cumbersome, unable either to respond quickly or pay proper attention to specific products or markets. Concentration of functional responsibility in one person, initially a virtue, now becomes a drawback.

To avoid dilution of effort, further specialization and more individualized attention to products and markets take priority. If you want to continue to achieve optimum results, duplication of functions is the price that inevitably has to be paid for growth.

Geographic Organization: Some managers choose to organize their market -driven efforts along geographic lines. A geographic subdivision can be organized easily because territorial borderlines are usually drawn along finite boundaries. Also, the sales effort is readily integrated into the marketing effort, since territories are already defined. However, geographic organization doesn't preclude you from defining different forms of buying behavior within a segment.

Product Management Organization: Product management becomes necessary when the complexity of the product mix threatens to overtax the functional system, resulting in a dilution of effort that leaves many products virtually unattended. The advent of product management brings order and focus to this disarray by clearly lodging responsibility for the fate of a specific product or product line with a single individual, ensuring it the attention it requires. This approach fosters individualized marketing programs for each product or product line – and often results in aggressive internal competition for funds and sales-force time.

The main advantage of the product management system is that every product or product line has its own advocate whose personal career is directly dependent on the success or failure of the line administered.

Market Organization: Focusing too strongly on an individual product or line may well detract from the main mission of your firm – namely, to serve the needs of its target customers and those of its existing products. Thus, executives continue to revamp their organizations to become customer-oriented instead of product-driven.

Whatever is lost in product expertise in such a reshaping of orientations is gained in market competence. Each market manager becomes a specialist in the particular needs and problems of a specific group of customers. In many other respects, a market-driven organization is comparable to a product organization: marketing managers also have to develop long-term and annual sales and profit plans and typically do not have their own support systems. As for the smaller firm where there is no individual with a marketing title, then the owner or general manager acts as the chief marketing executive

CHOOSING THE RIGHT SETUP

Given such a range of choices, it is not easy to decide on the optimum solution for your firm. The following guidelines should prove helpful:

- While a company with a small number of product lines can do well with a functional organization, a wide range of lines require product management.

- If your product mix is fairly homogeneous, you can rely on a functional organization, whereas a mixed collection of products warrants product management.

- Highly technical and complex products require product expertise, which is the cornerstone of the product management system.

- Mostly homogeneous markets can be served by a functional or product setup, while heterogeneous markets demand a market organization that responds to their unique needs and buying patterns.

- The size of your firm is another factor. If it is of small or medium size, a functional organization is likely to work well for you. The geographic dispersion of your markets should also be considered. If they are regional, or otherwise fairly concentrated, a product or market setup is a good choice. But if they are dispersed over a large area, you should look into the advantages of a geographic setup.

3.3 Your Company's Strategic Priorities

Your look at the internal workings of your company continues with an examination of how your firm, and in particular how your group, looks at its long-term strategic priorities – as defined in your SBP's strategic direction, objectives, strategies and business portfolio.

The level of market orientation is the focal point from which strategic priorities emerge. For instance, does a customer-driven mentality exist in your organization, or is it just given lip service? How much commitment is given to product quality and long-term market development?

You need to understand what makes your company tick. Success in the market place doesn't just happen. It usually evolves over years of absorbing hard-won skills and nurturing them into competencies to fit the explosive movements in your industry. In turn, they shape your firm's core competencies into strategic priorities.

Consumer-Oriented vs. Product-Oriented Concepts

As you develop your SBP, keep in mind that the consumer or market-oriented concept of marketing is a far cry from the old product-oriented philosophy, whereby the producer developed a product without input from the ultimate buyer and then used promotional pressure to persuade the consumer to buy it. In contrast to this one-way approach, the consumer-oriented concept is cyclical in nature, putting the consumer at the beginning and the end of the marketing process.

The product-oriented concept is shortsighted and usually distorts efforts to develop strategic priorities. It focuses on the needs of the seller and thus leaves a company vulnerable to the inroads of competitors who may be more sensitive to consumer needs and desires. Figure 3.1 contrasts the differences between the two concepts.

Accordingly, market research is a key element in sustaining a consumer-oriented organization. Based on consumer preferences and problems that have been researched, a company can specify with some confidence what features an upcoming product should include.

Instead of trying to create markets for products, you are now attempting to provide products for markets.

The entire thrust of your firm is now aimed at discovering and exploiting market opportunities. This reorientation is accompanied by another remarkable change: *Companies are no longer married to technologies and existing products, but rather to consumers and their evolving wants and problems.*

PRODUCT-ORIENTED	CONSUMER-ORIENTED
Focus on product	Focus on consumer
Emphasis on volume	Emphasis on profit
Insignificant marketing research	Thorough marketing research
Engineering self-guided	Engineering guided by market needs
Primarily interested in production economies	Primarily interested in providing need satisfaction
Aiming for short-term gains	Aiming for long-term relationships
Management engineering-oriented	Management market-oriented

TABLE 3.1: **CHARACTERISTICS OF THE TWO CONCEPTS OF MARKETING**

CHARACTERISTICS AND BENEFITS OF CONSUMER-ORIENTED PLANNING

Following this examination of the primary concepts that make up a consumer-oriented organization, let's take a closer took at its operational characteristics and impact. Table 3.2 highlights ways in which the concept penetrates every facet of your business effort and lists the benefits derived from its application.

By using such a systematic approach, you can pinpoint and improve areas of weakness. You may want to convert the specific action suggestions into a personal checklist.

AREA	ACTION	BENEFIT
Organization	Set up a separate marketing function under a vice-president who reports directly to the company president.	Stresses importance of marketing and puts it on equal footing with other functional areas, such as engineering and production.
Strategic Business Planning (SBP)	Base the SBP on systematic market research.	Keeps corporate effort truly attuned with markets.
	Try to project technological and market trends sufficiently far into the future.	Provides adequate lead-time for developing programs, products and facilities for future markets.
	Set objectives and communicate basic assumptions and objectives.	Creates a common framework for the SBP that becomes clearly goal-oriented.
Control	Institute tight feedback system to check results of the SBP.	Keeps your 'ear to the ground' and enables timely corrective action.
Research on consumer behavior	Investigate consumer wants, needs, desires, problems, habits, views, satisfactions and dissatisfactions.	Establishes necessary communication links to consumers and fine-tunes market strategies.

AREA	ACTION	BENEFIT
Legal aspects	Examine legal ramifications of planned strategies.	Determines legal requirements and framework for your market efforts.
Global marketing	Adjust strategies to specific environments.	Aligns business activities to particular market circumstances and increases chances of success.
Marketing strategy	Identify target markets that are emerging, neglected, or poorly served.	Pinpoints specific needs and wants in order to serve them better which, in turn, breeds loyalty.
Product	Base product specifications on market research.	Keeps product design in line with consumers' needs and problems.
	Make package appealing and distinctive.	Makes packaging a 'silent salesperson' on the shelf easily recognized and remembered.
	Select memorable, meaningful brand name.	
Pricing	Set prices in line with product's market value, as perceived by consumers.	Ensures optimum saleability because product is neither underpriced nor overpriced in consumers' eyes.

AREA	ACTION	BENEFIT
Promotion	Stress benefits that consumer will derive from product instead of glorifying its features.	Gives consumers good, convincing reasons to buy your product over others.
	Position product properly with respect to competition.	Gives product clear-cut profile in consumers' minds.
	Aid your dealers through displays, point-of-purchase materials and generous advertising.	Generates consumer business and dealer loyalty.
Selling	Advise your customers on how they can derive the most profit from your product instead of overloading them with stock.	Makes your salespeople welcome because they bring profits.
	Train your dealers in product knowledge and sales techniques.	Makes knowledgeable dealers do better long-term business.
Distribution	Be selective in choosing distributors, have them fit distribution policy objectives.	Associates your product with the right kind of outlet.
	Give your dealers adequate support in terms of product availability and service.	Gives dealers good reasons to buy from your company.

TABLE 3.2: **THE CONSUMER-ORIENTED BUSINESS CONCEPT AND MARKET BEHAVIOR**

IMPLEMENTING CONSUMER-ORIENTED MARKETING

How can you implement a market-driven concept if your firm is still using the old product-oriented approach? Table 3.3 presents an action program that you can include in your SBP for implementing the consumer-oriented concept. The result column gives information on the benefits of each step in the program.

You can use the table as a checklist for actions performed and benefits to be derived. (In your SMP, you might find it helpful to use the left-hand margin to indicate who will perform the action and the timeframe for its accomplishment.)

STEP	RESULT
1. Find out what your ultimate buyers' like/dislike about your product and the way in which it is marketed.	Provides invaluable assessment of what you are doing right/wrong.
2. Determine which changes and/or new products they would like to see.	Shows how you can protect your business and make more money.
3. Examine the differences that consumers perceive between your product and its better selling competitors, if any.	Enables you to evaluate and, possibly, correct your competitive positioning.
4. Draw up a plan aimed at improving consumer satisfaction and profits.	Setting objectives and aiming to achieve them is the only way to grow systematically.
5. Ensure top-level and full organizational support.	New strategies can only be successful if they enjoy the full support of the entire organization.
6. Initiate appropriate modifications and/or development projects.	Steady flows of tailor-made new products emerge.

STEP	RESULT
7. Test consumer reaction to new product(s).	You 'feel out' probable large-scale reception of your new product and can make final adjustments.
8. Launch new product(s) in market.	Full-scale presentation and availability of your innovation to your target market.
9. Follow up with consumer research to find out whether the changes you instituted paid off.	Feedback permits you to modify current situation and streamline future activities.
10. Keep attuned to evolving trends in the marketplace.	Helps you foresee changes and deal with them early.

TABLE 3.3: **AN ACTION PROGRAM FOR IMPLEMENTING THE CONSUMER-ORIENTED MARKETING CONCEPT**

The action program provides a comprehensive overview and permits further details to validate and support your firm's strategic priorities. Without a vigorous enactment program, the 'good idea' of the consumer-oriented concept, initially greeted with great enthusiasm, becomes too easily diluted, neglected and ultimately abused. It is easy to bask in the self-congratulatory, ivory-tower atmosphere of new product ingenuity and, in the process, forget the most important element – the consumer.

The consumer-oriented concept brings you back to the basics of sensitivity to consumer needs. Periodic reapplication of this action program can provide your company with invaluable survival insurance. That means, tune in to the dynamics of your marketplace because needs and problems change, as do attitudes and habits.

Catering to these changes differentiates your product in a consumer's mind from those of your competitors', thus creating a firm niche for it in the market-place. Failure to recognize or regard these changes could spell disaster for your product and your company.

3.4 Your Company Costs

The third component of looking at your company focuses on costs. If you conduct a cost analysis to maintain a balance of costs and expenditures that are synchronized with your SBP objectives, you don't have to compromise between market share and profitability goals.

Here are practical guidelines, with implications on how to maintain a balance among market share growth, costs and profitability:

1. While large expenditures are required to build market share, it takes less promotional expenditures as a percentage of sales to maintain market share.

2. Look at the criteria you use to evaluate market share. If you serve a segment rather than an overall market, there are implications for costs and profitability. For instance, examine market share based on customer type, region and the type of support provided through on-site technical service, overnight delivery, price contracts, guaranteed product performance, and so on.

3. It is less expensive to defend market share by investing in value-added services and differentiated products than it is to buy-back market share, after being pushed out by competitors.

4. Examine the following components that contribute to increases in market share and determine what actions would impact your cost structure and profitability:

   - **Customer penetration**. What would increase the total number of customers who would buy your product by segment, compared to reaching the overall market?

   - **Customer loyalty**. What would increase the purchase of your product compared to your customers' total purchases from all vendors of the same product?

   - **Customer usage**. How could you raise the quantity of your customers' purchases, compared to the average sized order from competitors?

   - **Price selectivity**. What would determine the profitability of your product at the average price charged, compared to the average price charged by all companies selling the product. (For meaningful comparisons, express all changes as percentages.)

To have a broader decision-base from which to select a strategy, you will need to understand cost from the standpoints of the *experience curve* and *sales forecasting*.

Experience Curve

Understanding the experience curve gives you an added dimension to look at costs as they relate to strategy options in SBP Section 3 (Growth Strategies) and 8 (Strategies and Tactics) for your own company, as well as of your competitors.

Much of the work on the experience curve began in the mid-1960s when the Boston Consulting Group (BCG), and others, conducted thousands of cost studies. The results showed that each time the cumulative volume of a product doubled, the total value-added costs – including administration, sales, marketing and distribution, in addition to manufacturing – fell by a constant and predictable percentage.

Further, the cost of purchased items usually fell as suppliers reduced prices as their costs fell, also due to the experience effect. This relationship between costs and experience is called the *experience curve*.

KEY FACTORS CAUSING THE EXPERIENCE CURVE

Knowing that costs will be reduced by a fixed percentage each time production doubles is only part of the equation. The other parts are in knowing which factors contribute to the experience curve and then consciously incorporating those factors in planning your strategy.

Some of the key factors include l*abor productivity, work methods, production* and *technology efficiency,* and *product design* and *materials.* Let's examine each:

Labor Productivity: Labor productivity goes beyond the factory floor to the white-collar jobs of middle management. During the 1980s and 1990s, there was a widespread trend to downsize and wipe out layers of employees, with the aim of reducing the organization into a 'lean and mean' operation.

In place of permanent workers, contingency or temporary workers were used on an as-needed basis, followed by an expanded use of outsourcing. These actions further reduced labor costs in such areas as employee benefits. Concurrent with the downsizing of organizations, continued productivity encouraged middle managers to become more innovative and entrepreneurial in planning and strategy development.

Work Methods: Paralleling labor productivity was the critical look at the methods workers used to complete a task. Outside consultants used reengineering techniques to examine and make recommendations about such methods. That approach also focused on problem-solving, with teams of workers using techniques from the numerous total quality programs, along with fresh applications of new technology to redesign and simplify work operations. Most importantly, the work methods had an overall effect of bonding with customers to strengthen relationships.

Production and Technology Efficiency: Tremendous progress has been made in factory automation with the use of robots, computer-aided design (CAD), computer-aided manufacturing (CAM), and integrated manufacturing techniques. While some companies faltered initially and did not experience cost reductions, the evidence became clear that such factory automation significantly reduced costs to the point that in many instances the unit cost of manufacturing dropped below that of the most inexpensive Asian labor. Executives at one of IBM's fully automated manufacturing plants claimed that it could produce computer printers at a lower cost and at a higher quality than those it previously purchased from Asian sources.

Product Design and Materials: Greater efficiency through experience is gained when product design and manufacturing work together. Also contributing to efficiency is the use of new space-age materials, such as ceramics, and new lightweight metals and epoxies. However, for an increasing number of companies, the efficiencies may not be realized completely if the trend continues toward separating product design from manufacturing through the shifting of production to overseas locations.

STRATEGY IMPLICATIONS

The implication of the experience curve is that it is prudent to accumulate experience faster than competitors do. One approach to accumulating experience suggests pursuing a first-into-the-market strategy and going for a large share of the market.

Another is to follow-the-leader into a market, assess the mistakes of the leader, and move rapidly to dominate an emerging, neglected, or poorly served market segment. If you can accumulate experience faster than competitors, with the corresponding reductions in costs, then you have the advantage of price flexibility to use as a weapon to attack a competitor's position.

The negative side of this scenario could result in becoming a slave to the experience curve by adopting a production-driven mentality rather than a market-driven orientation. For example, if the production-driven approach prevents responding to such changing consumer patterns as: demanding just-in-time delivery, accepting orders for short-run customized parts, or reacting to competitors' innovations, then the cost efficiencies will have a negative effect in a changing marketplace.

In summary, the marketing strategy implications of the experience curve are:

1. A competitive advantage is possible if you *accumulate greater experience than your competitors*. The resulting cost advantage can be used to plow back investment to achieve additional manufacturing efficiencies to improve products, shore-up the marketing effort, or build market share through lower prices. This advantage also serves to unbalance competitors' expansion moves.

   If your strategy calls for using a low price to buy market share rapidly, then it is essential that your company gains experience as rapidly as possible, certainly faster than your competitors. Further, the push for market share should begin early in the product's life cycle.

2. Within the context of identifying competitor behavior, it is important to examine your competitors' experience curves. It is not a simple task and certainly needs the cooperation of your production, purchasing and financial staff to create examples of different experience curves under a variety of pricing scenarios.

3. Experience curves can be used to forecast costs, which in turn can be used to set prices. However, costs and prices are usually calculated on the basis of a reasonably accurate sales forecast. The major quantitative contribution marketing people can make to these calculations is to provide a reliable sales forecast.

Sales Forecasting

Company sales normally result from the interaction of your company's marketing effort with market opportunities. Add to that any constraints imposed by the competition and the general economic climate. Taking all these contributing factors into account, it is the task of forecasting to furnish a set of alternative sales potentials derived from various market scenarios, along with the probable effect on sales under each condition.

As a manager, you can use these sales potentials as a frame of reference in developing your objectives in SBP Sections 2 and 7, and in assessing your market opportunities in Section 6. Estimating sales also helps in evaluating the payoffs of your business strategies under a variety of conditions. You can then deploy company resources to take full advantage of the opportunities open to you.

A well-managed forecasting program will make projections in time to allow you to alter your SBP, and develop alternative objectives and strategies before a negative situation is too far-gone. Such a program can also provide you with frequent comparisons of actual-to-forecast figures so you can revise your tactics during the forecast period.

FORECASTING TECHNIQUES

Although various computer models are available to do sales forecasts, time and budget restrictions may bar their use. Rather, executives still rely on a set of relatively simple, quick, do-it-yourself techniques that substantially reduce the time and money required in forecasting. There are a number of such forecasting techniques that, along with subjective judgment, add precision to sales estimates. However, it is advisable to use multiple approaches for arriving at estimated sales. If they all yield similar results, you can place great confidence in your figures.

The following non-mathematical forecasting techniques can be roughly subdivided into (1) judgmental methods, involving the opinions of various kinds of experts such as executives, salespeople and informed outsiders, and (2) market surveys using buyer surveys and market tests.

JUDGMENT FROM THE EXTREMES

Judgment from the extremes involves asking for an expert's opinion as to whether or not future sales are likely to be at an extremely high or extremely low level. If the expert's reaction is that neither seems probable, the range between the extremes is successively reduced until an approximate level of expected sales is reached. Resulting in a range rather than a single figure estimate, this approach is appropriate in situations where experts feel incapable of giving one-level forecasts.

GROUP DISCUSSION METHOD

As a quick check on figures arrived at by other methods, the manager frequently feels that a number of specialists should be invited to participate in forecasting.

Most often, the team meets as a committee and comes up with a group estimate through consensus.

This group discussion method has the advantage of merging divergent viewpoints and moderating individual biases. You should, however, guard against the potential disadvantage of one or more individuals dominating the discussion, or offering superficial responses where there is a lack of individual responsibility.

POOLED INDIVIDUAL ESTIMATES METHOD

While the pooled individual estimates method avoids the potential pitfalls of group discussions, it also lacks the benefits of group dynamics. A project leader simply merges separately supplied estimates into a single estimate, without any interplay with or between the participants.

DELPHI TECHNIQUE

An increasingly popular method for forecasting is the Delphi technique, which overcomes the drawbacks of both group discussion and pooled individual estimates methods. In this approach, group members are asked to submit individual estimates and assumptions. These are reviewed by the project leader, revised and fed back to the participants for a second round.

Participants are also informed of the median forecast level that emerged from the previous round. Domination, undue conservatism and argument are eliminated because of the written, rather than oral, procedure and the group members benefit from one another's input. After successive rounds of estimating and feedback, the process ends when a consensus emerges.

JURY OF EXECUTIVE OPINION

As mentioned, the experts consulted in one or more of these methods typically are recruited from one of three pools: executives, salespeople and informed outsiders. A jury of executive opinion is often composed of top-level personnel from various key functions such as sales, production and finance.

The major advantage of this type of source is that forecasts can be arrived at quickly. This advantage is, however, easily outweighed by the disadvantage inherent in involving people in the estimating process whom, in spite of their high rank, are relatively unfamiliar with the forces that shape marketing success.

COMPOSITE OF SALES-FORCE OPINION

The composite of sales-force opinion approach collects product, customer, and/or territorial estimates from individual salespeople in the field. Since they are in constant contact with customers, salespeople should be in a position to predict buying plans and needs. They may even be able to take into account probable competitive activity.

Few companies simply add up their sales-force's estimates to compute the sales forecast. Since sales quotas are frequently based on these estimates, a salesperson will tend to be conservative or pessimistic in estimating sales. This tendency can be partially corrected by rewarding accuracy and distributing company data, industry trends and records, showing the accuracy of past forecasts.

OUTSIDE EXPERTS

When it comes to outside experts, any knowledgeable source could be consulted – for example, trade associations or economists. Market researchers and industry consultants are another valuable resource, together with dealers and distributors. However, it is generally difficult to assess the degree of familiarity with industry conditions and evolving trends by such outsiders. Thus, they should be used with caution and only in a supplementary capacity.

CONSUMER SURVEYS

The judgmental methods just described involve estimates by people who are not themselves the ultimate buyers. Some observers consider this fact a weakness and suggest getting the word directly from 'the horse's mouth'.

Surveys of consumer buying intentions are particularly appropriate when past trends (such as energy consumption) are unlikely to continue or historical data (as for a new product or market) do not exist. This technique works best for major consumer durables and industrial capital expenditures, since these types of buying decisions require a considerable amount of planning and lead time, and the respondents are able to predict their own behavior with reasonable accuracy.

TEST MARKETING

The problem of accuracy can be remedied by using the test-market approach whereby a new product, or a variation in the marketing mix for an established one, is introduced in a limited number of test locations. The entire marketing program that is scheduled on a national basis is put into effect, scaled down to the local level but otherwise identical in every detail, including advertising, pricing, packaging and so forth.

The new marketing effort now has to compete in a real sales environment. Purchases are actual, not hypothetical. If carefully chosen and monitored, test markets provide a significant mini-picture of the full-scale reaction to the planned change. On the basis of actual sales results in the test markets, sales forecasts are simply scaled up by appropriate factors.

METHOD	NATURE	BENEFITS	DRAWBACKS
Judgmental			
Judgment from the extremes	Successive narrowing of high-low range	Range instead of single figure	Depends on individual estimating
Group discussion	Group consensus estimate	Merges divergent views, moderate biases	Domination by one individual, superficiality
Pooled and individual estimates	Averaging of individual estimates	Avoids group discussion pitfalls	Lacks group dynamics
Delphi technique	Successive written rounds of estimating with feedback from other participants	Eliminates domination, conservatism, superficial response	Lacks group dynamics

METHOD	NATURE	BENEFITS	DRAWBACKS
Jury of executive opinion	Top-level committee	Quick	Unfamiliar with market conditions
Composite of sales-force opinion	Adjusted estimates from individual salespeople	Front-line expertise, motivational tool	Bias due to impact on compensation, unfamiliar with economic trends
Outside experts	Merging of outside opinions	No bias due to personal interests	Difficult to assess degree of expertise
Market Surveys			
Consumer surveys	Consumer interviews about buying intentions	Directly from 'the horses mouth'	Hypothetical behavior
Test marketing	Sale in limited number of cities	Actual sales results	Costly, time-consuming, exposed strategy to competitors

TABLE 3.4: **COMPARISON OF NON-MATHEMATICAL FORECASTING METHODS**

3.5 Your Company's Portfolio of Products and Markets

Used in SBP Section 4, your company's business portfolio provides a systematic approach to assessing a competitive position and determining investment levels. In practice, portfolio analysis is used for self-contained organizational units – divisions, strategic business units, departments and product lines – in which you make investment decisions on a market-by-market or product-by-product basis.

Your job is to seek out the information needed for these portfolio approaches and determine which approach suits your business. The results can help in systematically analyzing your situation and in developing competitive strategies.

The following section describes three of the more popular models used in portfolio analysis and which can apply to your business: *BCG Growth-Share Matrix, General Electric Business Screen and the Arthur D. Little Matrix.*

BCG Growth-Share Matrix

With a technique developed by the Boston Consulting Group, this classic model has proven highly useful in assessing a portfolio of businesses or products. BCG Growth Share Matrix (Table 3.5) graphically shows that some products may enjoy a strong position relative to those of competitors, while other products languish in a weaker position.

Also, each product has its own total strategy depending on its position in the matrix. The various circles represent a product. From the positioning of these circles management can determine the following information:

- Sales – represented by the area of the circle.
- Market share – relative to the firm's largest competitor, as shown by the horizontal position.
- Growth rate – relative to the market in which the product competes, as shown by the vertical position.

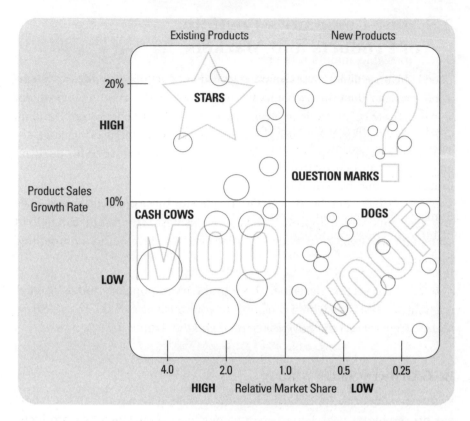

Existing Products   **New Products**

20%

HIGH

STARS

QUESTION MARKS

Product Sales
Growth Rate   10%

CASH COWS   DOGS

LOW

4.0   2.0   1.0   0.5   0.25

HIGH   Relative Market Share   **LOW**

3.5: BCG GROWTH-SHARE MATRIX

In addition, the quadrants of the matrix categorize products into four groups:

1. **Stars**: products that have high market growth and high market share. These products need constant attention to maintain or increase share through active promotion, product improvement and careful pricing strategies.

2. **Cash cows**: products that have low market growth and high market share. Such products usually hold market dominance and generate strong cash flow. The object: retain a strong market presence without large expenditures for promotion and with minimal outlay for R&D. The central idea behind the cash cow is that businesses with a large share of market are more profitable than their smaller-share competitors.

3. **Question marks** (also known as problem children or wildcats): products with potential for high growth in a fast-moving market but with low market share. They absorb large amounts of cash (usually from the cash cows) and are expected to reach the status of a star.

4. **Dogs**: products with low market growth and low market share, reflecting the worst of all situations. A number of alternatives are possible: maintain the product in the line to support the image of being a full-line supplier, eliminate the product from the line, or harvest the product through a slow phasing out.

As you review the growth-share matrix, note on the vertical axis that product sales are separated into high and low quadrants. The 10% growth line is simply an arbitrary rate of growth and represents a middle level. For your particular industry the number could be 5%, 12%, or 15% for example.

Similarly, on the horizontal axis there is a dividing line of relative market share of 1.0 so that positioning your product in the lower left-hand quadrant would indicate high market leadership, and in the lower right-hand quadrant, low market leadership.

The significant interpretations from the matrix are as follows:

- The amount of cash generated increases with relative market share. (This point was borne out in the section covering the experience curve.)

- The amount of sales growth requires proportional cash input to finance the added capacity and market development. If market share is maintained, then cash requirements increase only relative to market growth rate.

- From a manager's point of view, cash input is required to keep up with market growth. Increasing market share usually requires cash to support advertising and sales promotion expenditures, lower prices and other share-building tactics. On the other hand, a decrease in market share may provide cash for use in other product areas.

- In situations where a product moves towards maturity, it is possible to use enough funds to maintain market position and use surplus funds to reinvest in other products that are still growing.

In summary, the BCG Growth-Share Matrix permits you to evaluate where your products and markets are relative to competitors and what Investments are needed relative to such basic strategies as building share for your product, holding share, harvesting and withdrawing from the market.

General Electric Business Screen

The BCG Growth-Share Matrix focuses on cash flow and uses only two variables: growth and market share. The General Electric Business Screen (Table

3.6) on the other hand, is a more comprehensive, multifactor analysis that provides a graphic display of where an existing product fits competitively in relation to a variety of criteria. It also aids in projecting the chances for a new product's success.

The key points in using the GE Business Screen are:

1. **Industry attractiveness** is shown on the vertical axis of the matrix. It is based on rating such factors as market size, market growth rate, profit margin, competitive intensity, cyclicality, seasonality and scale of economies. Each factor is given a weight classifying an industry, market segment, or product as high, medium, or low in overall attractiveness.

2. **Business strength** is shown on the horizontal axis. A weighted rating is made for such factors as relative market share, price competitiveness, product quality, knowledge of customer and market, sales effectiveness and geography. The results show the ability to compete and, in turn, provide insight into developing strategies in relation to competitors.

Three color sectors divide the matrix: green, yellow and red. The green sector has three cells at the upper left and indicates those markets that are favorable in industry attractiveness and business strength. These markets indicate a 'go' to move in aggressively.

The yellow sector includes the diagonal cells stretching from the lower left to upper right. This sector indicates a medium level in overall attractiveness.

The red sector covers the three cells in the lower right. This sector indicates those markets that are low in overall attractiveness.

Arthur D. Little Matrix

Another time-tested portfolio analysis approach is associated with the consulting organization, Arthur D. Little Inc. In one actual application, a major manufacturer in the health care industry used this approach to analyze how its various products stacked up in market share. In Table 3.7, some of the company's products are used to demonstrate the function of this matrix.

First, note the similarities of this format to the other portfolio analysis approaches already discussed. The competitive positions of various products are plotted on the vertical axis according to such factors as *leading, strong, favorable, tenable, weak* and *non-viable*. On the horizontal axis, the maturity levels for the products are designated *embryonic, growth, mature* and *ageing*.

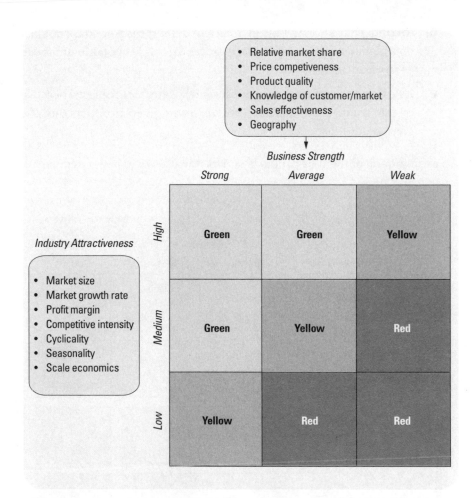

- Relative market share
- Price competiveness
- Product quality
- Knowledge of customer/market
- Sales effectiveness
- Geography

Business Strength

	Strong	Average	Weak
High	Green	Green	Yellow
Medium	Green	Yellow	Red
Low	Yellow	Red	Red

Industry Attractiveness

- Market size
- Market growth rate
- Profit margin
- Competitive intensity
- Cyclicality
- Seasonality
- Scale economics

TABLE 3.6: **GENERAL ELECTRIC BUSINESS SCREEN.**

The key interpretations for this matrix are:

1. **Non-viable**: the lowest possible level of competitive position.

2. **Weak**: characterized by unsatisfactory financial performance but with some opportunity for improvement.

3. **Tenable**: a competitive product position where financial perform-ance is barely satisfactory. These products have a less than average opportunity to improve competitive position.

4. **Favorable**: a competitive position that is better than the survival rate. These products also have a limited range of opportunities for improvement.

5. **Strong:** characterized by an ability to defend market share against competing moves without the sacrifice of acceptable financial performance.

6. **Leading:** incorporates the widest range of strategic options because of the 'competitive distance' between the given products and the competitors' products.

An examination of the four products shows how this matrix worked during a particular period in those products' life-cycle.

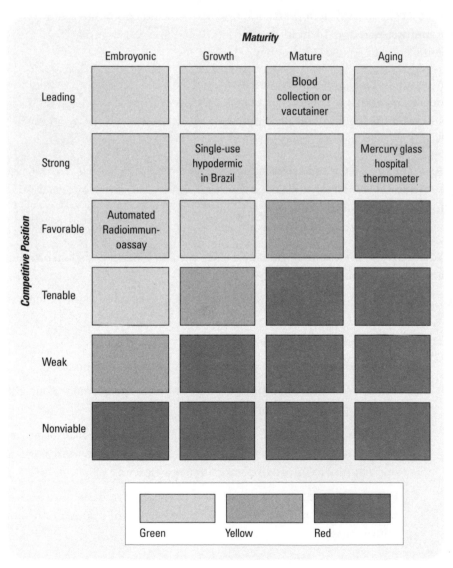

TABLE 3.7: **ARTHUR D. LITTLE MATRIX APPLIED TO PRODUCTS**

Automated radioimmunoassay (a sophisticated diagnostic product used in laboratories) was considered in its embryonic stage with a favorable competitive position at the time the analysis was prepared for the North American market. This favorable position offered the manager a range of strategy options as long as the decisions related to the overall corporate strategy.

Single-use hypodermic needles and syringes had a strong competitive position in a growth industry. Here, too, strategy options were fairly flexible and depended on competitive moves as well as on how quickly increases in market share were desired.

Blood collection system (Vacutainers) had a leading competitive position in a mature industry. To hold existing market share, the company's strategy centered on product differentiation.

Mercury glass hospital thermometers had a strong competitive position in a declining industry. This product had less price flexibility. However, by using service, repackaging and distribution innovations, the company attempted to maintain its strong position before giving in to price reductions.

As in the GE Business Screen, a green-yellow-red system is used to indicate strategic options: Green indicates a wide range of options; yellow signals caution for a limited range of options for selected development; and red warns of peril with options narrowed to those of withdrawal, divestiture and liquidation.

You can use this extremely valuable technique to evaluate your own product and market opportunities.

3.6 Your Company's Financial Resources

Financial analysis is an essential part of looking at your company and is part of SBP Section 9 (Budgets and Controls). It enables you to quantify your strategy decisions. Therefore, this section concentrates on those areas of financial analysis that a manager needs to understand about the internal condition of his or her company.

Specifically, evaluating financial performance is essential to managing your SBP for superior bottom-line results. Use these common measurements to achieve that goal:

- **Current-to-past sales comparisons**. To measure the performance of sales reps and sales territories, generate periodic reports on the quantities of products sold by product line, the profitability of territories and any quantitative data specific to measuring the overall selling efficiency of your operation.

- **Customer satisfaction evaluation**. This measure is vitally important when long-term customer relationships are the strategy of choice. Although a sales representative's likeability remains a factor, a more meaningful evaluation should assess outcomes and interests that are important to the customer. These may include being attentive to problems, overcoming technical obstacles and meeting delivery schedules.

- **Qualitative evaluation of sales representatives**. Use this measure to determine the representative's knowledge of your products, customers, competitors, territory; the economy and any other issues that are important to making a sale. Individual characteristics, such as dress, speech and personality, also become part of the evaluation.

What follows are the broader measurements of a financial analysis.

Financial Analysis

There are several approaches to calculating return on investment (ROI) depending on how 'investment' is defined in your company. The most often used is:

RETURN ON INVESTMENT

$$ROI = \frac{\text{Net Income}}{\text{Investment}} \times 100\%$$

RETURN ON SALES

$$ROS = \frac{\text{Net Income}}{\text{Total Sales}} \times 100\%$$

CASH FLOW

$$CF = (\text{Net Income} + \text{Depreciation}) - (\text{change in plant and equipment})$$
$$- (\text{change in working capital})$$

In some organizations, the term *cash flow* is used to identify cash flow from operations only, and does not include cash flow arising from balance sheet changes, as noted in the equation.

Market Share Analysis

While not used in traditional financial analysis, market share is useful because of its financial implications to ROI. Before a calculation can be made, you need to determine which of the four measures of market share will be used:[5]

- The company's overall market share in sales units or dollars, expressed as a percentage of total industry sales.

- The company's served market, stated as a percentage of the total sales to that market. The served market is a segment that can be reached and served by the company's marketing effort. It is particularly useful if your strategy aims to expand on a segment-by-segment rollout to other geographic regions or customer categories.

---

5 The list is adapted in part from Philip Kotler, *Marketing Management: Analysis, Planning and Control, 9th Edition* (Upper Saddle River, NJ, USA: Prentice-Hall, 1997, p767.) See professor Kotler's book for greater detail.

- The company's market share expressed as a percentage of the combined sales of the three largest competitors. This measure is especially valid when three or four companies command the major share of the market.

- The company's market share simply tracked as a percentage of sales of the leading competitor's sales. This measure is effective when the industry is fragmented with very small competitors and your growth is measured against the dominant competitor.

MARKETING EXPENSE-TO-SALES ANALYSIS

One key financial ratio to watch is marketing expense-to-sales. When you are monitoring different strategies in situations such as either defending market share or aggressively pursuing market share, it becomes a platform for projecting the financial impact of future strategy approaches.

The components of this ratio comprise sales-force-to-sales, advertising-to-sales, sales promotion-to-sales, marketing research-to-sales, and sales administration-to-sales. The ratios can be monitored either through a chart, which graphically shows deviation from budget, or from the more typical periodic budget variance reports.

BREAK-EVEN ANALYSIS

Another key financial consideration is the minimum sales revenue necessary to cover costs. This revenue is the product of two factors: *quantity* and *price*. The quantity factor is crucial here because it represents the number of units that must be sold just to recover costs. This quantity is called the *break-even quantity*.

To get the most out of break-even analysis, your cost accounting system must be able to separate each relevant cost category into its fixed and variable components. On a total cost level, the terms *fixed* and *variable* refer to whether or not the amount varies with the output. A cost item is considered fixed if its total amount is unaffected by the number of units produced – for example, advertising expenditures.

Variable cost, on the other hand, refers to items that are dependent on output. The most obvious examples are direct material and direct labor. These costs can be determined on a per-unit basis. Unlike fixed costs, they are not incurred when there is no production. In marketing, for example, sales-force commissions are an example of a variable cost.

3.7 Your Company's Strengths/Weaknesses

This last component of looking at your company, strengths/weaknesses, is actually an integration of input from both your company and your market analyses and is vitally important to SBP Section 1 (Strategic Direction.) It provides an excellent resource for examining the strengths and weaknesses of your own firm, compared to those of your competitors.

Numerous companies now appraise their strengths/weaknesses and core competencies before entering emerging markets, revitalizing mature markets, developing value-added products, and reacting to shifting customer-buying patterns. The resulting output of new product ideas, product enhancements and applications of technologies, are added to SBP Section 4 (Business Portfolio).

If specific skills are identified as vital to your success, but do not exist internally, you have the justification to locate outside alliances. At this stage, what may appear on the surface as a portfolio of disorganized products without a cohesive base, is in fact a well-ordered group of products built from basic strengths.

One special benefit of building a grouping of various strengths is that you can take a fresh look at so-called mature products – which, in effect, is admitting you've run out of product ideas. Whereas working with core competencies, you can use a building-block approach to bring about continuous product and service improvements.

The strengths/weaknesses analysis questionnaire presented in Chapter 4 consists of 100 questions that serve as a Business Audit (Figure 4.1.) They contribute to the total competitive analysis in two ways:

1. They look at business operations and key environmental factors affecting your company.

2. They assess your company's competencies and strategic capabilities and determine what strategies can be used to increase competitive advantage.

By using the Business Audit, you should be able to identify what makes your company, or division, or product outstanding. It helps you compare your overall distinctive competencies and specific strengths with those of your competitors. Similarly, you also pinpoint the weaknesses that would prevent you from achieving a competitive advantage.

Summary

Essential to developing an effective SBP are six basic components to looking at your company that taken together will give you a reliable picture of your organization.

1. **Performance** helps you evaluate the organization of your company or business unit. Whether you organize by function, geography, product, or market will depend on the size of your firm, your product mix and the character of the market.

2. **Strategic priorities** give you a more focused look at how well you are pursuing a *customer-oriented* strategy that puts the needs and wants of customers first. It highlights the essential lesson that you provide products for markets, rather than attempting to create markets for products as the preferred approach to exploiting profitable market opportunities.

3. **Costs** have two components: First, the experience curve shows you that as cumulative production (or experience with a product) increases, costs decrease. You can assess your experience by looking at labor productivity, work methods, production efficiency, and product design and materials.

    Second, you should engage in *sales forecasting* in order to predict and, therefore, control future levels of sales. Both of these factors give you a way to evaluate and manage costs.

4. **Portfolio** takes place in an organizational unit, such as a division, strategic business unit, or in most small businesses. It helps you assess your competitive position systematically in order to determine investment levels. The three popular portfolio models include the BCG Growth-Share Matrix, General Electric Business Screen and the Arthur D. Little Matrix.

5. **Financial resources** offer a range of quantitative techniques for identifying the financial implications of strategies. The major techniques include return on investment, return on sales, cash flow, market-share analysis, marketing expense-to-sales ratio and break-even analysis.

6. **Strengths/weaknesses** summarizes both the internal and external aspects of your analysis. It examines your strong and weak points in comparison with those of your competitors, so that you can concentrate in areas of the highest potential for market expansion.

Integrating Business Intelligence Into Your SBP

4.1 Why Integrate Business Intelligence Into Your SBP?

You cannot expect to develop a reliable SBP without a workable business intelligence system. Action without information leaves results to chance, as opposed to planning your course and attempting to control the outcome. Strategic business planning and the development of tactics require an effective and efficient information system.

Scores of companies worldwide are discovering that an on-going business intelligence system can turn into a potent strategic weapon. By using information outputs, organizations can better support their basic products, offer new value-added services that distinguish them from their competitors, and create new products and businesses that extend their markets. "In the next 10 to 15 years, collecting outside information is going to be the next frontier", declares management guru Peter Drucker.

Use the following framework for acquiring and organizing business information:

- **Use information from your internal records**. The most basic information should include reports on sales by segment, prices, inventory levels, customer activity and similar records. By analyzing this information, you can spot significant opportunities.

- **Develop a market intelligence system**. While internal records supply results data, a market intelligence system provides in-depth information to aid decision-making in such areas as setting advertising budgets, determining market saturation, assessing competitors' strategies and measuring customer satisfaction.

- **Systematize your approach to pursue business intelligence along four pathways:**

Overall exposure to information from newspapers, trade publications and your sales-force, where there is no special purpose in mind other than keeping current.

Controlled exposure to a clearly identified area of information by talking informally to customers, suppliers, distributors and other outsiders.

Informal research to obtain information for a specific purpose by attending trade shows, reading competitors' published reports, attending their open trade meetings, talking to their former employees, collecting competitors' ads, and so on.

A planned effort to secure specific information. This form of business intelligence is gathered through (a) syndicated-service research firms that supply periodic trade information; (b) custom marketing research firms; (c) specialty-line marketing research firms which sell specialized research service to others; and (d) online services that offer information at a modest cost.

To find new places to grow, utilize as many of the above sources as possible and organize the information into an intelligence system to capture the opportunity.

4.2 Information, Intelligence and Decision-Making

Your SBP must rely on accurate information. Yet, given the highly volatile and sometimes obscure signals from the operating environments, instinct and business intelligence must combine for effective business management. While it is not easy to work through the massive details often accompanying formal market intelligence, the alternative of 'flying by the seat of your pants' is hardly promising.

The purpose of an intelligence system is to improve, not replace decision-making. For example, the intelligence delivered by an information system will guide you in allocating scarce resources in a manner that will optimize profits. For that reason, the cost of acquiring intelligence is justifiable as long as it continues to improve decision-making.

Such a system can accomplish the following:

- Monitor competitors' actions to develop counter-strategies.
- Identify neglected or emerging market segments.
- Identify optimum marketing mixes.
- Assist in decisions to add a product, drop a product, or modify a product.
- Develop more accurate strategic business plans.

The World Wide Web

The rapid developments associated with setting up a business intelligence system are due to the dynamic expansion of the World Wide Web. With it, you can gain access to broad, multi-industry coverage of virtually every major sector of the business world.

You can locate company and industry overviews, management practices, regulatory decisions and executive changes. You can access information on industry trends, market share and size, mergers and acquisitions, new products and technologies, facilities and resources, sales and earnings performance, and R&D activities.

Important, too, is that the World Wide Web provides you with a barometer of popular culture. The databases enhance your search for trends in the following areas:

- Research on ways in which consumer products are marketed to specific ethnic groups.

- Life-style trends and changing attitudes among aging baby boomers about products related to fashion, entertainment, education, cosmetics, food and nutrition, personal fitness and home computing.

- Demographic information about users of various products and services associated with travel, toys, religion, personal finance, automobiles and music.

You can also develop a well-defined set of strategies that combines isolating your competitor's weaknesses and using your core competencies to greater advantage. You can do this by:

- Researching market needs, customer values and technologies that will support your business over the next 3 to 5 years.

- Selecting a favorable position consistent with your capabilities.

- Enhancing products and services to satisfy customers needs and place you in a more favorable position.

What You Can Expect From Your System

No business intelligence system can replace competent and effective line managers, but it can enhance their capabilities, help develop a quality SBP, run business operations more efficiently, and measure performance on a day-to-day basis.

Used properly, a system can track progress toward long-term strategic goals and alert you to significant structural and performance changes in your business as well as relevant environmental developments.

Table 4.1 summarizes what your system can and cannot do for you.

CAN DO	CANNOT DO
1. Track progress toward long-term strategic goals	1. Replace managerial judgment
2. Aid in day-to-day decision-making	2. Provide all the information necessary to make a flawless decision
3. Establish a common language between marketing and 'back office' operations	3. Work successfully without management support
4. Consider the impact of multiple environments on a strategy	4. Work successfully without confidence
5. Automate many labor-intensive processes, thus effecting huge cost savings	5. Work successfully without being adequately maintained and responsive to the user groups
6. Serve as an early warning device for operations or businesses not on target	
7. Help determine how to allocate resources to achieve strategic goals	
8. Deliver information in a timely and useful manner	
9. Help service customers	
10. Enable you to improve overall performance through better planning and control	

TABLE 4.1: **CAPABILITIES AND LIMITATIONS OF A BUSINESS INTELLIGENCE SYSTEM**

Marketing Research vs. A Business Intelligence System

Marketing research provides vital input into a business intelligence system, but it is not a substitute for total business intelligence. At times there can be misunderstanding and legitimate confusion between the two systems. For your purposes and to clearly distinguish for senior management the differences between marketing research and a business intelligence system, see Table 4.2.

MARKETING RESEARCH	BUSINESS INTELLIGENCE SYSTEM
1. Emphasizes handling external information	1. Handles both internal and external data
2. Is concerned with solving problems	2. Is concerned with preventing as well as solving problems
3. Operates in a fragmented, intermittent fashion on a project-to-project basis	3. Operates continuously as a system
4. Tends to focus on past information	4. Tends to be future-oriented
5. Is not always computer-based	5. Is a computer-based process
6. Is one source of information input for a business intelligence system	6. Includes other sub-systems besides marketing research

TABLE 4.2: **DIFFERENCE BETWEEN MARKETING RESEARCH AND A BUSINESS INTELLIGENCE SYSTEM**

4.3 Developing a Competitor Intelligence System

The urgency for acquiring specific competitor intelligence and the magnitude of the search earn it a distinct place in business intelligence. As already stressed, competitor intelligence results in competitive strategies, which is the essential output of your SBP.

Perhaps its importance is best described by the monitoring activities of four global companies overseas. In the 1980s, IBM, RCA, 3M and Corning Glass first set up offices in Japan to monitor competitors' activities and emerging technologies.

Further, to show how feverishly businesses are working to get information on competitors, according to one reliable source upwards of 50,000 electronic bugging devices are now hidden in the offices and meeting rooms of U.S. corporations, with 10,000 more planted every year, usually by rival corporations. In addition, estimates show that corporate spending on electronic surveillance is growing by 30% annually.

Assembling reliable intelligence helps you in the following ways:

You can develop defensive strategies to counter competitive moves. What's more, you can design offensive strategies that move you into new market segments by feeding information to product developers about customer trends and problems.

For example, one mid-size company developed an information system to monitor competition in its various product categories. Their system answers the following questions, which you may wish to modify for your own use:

1.   What are our competitors' current strategies?

2.   How are they performing? (By sales, profits, market share?)

3.   What are their strengths and weaknesses relative to our company?

4.   What action might they take in the future that would affect the company?

The same company's Competitive Information System then attempts to collect the following information about all major competitors:

Competitor's plans	Distribution facilities
Competitor's organization	Pricing strategy
Production strategy	Regulatory strategy
New product development	Major events
Investment strategy	Product-line strategy

Answers to the four questions, combined with the information contained in the above categories, create a profile that will offer insight into likely competitive actions.

Used as a source of competitor analysis, the following step-by-step process leads to effective strategies about:

1. **Competitors' size** – categorized by market share, growth rate and profitability.

2. **Competitors' objectives** – both quantitative (sales, profits, ROI) and non-quantitative (product innovation, market leadership, and international, national and regional distribution).

3. **Competitors' strategies** – analyzed by internal strategies (speed of product innovation, manufacturing capabilities, delivery, marketing expertise) and external strategies (distribution network, field support, market coverage and aggressiveness in defending or building market share).

4. **Competitors' organization** – examined by structure, culture, systems and people.

5. **Competitors' cost structure** – examined by how efficiently they can compete, the ease or difficulty of exiting a market, and their attitudes toward short-term versus long-term profitability.

6. **Competitors' overall strengths and weaknesses** – identified by areas of vulnerability to attack as well as areas of strength that can be bypassed or neutralized.

Finally, the primary lesson you can derive about market intelligence:

There is no reliable way to develop competitive strategies without accumulating and accurately interpreting total business intelligence, with special emphasis dedicated to competitor intelligence.

Responsibility for the competitor intelligence model generally sits with the IT manager, the chief marketing executive, and ultimately with any executive in charge of devising competitive strategies. In order to understand the flow of data, you need to examine the following intelligence-gathering procedure.

COLLECTING FIELD DATA

The sales-force represents one of the most valuable sources of competitor intelligence. When salespeople are trained to observe key events and oriented to believe their input fits into the competitive strategy process, these men and women are first-line reporters of competitors' actions.

Communications with salespeople can be maintained by periodically traveling with them, by conducting formal debriefing sessions to gain detailed insights behind the competitor actions, and by creating or expanding a section of the sales-force call reports to record key competitor information.

Another valuable source is the use of reverse engineering. That is, technical people and other product developers tear down a product and examine its components for methods of production, quality and other details. Then a purchasing agent and financial analyst calculate the costs of duplicating the product in order to provide insights into the competitors' operations.

COLLECTING PUBLISHED DATA

There are numerous sources of published information, from small-town newspapers, in which a competitor's presence makes front-page headlines, to large-city or national newspapers and magazines that provide financial and product information about competitors. Monitoring recruitment ads in print and over the Internet provide clues to the types of personnel and skills being sought.

Also, speeches by senior management of competing companies provide valuable insights into other firms' future plans, industry trends and strategies under consideration. At times it is astonishing how much sensitive information is leaked in speeches at trade shows and professional meetings, and that subsequently get into print.

ASSEMBLING THE DATA

Using tailored forms, individuals attending such key events as trade shows can observe and report accurately on competitors' activities, pricing, new products, or special promotions.

CATALOGING THE DATA

The varied sources of data come together at this point in the system. Depending on the facilities available to you, the data should be organized and maintained by a secretary or, more appropriately, by a marketing analyst, manager of marketing intelligence, or IT manager.

SUMMARY ANALYSIS

The first four procedures are mechanical ways of collecting, compiling and cataloging data. The analytical and creative aspects now apply as you begin to synthesize the data to detect opportunities. It is appropriate to call in key functional managers from finance, manufacturing and product development to assist in the analysis.

COMMUNICATIONS

There are various approaches to communicate the synthesized information: oral reports at weekly staff meetings and the increasingly popular competitor newsletter in the form of print or by e-mail.

COMPETITOR ANALYSIS FOR STRATEGY FORMULATION

As has been mentioned elsewhere, the whole purpose of looking at your market, your company and establishing a competitor intelligence system, is to develop competitive strategies and improve the quality of your SBP.

4.4 Application of the Competitor and Business Intelligence Systems

Your specific job in applying competitor intelligence is to provide accurate information about your competitors' strengths and weaknesses. The overall aims: attack areas of competitors' weaknesses, unbalance the competing managers into making mistakes, and generally weaken their resistance to withstand your efforts.

As in so many encounters in an unrelenting competitive marketplace, it may not be your brilliance that wins the day; rather, it is the errors in judgment made by your opponent. As an outcome of diligently gathering and applying intelligence, therefore, you gain your objectives without costly market confrontations that otherwise would consume resources with little or no gain.

Above all, when going outside your prime markets, use Competitive Intelligence (CI) to determine your opponents' strategies.

Take into account the following criteria:

- CI must be **accurate**. Critical decisions affecting expenditures of money, human resources and time are at stake.

- CI must be **timely**. Events have time-cycles. Past a certain point, an opportunity may not occur again – or, competitors may seize the opportunity.

- CI must be **usable**. Data without application becomes irrelevant.

- CI must be **understandable**. Information that cannot be interpreted with relative ease by the average manager and then applied to developing strategies and tactics, is nearly useless.

- CI should be **meaningful**. If it cannot be translated into scenarios that offer strategy options, it's just nice-to-know information.

While it is in your best interest to become the driving force behind installing a business intelligence system, your most important role is to know where to apply the information. For instance, looking to such key issues as withdrawing from an existing market or expanding into a new market can be viewed through (1) market segmentation analysis, (2) product life-cycle analysis, and (3) new product development.

For *market segmentation analysis,* business intelligence systems can be used to:

- Identify segments as demographic, geographic and psychographic (lifestyle); as well as by product attributes, usage rates and buyer behavior.

- Determine common buying factors within segments.

- Monitor segments by measurable characteristics – for example, customer size, growth rate and location.

- Assess potential new segments by common sales and distribution channels.

- Evaluate segments to protect your position against competitor inroads.

- Determine the optimum marketing mix for protecting or attacking segments.

At the introduction stage of a product life-cycle analysis, system output can be used to:

- Determine if the product is reaching the intended audience segment and what the initial customer reactions are to the offering.

- Analyze the marketing mix and its various components for possible modifications – for example, product performance, backup service and additional warranties.

- Monitor for initial product positioning to prospects – that is, to determine if customer perceptions match intended product performance.

- Identify possible points of entry by competitors in such areas as emerging or poorly served segments, product or packaging innovations, aggressive pricing, innovative promotions, distribution incentives and add-on services.

- Evaluate distribution channels for market coverage, shipping schedules, customer service, effective communications and technical support.

- Compare initial financial results to budget.

At the growth stage, system output can be used to:

- Analyze product purchases by market segment.

- Identify emerging market segments and any new product applications.

- Conduct a competitor analysis and determine counter strategies by type of competitor.

- Adjust the marketing mix to emphasize specific components; for example, change product positioning by shifting from a pull-through advertising strategy directed to end users, to a push advertising program aimed at distributors.

- Decide on use of penetration pricing to protect specific market segments.

- Provide new incentives for the sales-force.

- Monitor financial results against plan.

- Provide feedback on product usage and performance information to R&D, manufacturing and technical service for use in developing product life-cycle extension strategies.

At the maturity stage, system output can be used to:

- Evaluate differentiation possibilities to avoid facing a commodity type situation.

- Determine how, when and where to execute product life-cycle extension strategies – for example, finding new applications for the product to locating new market segments.

- Expand product usage among existing market segments or find new users for the product's basic materials.

- Determine potential for product-line extensions.

- Continue to monitor threats at market segments on a competitor-by-competitor basis; then use competitor intelligence to develop strategies to protect market share.

- Evaluate financial performance, in particular profitability (if all went well you should be in a cash cow stage of the cycle).

At the decline stage, the business intelligence system can be used to:

- Evaluate options such as focusing on a specific market niche, expanding the market, forming joint ventures with manufacturers or distributors, and locating export opportunities.

- Determine where to prune the product line to obtain the best profitability.

- Monitor financial performance as a means of fine-tuning parts of the marketing mix.

- Identify additional spin-off opportunities through product applications, service, or distribution networks that could create a new product life-cycle.

For *new product development*, business intelligence output can be used as a preliminary screening device to:

- Identify potential market segments as an idea generator for new product development.

- Determine the marketability of the product.

- Assess the extent of competitors' presence by specific market segments.

- Develop a product introduction strategy from test market to rollout.

- Develop financial performance.

Applying Marketing Research to Your SBP

5.1 Why Apply Marketing Research to Your SBP?

When you use business intelligence to plan competitive strategies, marketing research provides the primary input to reduce the risks inherent in decision-making. Such research is invaluable during every phase of the planning process, from the onset of a new product or service idea through the stages of its evolution and market life, and, finally, to the decision to discontinue the product or service.

Marketing research acts as the primary tool for bridging the communications gap that enables managers to stay in touch with their markets. Better and more successful strategy decisions can be made when based on facts rather than hunches. These facts are the output of marketing research, which act as a listening post between your company and the customer.

> *Marketing research is the mechanism to improve the effectiveness of your business decisions by furnishing accurate information about consumer needs or problems through which you can base your recommendations.*

Further, marketing research is the systematic gathering, processing and analyzing of relevant data to develop your firm's long-term and short-term objectives in SBP Sections 2 and 7. It also aids in pinpointing potential market opportunities in Section 6. Ideally, your research efforts should be *systematic, comprehensive* and *objective*.

They should be systematic because an unplanned undertaking cannot be interpreted quantitatively. They should be comprehensive because having only some of the truth can be misleading. And they should be objective because research is worthless if it is not reproducible and aimed at discovering the truth.

To justify the expenditure of time and money, consider the following benefits of market research. You can:

- Single out market segments for growth and expansion, as well as protect an existing market position against competitors' inroads.
- Shift emphasis in your product, price, promotion and distribution mix to target special groups of buyers with greater precision.
- Generate reliable customer feedback so product developers can coordinate their efforts to improve a product's usage, performance and reliability.
- Avoid the threat of your product facing an indistinguishable commodity situation by accurately defining differentiation strategies.
- Suggest meaningful options for growth as you evaluate market data and seek out viable export markets.
- Target poorly served customer niches as fresh opportunities to accumulate incremental sales.
- Reverse a sales decline, polish a tarnished product image, or re-establish customer relationships.

5.2 Marketing Research Guidelines

You can obtain the data needed for marketing research either by generating your own (primary data), or by turning to existing information (secondary data). Initially, you should avoid a primary research study for reasons of time and cost. Instead, many market-related questions can be answered satisfactorily by utilizing secondary data. Only if this avenue proves inadequate should you consider primary research. Let's examine each approach.

5.3 Generating Primary Data

If you come up with 'what if' questions, secondary data are no longer useful. They cannot address the issues of new product information, reactions to advertising, the impact of alternative pricing approaches, or the effect of a package change, among others. It then becomes unavoidable to generate your own data for the specific research purpose at hand.

You have three major methods at your disposal that has been refined to a high degree of sophistication: *experimentation, observation* and *interviewing.*

Experimentation

Experimental research aims to discover the impact on changes of two variables that, in turn, can help you optimize your marketing mix. It involves the creation of artificial situations in which all variables except the one to be tested are kept constant.

The one experimental variable is deliberately manipulated to test its effect on the outcome, usually measured in terms of sales. An example of an experiment is a test-market setup in which different prices are charged for the same product in different cities to test the direct effect of price on sales.

To be meaningful, experimentation requires controlled situations, either in the field or in a laboratory-type setting. If influences from uncontrollable variables are found (for example, dealer display), the data can be adjusted accordingly.

To ensure the reliability of the experimental research, it is always advisable to employ *control groups,* in which no changes are introduced. For best results, experiment must be designed and tailored to meet the specific needs of your project.

Observation

Should you want to know the reactions of consumers to your product, packaging, advertising, or some other aspect of your marketing mix, observation can supply the input. Researchers and marketing managers would personally watch a test to get a firsthand look at the consumer's reaction to an intended change before implementing it on a large-scale.

Observation involves recording the behavior of people. Sometimes it is done without the knowledge or consent of the subjects, thereby allowing them to behave naturally.

The content of an observation can be recorded either by a person or by an electronic device. For example, you could personally observe the behavior displayed by consumers in selecting toys. In contrast, a surveillance camera and lie detector are examples of electronic devices used to record consumer reactions.

Auditing and visual assessment, often referred to as 'looking' research, is another kind of observation. By generating a count of the merchandise most recently moved through the nation's supermarkets, observation research gives you a capsule overview of the competitive framework for your product at a particular point in time. Much of the merchandise count is now computerized, along with valuable data gathered through bar-coding technology.

As in experimentation, observation can be carried out either in the marketplace (traffic counts) or in a laboratory setting (eye movement studies applied to advertising and packaging). Whatever the circumstances, use observation to find out what people do. Its big limitation is, of course, that it cannot tell you why they do what they do.

Interviewing

Interviewing is asking questions of selected respondents who might possess valuable insights and would represent the group under investigation. Such survey research can be conducted formally or informally, structured or unstructured, and disguised.

If informal, the results cannot be extended to the underlying population, if structured, a formal questionnaire is used, and if disguised, the true purpose of the research is concealed from the interviewee. An example of an informal questioning technique is the focus group interview, while a mail questionnaire is a formal technique.

Interview research that you conduct can extend over a period of time to monitor changes in your competitive environment. Or it can provide a one-time snapshot of your market highlighting, for instance, the impact of a particular advertising campaign. As with the other two methods, you can interview either in the field (in shopping malls, offices, or homes) or in the laboratory (inviting selected consumers into a research facility).

A key rule in interviewing is to ask only necessary questions, because every additional question takes time and increases the risk of consumer refusal. You should, therefore, refrain from asking questions that interest you personally but contribute little to the understanding of the subject at hand.

THREE APPROACHES

Depending on the nature of your research task, the amount of money and time available, and the accessibility of the target group to be surveyed, conclusive interview research may take one of three forms:

1. In-person interview: Interviewer questions the respondent face to face (a) in the privacy of the interviewee's home or office, or (b) in a central location by intercepting the consumer in a shopping mall or on the street.

2. Telephone interview: Interviewer conducts the survey over the telephone (a) in a local market, or (b) nationwide over telephone lines.

3. Mail interview: A survey questionnaire is mailed to selected respondents and returned by mail.

In choosing one approach over another, look not only at your budget and timeframe, but also the likely rate of response and response bias. The rate of response is the ratio of those who respond to the total number of people contacted.

Response bias, on the other hand, is the distortion inherent in the answers given, due to misinterpretation of the questions or deliberate misrepresentation. You will want to keep the rate of return as high, and the response bias as low, as the constraints of time and budget will allow.

Table 5.1 represents a comparison of the three interviewing techniques on the basis of a variety of criteria. It is designed to assist you in examining their relative merits and choosing the approach best suited to your particular research objectives.

	IN PERSON	TELEPHONE	MAIL
Flexibility in data collection	Most flexible; can use visual aids, depth probes, various rating-scales; can even alter direction of interview while still in progress	Fairly flexible, although visual aids and extensive rating-scales cannot be used	Least flexible, but pictures and rating-scales that do not require investigator assistance may be incorporated into a questionnaire; too many open-minded questions reduce response rate
Quality of data obtainable	Fairly extensive data may be obtained, subject to respondent-investigator rapport	Generally limited by short duration of interview	Long questionnaire adversely affects response rate and is not recommended
Speed of data collection	Process of personally contacting respondents is time-consuming	Data available almost instantaneously; ideal for ad-recall and similar studies	Delays result from slow and scattered returns
Expense of data collection	Generally most expensive	Less expensive than in-person interview	Least expensive, depending on return rate
Investigator bias	Respondent-investigator interaction may significantly modify responses	Investigator bias, while present, is less serious than with in-person interview	No investigator bias
Lead time for respondents	Need to respond quickly to questions may result in incomplete or inaccurate data	Same problem as with in-person interviews	Respondents have time to think things over and do calculations to provide more detailed and accurate information

	IN PERSON	TELEPHONE	MAIL
Sampling considerations	In-person interviews require detailed addresses of all respondents; problem may sometimes be overcome by using area and systematic sampling procedures	Problems resulting from imperfections in telephone directory may be controlled to some extent by using 'random digit dialing' or other computerized procedures	Mailing list is required; samples generated from unreliable lists introduce substantial selection bias
Non-response bias	Refusal rate is generally somewhat higher than with telephone interviews	Callbacks can reduce non-response bias and are fairly inexpensive	Non-response bias could be very serious in cases where those who return the questionnaire differ substantially from those who do not
Sequence bias	No serious problem; investigator can record any changes respondents make to previous questions as interview progresses	Same problem as with in-person interviews	Respondents can see entire questionnaire and modify their responses to individual questions
Anonymity of responses	In-person, eye-to-eye contact may stifle frank interchange on sensitive issues	Obtaining frank responses is a problem, although less so than in in-person interview situations	Frank responses on sensitive issues can be obtained by guaranteeing anonymity
Identity of respondents	Easily available for future reference	Name and telephone number are available for future reference	May not be available in many cases; questionnaire may even have been filled out by someone other than intended respondent

	IN PERSON	TELEPHONE	MAIL
Field control	Difficult and expensive	Centralized control is no problem; better-quality data result	Generally not a problem
Difficulty of reaching certain segments of population	The very rich are hard to reach, and investigators dodge very poor areas; most working men and women cannot be reached during normal working hours	Non-telephone-owning households cannot be reached; most working men and women are unavailable unless interviews are conducted in the evening and at weekends	Individuals with a low literacy level cannot be reached
Geographic coverage	Generally limited by cost considerations	Telephone facilities permit wide coverage at reasonable cost	Geographic coverage is no problem
Investigator assistance	Easily available to explain instructions, provide help with unfamiliar terms and research procedures	Available, although not to the same extent as in in-person interviews	Not available; instructions may be misinterpreted; incomplete answers or blanks are fairly common

TABLE 5: **COMPARISON OF RELATIVE STRENGTHS AND WEAKNESSES OF THE THREE PRINCIPAL INTERVIEWING TECHNIQUES**

IN-PERSON INTERVIEWING

In-person interviewing produces not only a relatively high rate of response, but also an unusually high proportion of usable responses. It is the most flexible of the techniques. For instance, it can respond spontaneously to the unique conditions of each interview and also incorporate a variety of visual cues such as environmental situations, facial expressions, gestures and body language.

Also, it allows for follow-up questions to clarify and specify answers given. Once a respondent agrees to interview in this mode, a considerable amount of time can be spent and extensive information obtained. However, in-person interviews are the most expensive questioning technique and can be rather time-consuming to complete because they involve travel.

All things considered, in-person interviewing is, in most instances, the best research method because it combines flexibility with depth and visual monitoring.

TELEPHONE QUERIES

With the proliferation of telephones in most households within industrialized regions, lack of accessibility is not a serious problem. Phone interviewing is the least time-consuming of the three questioning techniques. You can survey a relatively large number of people within a short period of time. This makes the telephone query particularly suitable for measuring customer reaction to your product and that of a competitor.

With telephone interviewing, the response rate is good and callbacks are easy. Also, travel is eliminated and interviewer bias is reduced. However, you cannot ask intricate or intimate questions over the phone without the risk of people hanging up on you, and you have to be watchful of the time of day calls are made, particularly in areas where all adult members of the household work outside the home.

All things considered, because of ease of administration, speed of response, flexibility and wide coverage, phone interviews still remain popular among researchers.

MAIL SURVEYS

Although it is the slowest technique, and the most susceptible to internal questionnaire bias, mail survey research offers one of the most cost-effective methods available. It has the great advantage of generating input from many people at relatively little cost. No interviewing staff is required, and no training or travel expenses are incurred.

Probably the most serious problem with mail surveys is motivating people to fill out the questionnaires. If the response rate is less than 20%, it will raise questions about how truly representative your results are with respect to the underlying population. Since respondents tend to differ from non-respondents, you cannot remedy the situation simply by increasing the size of your sample.

To increase your response rate, you should follow up your original sample by sending them another copy of your questionnaire with a different cover letter. You can also provide a modest financial incentive. These actions tend to increase returns significantly.

In spite of some handicaps, mail surveys are widely used because they can reach thousands of participants at a reasonable cost, offer wide geographic coverage, and can address issues that would otherwise be too sensitive.

5.4 Focus Groups

Focus group interviews are a flexible, versatile and powerful tool for the decision -maker. These interviews can furnish valuable information on a variety of competitive and market problems in a short span of time and at a nominal cost. But you have to keep in mind their limitations. Focus groups are a *qualitative* research technique and should not be a device for head counting.

The results of focus group interviews cannot be projected to your target market at large. They may not even be representative and, certainly, cannot replace the quantitative research that will supply you with the necessary numbers.

Yet the interviews can improve the quality of your quantitative research significantly. When there is no time for a well-planned formal project, you can call upon this technique to supply factual and perceptual input for making reasoned decisions, which otherwise would have to rely exclusively on executive speculation.

Focus group interviewing involves the simultaneous interviewing of a group of individuals – physicians, homemakers, engineers, purchasing agents, or any other group of potential buyers or specifiers representative of your market. A session is usually conducted as a casual roundtable discussion with six to ten participants. Fewer than six poses the danger of participants feeling inhibited. More than ten could result in some members not being heard. The idea, of course, is to get input from everybody.

Although the length of a focus group interview varies, an average session lasts about two hours. Traveling within your market area, you can collect a good geographic cross-section of opinions within a relatively short period of time. Thus, focus groups offer a quick and relatively inexpensive research technique.

Use focus group interviews to:

- Diagnose your competitor's strengths and weaknesses.
- Spot the source of marketing problems.
- Spark new product lines.
- Develop questionnaires for quantitative research.
- Find new uses for your products.
- Identify new advertising or packaging themes.
- Test alternative marketing approaches.
- Streamline your product's positioning.
- Utilize the Internet more effectively.

The key figure in a focus group interview is the moderator who introduces the subject and keeps the discussion on the pre-determined topic. The moderator could be you or someone employed by an outside marketing research firm. The job of moderator is not an easy one and much preparation is necessary, but the information obtained can be substantial and well worth the effort.

The focus group interview does not follow a strict question-and-answer format. Rather, questions presented by the moderator serve essentially as catalysts for effective group discussion. Typically, answers point out areas that merit deeper probing by the moderator through ad-lib questioning.

A successful session leads to thoughts and ideas that were not anticipated. Consequently, it is crucial that the moderator create an atmosphere conducive to spontaneity and candor. This format allows for flexibility and enables the moderator to pursue leads suggested by participants.

5.5 Image Research

The consumer and the industrial purchaser buy an image as well as a product or service.

> *An image is the complex of attitudes, beliefs, opinions and experiences that makes up an individual's total impression of a product, service, or organization.*

An image represents a 'personality' with which the prospective buyer either can or cannot identify. How your company, product line, or service is perceived in the marketplace should take center stage in your SBP priorities. Toward this end, you should conduct image research.

Developing an Image

An image evolves from a multitude of factors. It can be outcomes of a company's own efforts as well as those of its competitors. It can result from the choice of company or brand name, the symbolism used, or any other part of the entire promotional effort, including product design, pricing and distribution. The symbolism may include logos, slogans, jingles, colors, shapes, or packaging.

Therefore, if you want to strategically shape your product's image, Table 5.4 offers some useful insights and guidelines. It presents a dozen image ingredients that are under your control and briefly highlights their respective roles in determining your product's overall image.

CONTROLLABLE IMAGE INGREDIENTS	WHAT THEY CAN DO
Design	Provides esthetic appeal
Color	Sets a mood
Shape	Generates recognizability
Package	Connotes value
Name	Expresses central idea
Slogan, jingle, logo	Create memorability
Advertising, personal selling	Communicate benefits
Sales promotion	Stimulates interest
Price	Suggest quality
Channels of distribution	Determine prestige
Warranty	Establishes believability
Service	Substantiates product support

TABLE 5.4: **MARKETING MIX AND PRODUCT IMAGE**

Researching an Image

In view of their largely emotional nature, images are best researched by using projective techniques that present the respondents with a stimulus (such as a cartoon character) and ask them to interpret it. While ostensibly talking about this stimulus, the interviewees will unknowingly project their own feelings into the interpretation, thus revealing a true image that could not be obtained by straightforward questioning.

The three projective techniques most frequently used in marketing research are *sentence completion, word association* and *picture association*.

SENTENCE COMPLETION

This test is made up of 10 to 20 sentence fragments that give only a partial direction of thought and encourage the respondents to complete the sentences in any way they think appropriate. The statements should be balanced with respect to personal ('I think CitiBank is…') and neutral ('Colgate toothpaste is…') direction.

An equal balance should be achieved between negative ('The least useful feature in the Toyota is...') and positive ('The most used feature in the Toyota is...'). The major benefit of this technique is that respondents express their own feelings in their own words. Sentence completion tests can be administered either by personal interview or by the pencil-and-paper method.

WORD ASSOCIATION

This test is a high pressure technique that presents an interviewee with key words, terms, or names one at a time and insists on the respondent's immediate reporting of whatever comes to mind upon hearing a given word. In order to avoid second-guessing, the subject is not granted any time for reflection or deliberation.

A brief series of about five responses per trigger word is generally registered. The main advantage of this method is that it produces spontaneous association. This technique must be administered by means of personal interview.

PICTURE ASSOCIATION

This test presents respondents with drawings or photographs of different people representing potential product users. The interviewees are asked to identify the prospective users of products A, B and C. The interviewer then probes for characteristics of the pictured people, thus developing a personality profile of the perceived typical user of a particular product, which reflects its image.

The prime payoff of this approach is that it elicits a wealth of uninhibited information that would otherwise be impossible to obtain. Like the word association test, picture associations are best administered by personal interview.

Guidelines to Image Management

Here are some of the key questions that you may want to ask yourself with respect to your image management responsibilities and efforts:

- What do we know about the image of our company/product/service in the eyes of actual or potential buyers?
- Do we have any image at all? Are we well known?
- Is our image positive or negative?
- Is the perceived image accurate or inaccurate? Are we better than our reputation?

- What does our name suggest? Is it appropriate? Have we outgrown it?

- How does our image compare with that of our competition?

- What are our perceived strengths and weaknesses?

- How can we improve our image?

Favorable images serve to attract investment, talent and buyers. A company's image can make products stand out that are otherwise indistinguishable. Mostly, however, good images lead to a competitive edge.

5.6 Generating Secondary Information

There are numerous sources open to you. These categories include national and regional government agencies, service organizations and publications. Perhaps the most useful source of information is through the vast reaches of the Internet. Sitting at a computer terminal, you can gain updated information about a public company's financial data. You can visit a company Website for revealing information about its mission, new product data, listings of executives with details of their work and education backgrounds, and other key pieces of information. (See following details on using the Internet.)

Then, there are voluminous amounts of information about demographic, economic, social and other aspects of an area's economy; including data on population, education employment, income, housing, product usage and retail sales.

Industry Studies

Research organizations, management consultancies, trade associations, and stock brokerage houses conduct a variety of broad and industry-specific studies. These studies provide varied data from products and brands sold through retail outlets and profiles of television audiences, to demographic and behavioral information on a magazine's circulation.

One caution: Make certain you do not take broad generalizations from a study and apply them indiscriminately to your situation without verifying their appropriateness to your business.

Reducing the Risk of New Market Entry

To reduce some of the risk before entering a new market, use the techniques of market intelligence and market research covered in these Help Topics. Overall, the central methods for gathering market intelligence include the following:

- **Competitive audits**: Measures market share and finds out how competitors 'stack up' against each other in product quality, performance, delivery, price and distribution – as well as any other areas of particular significance to your industry and to prospective customers.

- **Customer satisfaction studies**: After you have made your initial entry, track your company's performance over a period of time and measures progress (or lack of it) toward becoming a better supplier.

- **Testing new products at the conceptual stage**: Avoids investment in products with no or very little acceptance in the marketplace; prioritizes those that do have a chance.

5.7 The World Wide Web – A Boon to The SBP

Perhaps the biggest breakthrough in conducting commercial marketing research is the World Wide Web and its easy-to-use browser interface. As indicated, the Internet is a viable platform for online research services, database producers, and primary publishers of all types.

- Corporate directories identify and screen customers, prospects and competitors, and provide quick profiles of particular firms and their lines of business, management structure, staffing levels and sales.

- Detailed financial reports help assess the financial health of an individual company, as well as overall industry trends.

- Press releases highlight new product announcements, staffing changes, and quarterly financial results.

- Trade journals and general business publications provide a wealth of information, including company profiles, case studies and analyses, interviews with executives, industry surveys, and overviews on emerging technologies.

Table 5.5 describes typical examples of multi-industry coverage advertised by one online service.

Company activities and events	Professional business activities
Industry trends and overviews	International trade
Economic/demographic information	Company stock performance
Management theory and practice	Editorials
Legislative/regulatory information	Biographies
Product evaluation and reviews	Financial exchange information
Executive changes and profiles	

TABLE 5.5: **MARKET RESEARCH ON THE INTERNET**

Altogether, the World Wide Web opens up an unparalleled source for detailed information on industries, companies, company individuals, competitors and consumer behavior that can add greater precision to your SBP.

Summary

There is an overwhelming amount of information available for input into a business intelligence system. Yet, as a practical matter for many managers, there is not enough time or money to conduct all forms of market research. The prudent approach for determining what specific research to undertake is to look at your SBP and identify any gaps of information and what additional information is needed to make intelligent decisions.

Selecting Market Strategies

6.1 Why Select Market Strategies?

To look at your market in its totality is especially relevant as you develop your portfolio of markets and products in SBP Section 4. Meaning: First, consider the size of the market and types of segments that interest you. Also determine what market entry procedures you intend to use, the amount of commitment of resources you intend to make, the level of product demand, and what opportunities there are to diversify.

Second, decide if you want to participate in a particular market. If so, how much of it do you want? How you are going to hold on to it? And how are you going to manage the market for long-term profitable growth? Let's consider all of these issues.

6.2 Market Size

Once you determine the size of the market you can handle successfully against competition, then concentrate your selling power in a form that offers the greatest chance of success. Avoid spreading resources that may result in becoming vulnerable to competitors. When growth opportunities become available, branch out to additional markets – as long as those opportunities conform to your strategic direction (Section 1).

In addition to the above guidelines, refer to the detailed discussion of segmentation in Help Topics, under Analyzing Customer Groups. Review how to segment a market and how to apply segmentation criteria. There are a variety of strategy applications from single-market concentration, to product specialist, to market specialist, to selective target niches and to total market coverage.

For example, you may have identified a poorly served, neglected, or emerging market niche and introduced a dedicated product or service. Having established a foothold in a niche, you have a series of choices:

1. You can become a product specialist and expand your product line.

2. You can serve as a market specialist in, for example, the banking industry with a diverse grouping of products and services.

3. You can choose a highly selective niche strategy concentrating in areas of most favorable opportunities.

4. You can select full market-product coverage. For example, Seiko watches started in a single niche and spread into full market coverage with 2,400 models of watches.

6.3 Market Entry

The over-riding issue of market entry deals with deciding on a strategy of *first-in to the market, follow-the-leader,* or *last-in to the market* with a new product or technology.

A first-in strategy has the potential advantage of identifying a company as the market leader. Often, the companies that decide on the follow-the-leader and last-in strategies must conform to the market leader. In those situations, managers have several options: Creating a competitive advantage by using product differentiation, price incentives, promotion originality, service add-ons, or distribution innovations to overcome the leader's advantages. They also have the choice of targeting poorly served or emerging market segments left vacant by the first-in competitor.

Entry Options

FIRST-IN STRATEGY

The first-in strategy enjoys the advantage of locking up key distributors and customers and possibly gaining a reputation of market leader. In a study by McKinsey & Co., the management consultants indicated that being first to introduce a new product, even if it is over budget, is better than coming in later but on budget. The downside is that rushing to the market before the product is thoroughly debugged can result in a negative image.

FOLLOW-THE-LEADER STRATEGY

Here, a firm might time its entry closely to the first-in competitor. Both companies would gain from the promotional impact of advertising the product category, and they would share the overall promotional costs of the launch.

LATE ENTRY

Delaying a product launch until a competitor has already entered has some clear-cut advantages: At the outset, the first-entry company will have borne the cost of educating the market. The late-entrant also can avoid product flaws and take the time to appraise the size of the market, profile the buyer, and target still viable segments that remain untapped.

To a great extent, your market entry strategies are preset at the time of product launch. By grasping the full significance of the first-in, follow-the-leader, or last-in strategy choice, you will gain additional insight as you make market decisions, and develop and refine your SBP.

Ultimately, the decision in market entry depends on your resources, your ability to sustain a competitive edge (particularly if you are first-in), and your long-term objective as it relates to amount of market share and your position in the market.

6.4 Market Commitment

Company priorities and resources determine the degree of commitment to a market. Consider if heavy involvement should characterize the thrust of your growth strategy. Or if less involvement is the best course of action to protect your other market commitments.

There are two dimensions to market commitment: yours and your competitors'. Competitive strategy requires that you use your strengths against the weaknesses of the competitor. Therefore, through a side-by-side analysis determine how much commitment will be given to key areas such as: extent of new product development, amount of market share desired and willingness to sustain an aggressive promotional effort against competitors.

You also need to know your competitors' patterns of behavior and how they are likely to respond to your level of commitment. Finally, you need to consider how and what you communicate to the marketplace – to your customers and competitors – about the amount of commitment you will make, i.e., major, average, or limited.

6.5 Market Demand

Managing market demand is a key factor to successful performance. You need to know at what point to prune markets if demand slackens, when to concentrate on key markets when demand increases, and how soon to harvest profits should sales plateau and cash flow is needed.

The following guidelines will help you align your product introductions with your market demand strategy:

1. **Selecting Markets**. Whether domestic or international markets, be certain those you select align with a long-term demand strategy. Then determine your capabilities to sustain a steady product flow of new or enhanced products. In addition, determine the commitments of competitors to match or exceed your product introductions.

2. **Entering Markets**. Study the markets for points of entry. That is, determine geographic locations of available distribution networks and their capacity to handle your products. Also evaluate what product advantages you can tout, such as lower price, more features, or some other value-added benefits that are strong enough to displace competitors' products in favor of yours.

3. **Building Market Share**. Depending on your resources, explore the potential of a rolling strategy: (a) producing your product as a private brand; (b) followed by establishing your own brand name; (c) then continuing with product improvement, product upgrading and supporting services.

4. **Protecting Market Share**. This strategy assumes the best defense is an offense. Begin with continuous observation of competitors' products and strategies. Then monitor how customers' judge your products and observe their changing needs. Lastly, recognize that timing new product introductions are not isolated activities, but are integral parts of your total market demand strategy.

Managing market demand requires flexibility, good timing, and extensive use of competitive analysis. For its application, it connects directly to the strategies of concentration and segmentation as they relate to expanding or contracting your presence in a selected market.

6.6 Market Diversification

You should be aware of opportunities to add new businesses that relate to existing production or distribution capabilities – known as horizontal diversification. Or about opportunities to add another stage of production or distribution to existing operations, one that either precedes or follows the ultimate path to the consumer – called vertical diversification. And also the possibility to diversify into unrelated businesses using new technology and marketing strategies – called lateral diversification.

Therefore, market diversification presents many opportunities for middle and upper-level managers to exercise innovation and entrepreneurial thinking. Let's consider the three categories of diversification in more detail:

Horizontal Diversification

Procter & Gamble is expert in horizontal diversification. Originally a soap company, Procter & Gamble has long since expanded horizontally into such diverse products as cake mixes, potato chips, coffee, paper products, toothpastes, deodorants and detergents.

What P&G has discovered is that great economies can be derived from using the same sales-force to sell new product categories to the same retail outlets, simply by applying already developed marketing skills. Because it involves building on an existing strength, either in technology or in marketing, horizontal diversification is the most promising and least risky of the market diversification strategies.

Vertical Diversification

Hart Schaffner & Marx, the manufacturer of such famous clothing brands as Hickey-Freeman and Christian Dior, acquired a chain of retail stores in the early 1980's to add to its existing stores. This type of vertical diversification has attracted a variety of companies.

Some large retailers that produce some of the goods they sell practice another form of vertical diversification. For instance, Sears makes some of its own appliances, or has large ownership interests in manufacturers. In the industrial sector, Ford has long owned its steel-making facilities.

Vertical diversification (or integration) in some instances increases the level of risk because the management of one level of business (retailing) may not have enough expertise at another level (manufacturing).

Lateral Diversification

Lateral diversification is the most extreme form of diversification because it usually represents a complete departure from current operations. The only connection is that the same parent owns diverse businesses. The resulting group is called a conglomerate and was made popular in the 1960's by such corporate names as LingTemco-Vought, ITT Corporation, Litton Industries, Inc., and Gulf + Western, Inc.

While this form of diversification still occurs through holding companies, the current trend is more restrained, and the business portfolio (SBP Section 4) is developed with greater attention to the overall strategic direction of the company.

Diversifying Globally

Finally, where you wish to diversify globally, or move into another stage of business, there are additional issues you will also deal with in developing your SBP. Use the following guidelines:

1. Don't distance yourself from customers, regardless of the types of alliances you form. In global markets, where possible, set up indigenous operations staffed with the nationals of each country.

2. Don't permit distributors to shoulder the entire load of contacting prospects, selling your products and servicing the customer. Take the time to learn the intricacies of distributing to local markets. (This point is as true of domestic markets as it is for global ones.)

3. Watch the actions of your competitors. Identify territories where foreign competitors buy a distributor as a quick way to enter a market and circumvent barriers to market entry.

Selecting Product/Service Strategies

7.1 Why Select Product/Service Strategies?

Reviewing your products offers a dual opportunity. First, you tune in to the changing needs and wants of customers. Second, you decide how and when to remove losing and marginal products.

The seven major areas of product considerations – positioning, product life-cycle, product competition, product mix, product design, new products and product audit – provide a systematic framework for reviewing your products and developing competitive strategies.

7.2 Positioning

Al Reis and Jack Trout popularized positioning during the 1980s as "Not what you do to a product. Positioning is what you do to the mind of the prospect. That is, you position the product to the mind of the prospect."

Professor Philip Kotler (Northwestern University) says, "Positioning is the act of designing the company offer and image so that it occupies a distinct and valued place in the target customers' minds."

What follows, then, is to find out how customers perceive your product by examining the image it projects and the needs it satisfies. Next, monitor those perceptions through observation and research. If they are undesirable, change them. Then locate an open position in the market and in the customer's mind. Occupy that new position and protect it against competitive inroads.

To consider the broader aspects of positioning, use the following guidelines:

1. **Keep focused**. Position your products in those niches where there is an above average chance to rank among the leaders. Where possible, avoid the commodity segments. Ideally, find a technology, product design, distribution system, or service that differentiates you and leads to a favorable position compared to that of competitors.

2. **Establish flexible work teams**. Cross-functional teams now create the vital linkage between customer and successful product development. To succeed, however, teams must have a clear definition of how the company wants to be positioned and be able to implement the desired position through the SBP.

3. **Solve customers' problems**. The extent to which you are able to solve customers' problems and thereby make your customers more competitive, the greater chance you have for survival and long-term growth. Therefore, look for new product applications, value-added services, and new market segments that were overlooked in the initial stages of product development.

4. **Look globally**. Trade barriers continue to crumble. Push your product ideas and technologies wherever they apply in the world. However, follow the principles indicated above. That is, make sure you are positioned to offer a specialty or customized product that will satisfy local needs, and not use foreign markets as a means to unload a standardized product.

The primary goal of positioning, then, consists of a two-pronged strategy: Create a long-term desirable position for your product in the customer's mind and secure a strong advantageous position against your competition.

Developing a Positioning Strategy

If the picture of your market reveals an undesirable position for your brand, the following procedure may help you improve your situation in the marketplace:

STEP 1

Identifying your product's actual position invariably requires individual consumer interviews, generally in the form of a questionnaire. (See Help Topics for marketing research techniques.)

STEP 2

The easiest way to select an ideal position is to accept your brand's current position, providing it commands a strong position in its field. A second method is to select a position that nobody else wants.

STEP 3

In attempting to achieve an ideal product position, your firm has two principal options. It can (1) move its current product to a new position, with or without a change in the product itself, or (2) introduce another product with the necessary characteristics for new positioning, while leaving the current product untouched, or possibly withdrawing it from the market.

Once you discover that your product's position is far from ideal, your advertising has its job cut out for it. Together with the other elements of your promotional mix – namely, personal selling, publicity, the Internet and sales promotion – your advertising will have to shoulder the burden of creating a new position for your product.

STEP 4

After developing several alternative strategies for achieving your ideal product position, select one of them to implement in the marketplace. In making your decision, be guided by your company's overall objectives, resources and capabilities. Consider, too, how long and how firm a commitment your company is willing to make, and how much money it is ready to put behind such a commitment.

Achieving a lasting and favorable position is an expensive, time-consuming proposition. Unless your company's management is firmly committed to this strategy, it is best not to tamper with your brand's position. You might do more harm than good if the effort is half-hearted, or is terminated halfway into the program.

STEP 5

While tracking your competition, monitor the impact of your positioning on the customer's mind, where it counts most. Follow-up research must examine and compare your product's actual position with its desired ideal position. After all, it is possible that your program will not produce the intended results. In this event, a review of your strategy may be necessary.

7.3 Product Life-Cycle

The product life-cycle has particular relevance for SBP Section 1 (Strategic Direction), with specific application in Section 4 (Business Portfolio) and the various strategies that extend the sales life of products are the pillars for successful growth (Table 7.1).

You will find these life-cycle extenders are the safest and most economical strategies to follow. To identify the best extension opportunities, seek the cooperation of product developers, manufacturing, finance, distribution, marketing and sales personnel.

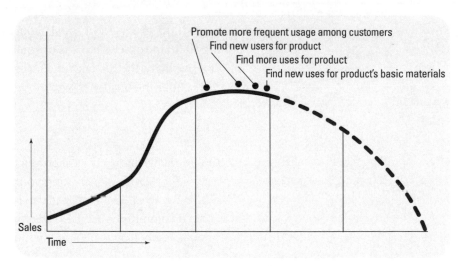

TABLE 7.1: **STRATEGY APPLICATION FOR EXTENDING A PRODUCT'S LIFE CYCLE**

The product life-cycle offers a reliable perspective for observing a 'living' product moving through dynamic stages, influenced by outside economic, social and environmental forces – as well as by inside policies, priorities and resources.

For many companies, monitoring the life-cycle curve often prevents the severe consequences of allowing a product to reach a commodity status, where price is often the solitary weapon in the strategy arsenal. Consequently, the classic product life-cycle model remains a highly effective framework for devising strategies and tactics at various stages of the curve.

Examples abound of organizations successfully extending the sales life of their products. The classics include nylon, Jell-O brand gelatin desserts and Scotch-brand tape. All have had enjoyed life-cycles of more than 60 years and are still going strong.

Measuring the Product Life-Cycle

If the product life-cycle is of any strategic value to you and your firm, you have to determine where in the life-cycle your product is at any given time. You can determine the stage of your product category's life-cycle by identifying its status on the three curves shown in Table 7.2.

These curves are:

1. Market volume, expressed in units to avoid any distortion resulting from price changes.
2. Rate of change of market volume.
3. Profit/loss, illustrating the differences between total revenue and total cost at each point in time.

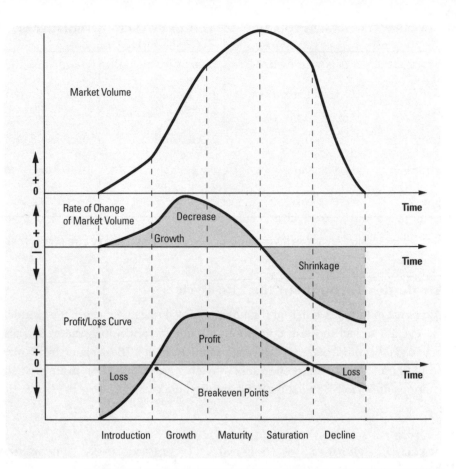

FIGURE 7.2: **CURVE TRENDS USED TO MEASURE LIFE-CYCLE POSITION**

Successful management of your product's life-cycle requires careful planning and thorough understanding of its characteristics at the various points of the curve. Only then can you respond quickly and advantageously to new situations, leaving competitors in your wake.

LIFE-CYCLE STAGE	SALES VOLUME	RATE OF CHANGE OF SALES VOLUME	PROFIT/LOSS
Introduction	Slow growth	Increasing	Loss
Growth	Rapid growth	Increasing/ Decreasing	Very high profit
Maturity	Growth	Decreasing	Decreasing profit
Saturation	Stagnation	Negative	Decreasing profit
Decline	Decrease	Negative	Loss

TABLE 7.3: **IDENTIFYING YOUR PRODUCT'S POSITION IN THE LIFE-CYCLE**

Strategies Throughout the Life-Cycle

As shown in Table 7.3, different conditions characterize the stages of the product life-cycle. This fact suggests continuous monitoring and appropriate changes in your tactical approach, if you are to optimize results. These changes include adjustments in your marketing mix at each stage (Table 7.4). In turn, such changes apply to SBP Section 8 (Strategies and Tactics).

LIFE-CYCLE STAGE	PRODUCT	PRICING	DISTRIBUTION	PROMOTION
Introduction	Offer technically mature product, keep mix small	'Skim the cream' of price insensitive innovators through high introductory price	'Fill the pipeline' to the consumer; use indirect distribution through wholesales	Create primary demand for product category, spend generously on extensive and intensive 'flight' advertising
Growth	Improve product; keep mix limited	Adjust price as needed to meet competition	Increase product presence and market penetration	Spend substantially on expansion of sales volume

LIFE-CYCLE STAGE	PRODUCT	PRICING	DISTRIBUTION	PROMOTION
Maturity	Distinguish your product from competition; expand your product offering to satisfy different market segments	Capitalize on price-sensitive demand by further reducing prices	Take over wholesaling function yourself by establishing distribution centers and having your own sales-force call on retailers	Differentiate your product in the minds of prospective buyers; emphasize brand appeal
Saturation	Proliferate your mix further, diversify into new market	Keep prices stable	Intensify your distribution to increase availability and exposure	Maintain the status quo; support your market position
Decline	Prune your mix radically	Carefully increase price	Consolidate your distribution setup; establish minimum orders	Reduce advertising activity to reminder level

TABLE 7.4: **STRATEGIES THROUGHOUT THE PRODUCT LIFE-CYCLE**

INTRODUCTION

In the introduction stage, it is the task of the pioneer to create primary demand – namely, demand for the new product category. Creating primary demand is an educational process that involves activating people's needs and focusing them on the product in question.

Initially, keep the product mix small to provide a clear focus and keep costs under control. Also, confine the mix to just a few variations that reflect the underlying concept of the entire category.

Your channel decisions are crucial because they lock your firm into long-term commitments to a selected group of middlemen that cannot be changed easily, if at all. The degree to which you know how to secure maximum availability of your product in the right outlets can make or break your participation in the ongoing growth of a new market.

If you have an established sales-force and ongoing business relationship with prospects, you still have to sell them on the merits of your innovation, which is no easy task. To this end, you have to motivate your sales-force with a dramatic show that gets the adrenaline flowing.

Also essential is the support given to your product in the form of advertising. Anything less than generous funding and an all-out advertising effort will reduce the product's chances for survival. Giving a new product lukewarm advertising support is generally tantamount to dismal if not failed sales performance.

As for price, you can set it fairly low. A strategy called penetration pricing aims at creating a mass market and discouraging competitive imitation through low unit profits and large investment requirements. Or, you may consider a skim strategy that starts out with a comparatively high price and attempts recovery of the initial outlays for development and market introduction, before competitive pressure erodes your temporary advantage.

GROWTH

In the growth stage, you will want to modify your basic product to take care of any problems discovered through initial consumer reactions. However, if the product is selling well, the product mix can remain small.

With channels of distribution your goals will include persuading current channel members to buy more, and to sign up new channel members.

Your salespeople will continue to sell along the same lines as before, building upon the emerging success story of your innovation. Your advertising emphasis is likely to shift somewhat from creating product awareness to expanding market volume. Prices soften as price-cutting competitors enter the market.

MATURITY

Moving into the maturity phase now turns into a fight for market share against other competitors. At this time, it pays to redesign your product to make it more distinctive and easier to differentiate from competitive offerings. It is also advisable to adopt a strategy of market segmentation to satisfy the unique needs of these fairly homogeneous groups within the market.

Consider your channel strategy as it relates to effective market coverage, costs and control. If you employed the services of wholesalers in your introductory thrust, think about eliminating some and shifting support to the remaining ones to push your product harder and cut costs.

Your advertising has to communicate and enhance your drive to differentiate your product. It should put heavy emphasis on brand appeal to pre-sell the product, so that the prospect recognizes and prefers your product even in a competitive environment. The effectiveness of your promotional efforts, however, is likely to decrease sharply as demand becomes less responsive to promotion because of growing brand loyalty and resultant market resistance.

Since actual differences between substitute products are very slight and price sensitivity of demand is high, price variations between your firm's products and those of your competitors gain in importance. Prices will tend to drop further, but stabilize toward the end of the stage as a result of cost pressures. Insofar as your company has been able to create brand loyalty among its buyers, you can permit price adjustments when necessary without losing a substantial amount of sales.

SATURATION

As your product enters the saturation stage of its life-cycle, typically, a no-holds-barred fight develops for market share. Because market volume has ceased to improve, the growth of individual firms' sales volume is achieved at the expense of competitors.

In your product strategy, attempt to differentiate further by offering even more choices. Because of the limited growth potential, it will pay to pursue a strategy of diversification. For instance, it might be worth moving into other geographic markets where your product could be at the introduction or growth stages of a new life-cycle.

Your channel strategy remains unaltered in the saturation phase. You should attempt to gain even more intensive distribution and, thereby, maximize avail-ability and exposure. Toward this end, your salespeople will have to make a well-planned, concerted effort to obtain more trade cooperation.

Your advertising strategy at this point is to maintain the status quo. Little new ground can be broken, so advertising of the reminder or reinforcement type is needed. Elasticity of demand reaches its highest point at this stage. This fact is of little strategic consequence, however, since most possibilities for cost reduction have been exhausted.

DECLINE

With consumer interest on the wane, competitors drop out of the market in droves. If you are still in the market, you will trim your product offerings, vigorously weed out weak products and concentrate on a few unchanged items.

Similarly, you will attempt to reduce distribution cost by consolidating warehouses and sales offices, as well as establishing minimum orders to discourage small shipments. Your sales effort will tend to be low key, with emphasis on retaining as much of your market as you can. Advertising support will diminish to the low-budget, infrequent-reminder type. Your prices will stay right about where they are.

Finally, studies show that the classic product life-cycle pattern just described conforms reasonably well to reality. Therefore, as you develop your SBP, take note of the strategies at each stage of the product life-cycle and incorporate them into the appropriate sections of your plan.

7.4 Product Competition

Also relevant to SBP Section 4 (Business Portfolio) is to gain a larger share of a total market by introducing additional products as competing lines or as private labels. The additional products provide a solid front against competitors. Overall, the strategy aims at generating higher revenue than does the use of only a single product.

To develop competing products, however, be certain you apply a differentiation strategy so that you don't cannibalize sales from one line to another. Here are useful guidelines:

- **Features and Benefits**: Select saleable features and benefits that complement the product's basic functions. Start with your basic product. Then envision adding unique features and services; ideally, ones based on users' expectations.

- **Performance**: Relate this factor to the optimum level at which the product operates – including quality.

- **Acceptance**: Measure this characteristic by how close the product comes to established industry and customer standards or specifications.

- **Endurance**: Relate this factor to the product's expected operating life.

- **Dependability**: Measure this attribute to the probability of the product breaking or malfunctioning within a specified period.

- **Appearance**: Look at numerous considerations ranging from image, function, look, or feel. Different from performance, appearance integrates the product with all its differentiating components, including packaging.

- **Design**: Combine the above differentiating components into this factor.

While design encompasses the product's appearance, endurance and dependability, there is particular emphasis placed on ease of use and the appropriateness to the function for which it was designed.

Procter & Gamble, with its array of brands of detergents and other product categories, is the master at executing a product-competition strategy. Likewise, Becton Dickinson, the large health care firm, produces its famous brand of Ace bandages as the premium brand. It also makes a competing brand, the lower-priced line of Bauer & Black bandages.

You have to be careful with competing brands, though; to be sure there is a minimal amount of taking sales from one product to another. The intent is to segment and position your product with as much precision as possible.

Care must be taken because the supplier shoulders a high-risk position should the relationship deteriorate. In its worst-case scenario, such a firm could be out of business overnight. One possible remedy is to have a long-term supply contract with the customer – or open an alternative channel of distribution.

7.5 Product Mix

The intent here is to evaluate the profit advantage of a single product concentrated in a specialized market. Then, for growth and protection from competitors, also consider a multiple-product strategy, which could include add-on products and services.

In doing so, keep in mind the definition of a new product: A product is new when it is *perceived* as new by the prospect or customer. Therefore, new products can cover a range of innovations – from minor change to new to the world – if the changes are perceived as new. For example: *new* could mean modifying products for specialized applications, or developing new forms of packaging, or devising a convenient system for storage and retrieval.

Further, you can give the impression of *new* by adding value through improved field technical assistance, computer-linked inventory systems, and technical/advisory telephone hookups. The following checklist can get you started on developing your product mix:

STEP ONE

Review your company's strategic direction (SPB Section 1) or overall product line objectives (SBP Sections 2 and 7). You thereby guard against venturing into line extensions that do not relate to your core business.

STEP TWO

Define your market by sales and profit volume, customer usage, purchasing patterns, anticipated market share, and investment required.

STEP THREE

Determine product development requirements, such as: using existing company technology, obtaining new technology, licensing finished products, or subcontracting an entire project.

STEP FOUR

Evaluate competitive offerings. Determine how to differentiate your new product to avoid a direct confrontation with look-alike products.

STEP FIVE

Determine the proposed product's position. Will it be positioned to *defend* a market niche or be placed on the *offensive* to secure additional market share? Will it be used as a *probe* to enter an emerging market or as a *pre-emptive* attack on competitors to discourage their entry?

The product mix strategy overlaps with other considerations, such as those already discussed for market dimension, market entry and market commitment strategies. As always, you should also orient your competitive thinking to your competitors' product mix and how you intend to position your product line in relation to them.

7.6 Product Design

To deal with product design decisions, instill a mindset within yourself and those with whom you work that keeps your customers' needs in the forefront of product development and service. Sustaining such an attitude is one part of the success formula. The second, and more critical part, is to install a systematic approach that permits you to learn about your customers' business.

Here's one system that works: Explore customers' needs and problems in two broad categories that would appeal to their self-interests: *revenue-expansion* and *cost-reduction* opportunities. To conduct the analysis, ask the following questions:

Revenue Expansion Opportunities:

- What approaches would reduce customer returns and complaints?
- What processes would speed up production and delivery to benefit your customer?
- How can you improve a customer's market position and image?
- How would adding a name brand impact your customers' revenues?
- What product or service benefits would enhance your customers' operation?
- How can you create differentiation that gives your customers' a competitive advantage?
- How would improving re-ordering procedures impact revenues?

Cost Reduction Opportunities:

- What procedures would cut customers' purchase costs?
- What processes would cut customers' production costs?
- What systems would cut customers' production downtime?
- What approaches would cut customers' delivery costs?
- What methods would cut customers' administrative overheads?
- What strategies would maximize customers' working capital?

Several of those areas reach many functions of the organization. Therefore, use your cross-functional planning team to interpret findings and translate them into product design solutions.

Finally, implementing the process is a sticky problem, particularly when it comes to involving individuals from various specialties into actively thinking about such areas as customers' needs, market growth and competitive advantage.

For starters, however, enlist the assistance of the senior executives in your group or company. Have them brief team members on the benefits of paying attention to market-driven issues for the welfare of their company as well as their personal career growth – and even survival. If that doesn't work, recommend an orientation/training seminar to help instill the appropriate attitudes.

7.7 New Products/Services

In this category, you take into account strategies related to product innovation, modification, line extension and diversification. Each of which requires changing the product either slightly or extensively. Also, as you consider new products, look at the opportunities for re-merchandising and market extension. These strategies don't alter the product but permit a perception of a 'new' product.

Categories of New Products

New products come in many different forms. This diversity can be reduced to varying degrees of technological and market newness. In terms of increasing degrees of technological change, you may want to distinguish among modification, line extension and diversification.

For increasing degrees of market newness, you can differentiate between re-merchandising and market extension. Table 7.5 presents the differences among these five categories of new products and points out the benefits of each.

CATEGORY	DEFINITION	NATURE	BENEFIT
Modification	Altering a product feature	Same number of product lines and products	Combining the new with the familiar
Line extension	Adding more variety	Same number of product lines, higher number of products	Segmenting the market by offering more choice
Diversification	Entering a new business	New product line, higher number of products	Spreading risk and capitalizing on opportunities
Re-merchandising	Marketing change to create a new impression	Same product, same markets	Generating excitement and stimulating sales
Market extension	Entering a new market	Same products, new market	Broadening the base

TABLE 7.5: **CATEGORIES OF NEW PRODUCTS**

Combined Approach for New Product Categories

Rarely will the five categories of new products presented here be used separately. They lend themselves to combined applications for maximum impact. Moreover, you will probably want to avail yourself of a package approach if you wish to maintain steady growth in a rapidly changing environment.

Line extension, for example, is often used with re-merchandising or market extension. Diversification is often combined with market extension. The use of one category does not preclude the application of other approaches at the same time, possibly within the same market. What remains essential, though, is that the prospective customer perceives a difference worthy of consideration.

Steps in the Evolution of a New Product

A new product results from a process called new product evolution. The steps are presented in Table 7.6, together with their respective results.

PROCESS STEPS	RESULTS
Initiative	
1. Initiating forces	Get action under way
2. Perception and identification of problem or opportunity	Realize and pinpoint nature of challenge
Decision-making	
1. Definition of objectives and criteria	Set frame of reference
2. Start of comprehensive marketing research program	Feed decision-maker relevant information on continuous basis
3. Examination of market data	Provide factual input
4. Idea generation	Map out alternative courses of action
5. Screening	Weed out unpromising alternatives
6. Business analysis	Subject surviving proposals to in-depth scrutiny
7. Product development	Convert ideas into products
8. Market testing	Examine market acceptance
9. Finalize marketing program	Prepare for rollout
10. Pilot production	Fill the pipeline
Execution	
1. Full-scale launch	Begin market introduction
2. Product life-cycle	Analyze sales and profit changes
Control	
1. Continuous feedback of results	Compare planned and actual figures
2. Corrective action	Keep on course

TABLE 7.6: **THE PROCESS OF NEW PRODUCT EVOLUTION**

Initiative

New products don't emerge in a vacuum. Rather, the initiating force is likely to reside with some astute individual within your organization who perceives a product concept and triggers the process that results in a profitable addition to your product mix.

Numerous external or internal factors (discussed in these Help Topics) can inspire a new product initiative. They may reflect market, technological, competitive, or company developments. In any case, they constitute the motivating forces behind the evolutionary process.

Some companies even retain the services of an elite group of planners to speculate about such future scenarios. Yet, there are more basic approaches for obtaining significant insights into market trends. One is to carefully examine consumer preferences and life-styles, competitive new product activity, distribution patterns and – most basic of all – sales and profit data.

Technological developments can be just as stimulating. For example, new applications of lasers, glass fibers and superconductors offer a host of opportunities for the imaginative manager, and there is the immense potential of technology transfer, that is, applying to one field the technology developed in another. For example, Rockwell International Corp., a major space contractor, used technology developed for the U.S. space program in designing anti-skid devices for truck braking systems. There is also the discovery and development by the U.S. Military of the Internet, which has been commercialized throughout most of the world.

In a more down-to-earth scenario, events within your firm may also be the source of a new product initiative. These may include employees' suggestions about improving existing products or developing entirely different ones, or purchasing problems involving limited availability of key materials, or price increases may motivate a rethinking process.

Decision-making

The sequence of new product evolution begins with goal setting and ends with initial production. In between is a series of crucial steps that will determine the success of your venture in the marketplace. Close attention to each of the following steps is essential:

DEFINING OBJECTIVES AND CRITERIA

Well-defined objectives not only give direction and orientation to your effort, but they serve as a measure of actual achievements. Typically, new product objectives involve growth targets with outcomes measured by increases in sales volume and market share. However, they often remain non-operational, since they are interpreted by criteria.

RESEARCH AND EXAMINATION OF MARKET DATA

While it is the role of objectives and criteria to guide the evolutionary effort and keep it on course, it is the job of ongoing market research to supply the decision-maker with the relevant facts. The task, then, is to hook up with the consumer and establish communication links that keep the evolutionary process going efficiently and on course.

The body of data generated in the first round of this research program is then screened for usable information capable of triggering dynamic thinking. The following process, attributed to management consultants Booz, Allen & Hamilton, is a reliable product development system you can emulate:

- **Phase 1: Idea Generation**. Once a database has been established, idea generation begins. At this early stage, many ideas are necessary for an ultimate yield of one successfully commercialized product. Booz, Allen & Hamilton put this ratio at 58:1. Scrutiny becomes more and more rigorous as a product idea advances from its source. That translates to generating as many ideas as possible at the outset.

  Tap a wide range of sources for product ideas: internal sources such as top management, research and development people, marketing personnel and other employees. Also use a variety of external sources such as consumers, middlemen, competitors, scientists, inventors, research labs and suppliers. The techniques employed in activating these sources range from brainstorming to various surveying methods.

- **Phase 2: Idea Screening**. Assuming you have generated a wealth of new product ideas, then subject them to a screening procedure. This step aims to weed out unpromising ideas before they become costly in time, effort and money. Thus, the goal at this step is to eliminate from further consideration as many ideas as possible. Two thirds to three-quarters of the original ideas vanish at this point.

  The focus now is to examine questions of feasibility and profitability. Neither of the two, after all, can exist without the other: feasible products that are not profitable are simply giveaways; profitable products that are not feasible are fiction.

- **Phase 3: Business Analysis**. The few chosen ideas that pass the screening test enter the business analysis stage. They now receive in-depth scrutiny. The purpose of this step is to advise top management whether it should authorize certain proposals as development projects. Therefore, a careful impact statement has to be developed for each concept, with thorough projections of what would happen if it were adopted and converted into a real product.

  Management must know the consequences to your firm in terms of required technological know-how, production and sales-force utilization, image, morale and – most of all – finances. Testing the product concept through market research can help you assess consumer reaction and preference at this point.

- **Phase 4: Product Development and Market Testing**. Once a particular idea has tested well and has received top management's blessing, it is assigned to personnel for conversion into a tangible product. Here, your technical and production people go to work with clear-cut specifications spelled out by you on the basis of several rounds of market research. They will develop rough drafts that will then be laboratory tested and refined, until they have developed a product that is completely debugged and ready for full-scale production.

  Of course, before you begin full-scale production, you have to test a sample quantity among users, asking them to try your product at your expense and then suggest changes to improve its performance or enhance its appeal. This procedure – product testing – is intended to help you modify and finalize the product design.

- **Phase 5: Final Marketing Program and Pilot Production**. Completion of market testing enables you to put the finishing touches on your product-launch program by adjusting certain elements of your marketing mix for maximum effectiveness. This adjustment permits you to get ready for a full-scale rollout.

  Of course, you first have to go through pilot production; that is, produce enough merchandise to satisfy initial demand. This step completes the decision-making phase of new product evolution.

- **Phase 6: Execution and Control**. Once you complete the internal development and external testing of your new product, you are ready to launch its full-scale market introduction. Your revised introductory program should now set in motion the start of your product's life-cycle.

  As no one is all-knowing and even the best planning cannot foresee all possible events, continuous feedback to monitor the effectiveness of your product strategy is necessary. This feedback enables periodic comparisons between planned and actual figures. In turn, you can take corrective action to keep your program on course.

7.8 Product Audit

Knowing when to pull a product from the line is as important as knowing when to introduce a new one. Consider such internal requirements as profitability, available resources and new growth opportunities. Examine external factors of sales-force coverage, dealer commitment and customers' needs to determine if a comprehensive line is required.

One easy-to-install procedure with direct impact on profitability is the *product audit*. Just as regular physical examinations are essential to maintain the body's good health, likewise, products require regular examination to determine whether they are healthy, need re-promotion, or should be allowed to phase out.

Begin your product audit by setting up a Product Audit Committee (see details below). The product audit can assist you in accomplishing the following:

1. Determine your product's long-term market potential.

2. Assess the advantages and disadvantages of adding value to the product.

3. Alter your product's market position compared to that of a competitor's comparable product.

4. Evaluate the chances of your product being displaced by another product or technology.

5. Calculate the product's contribution to your company's financial goals.

6. Judge if the product line is filled out sufficiently to prevent your customers from shopping elsewhere.

In addition to the above criteria, consider such issues as availability of money and human resources, assessment of new product and market growth opportunities, and even the effective use of your executives' time. Also, add such factors as your firm's willingness to sustain sales-force coverage, dealer commitment and ongoing eagerness to respond to changing customers' needs.

Finally, phasing out weak products or exiting a market requires careful consideration of your company's obligations. For instance, there may be significant costs related to labor agreements, maintaining capabilities for spare parts, contractual relationships with dealers and distributors, financial institutions and so on. In sum, the product audit provides a practical approach to the profitability and the decision-making process.

Establishing a Product Audit Program

The first step in establishing a regular product evaluation program is to create a Product Audit Committee. The committee may consist of members of the planning team or a separate group.

This core group, comprised of the top people in the marketing, finance, engineering and purchasing departments, should control decision-making authority about the design of the company's product mix. Depending upon the dimensions of the product mix and the significance of the products, or developments involved, the Product Audit Committee should meet monthly and every product should have at least an annual review.

How does such a committee operate? To do justice to each product and to have an objective basis for product comparisons, a common rating form should be used. For products that appear dubious and thus demand careful evaluation, you can use a product audit form using a simple 1 to 5 scoring system using the above six criteria.

Phasing out weak products, following the decision to drop them, requires careful consideration of your company's obligations to the various parties effected by the decision. Supplier and customer notification and an adequate stock of replacement parts may be necessary.

FIVE: PART 8
Pricing Strategies

8.1 Selecting the Pricing Process

Pricing is a component of the marketing mix and thereby is not treated in isolation from the broad objectives you developed in your SBP Section 2, which might include high return on investment or high market share.

Also look at the threat of tough pricing competition, by examining all possible alternatives, such as product improvement, promotion and distribution strategies, before getting involved in pricing wars. The essential point: Pricing must work in harmony with all of these strategies.

8.2 The Pricing Process

When pricing new products in your line, ask: Can low price and high price be compatible? Do you create a conflict in the customer's mind? What perception or image do customers hold in their minds about your product?

Do give careful consideration to these questions when positioning a product into a new category and devising a pricing strategy. For instance, some organizations recognize image as a precious factor and will create a new name brand within a low-price category, just to avoid conflict rather than run the risk of damaging the image of its upscale product.

In general, it is difficult to regain a premium price position for the same brand once it has been diluted by low price promotions through mass merchandising outlets. Therefore, as you shape a strategy for a new product entry, it is wise to maintain ongoing feedback about the market position you want. In turn, the market position you select ultimately has consequences on your product's image.

The following process increases your chance for success:

1. Establish your pricing objectives. These might be to maximize profits, increase sales revenues, increase market share rapidly, or position your product advantageously among competitive look-alike products.

2. Develop a demand schedule for your product. Specifically, forecast the probable quantities purchased at various price levels.

3. Examine competitors' pricing. This review will determine where you can slot your price to achieve your market objectives.

4. Select your pricing method. Use the following strategies for use in SBP Sections 3 and 8.

8.3 Pricing Strategies

Skim Pricing

Skim pricing involves pricing at a high level to hit the 'cream' of the buyers who are less sensitive to price. The conditions for using this strategy are:

- Senior management requires that you recover R&D, equipment, technology and other startup costs rapidly.

- The product or service is unique. It is new (or improved) and in the introductory stage of the product life-cycle. Or it serves a relatively small segment where price is not a major consideration.

- There is little danger of short-term competitive entry because of patent protection, high R&D entry costs, high promotion costs, limitations on availability of raw materials, or because major distribution channels are filled.

- There is a need to control demand until production is geared up.

A typical example is the electronics industry, which usually employs skim pricing at the introductory stage of the product life-cycle to the point that consumers and industrial buyers expect the high introductory-pricing pattern. There are exceptions, however. One company introduced its much-touted storage device for computers with the capability of not losing stored data when power is cut off. Even with the impressive technology, sales were initially disappointing because potential users were not willing to pay the high introductory price and were willing to wait for price reductions.

Penetration Pricing

Penetration pricing means pricing below the prevailing level in order to gain market entry or to increase market share. The conditions for considering this strategy are:

- There is an opportunity to establish a quick foothold in a specific market.

- Existing competitors are not expected to react to your prices.

- The product or service is a 'me too' entry and you have achieved a low-cost producer capability.

- You hold to the theory that high market share equals high return on investment, and management is willing to wait for the rewards.

Penetration pricing has been the strategy of choice for Japan throughout the latter part of the 20th Century to gain footholds throughout Europe and North America. In the 21st Century companies in China, and other countries along the Pacific Rim with low-cost labor, have adopted the same strategy.

Psychological Pricing

Psychological pricing means pricing at a level that is perceived to be much lower than it actually is: For instance, $99, $19.99, and $1.98. Psychological pricing is a viable strategy and you should experiment with it to determine its precise application for your product. The conditions for considering this strategy are:

- A product is singled out for special promotion.
- A product is likely to be advertised, displayed, or quoted in writing.
- The selling price desired is close to a multiple of 10, 100, 1,000 and so on.

While psychological pricing more likely applies to consumer products, there is an increasing use of the strategy for business-to-business products and services, as in the example of a machine priced at $24,837.00. Note in this example that the traditional '9' is not used. Tests by such organizations as Sears reveal that the '9' doesn't have the psychological impact it once had. In various combinations the '7' has come out on top. In instances where a prestige product or service is offered, a psychological price may be expressed as 'one hundred dollars' to give an elitist impression.

Follow Pricing

Pricing in relation to industry price leaders is termed follow pricing. The conditions for considering this strategy are:

- Your organization may be a small or medium-size company in an industry dominated by one or two price leaders.
- Aggressive pricing fluctuations may result in damaging price wars.
- Most products offered don't have distinguishing features.

The most visible example of follow pricing is found in the computer market, in which IBM still holds a relatively high worldwide position. At one time,

IBM set the pricing standards by which its competitors priced their products. However, this situation turned out to be a two-edged sword.

The IBM-compatible computers priced at 20% to 40% below IBM reached such high proportions that IBM was forced to reverse its role and use follow pricing against aggressive competitors as a means of protecting its share of the market. However, IBM's use of follow pricing was a holding action in its broader strategy of attempting to regain leadership with the introduction of new products, systems, and especially, services.

Cost-Plus Pricing

Cost-plus pricing means basing price on product costs and then adding on components such as administration and profit. The conditions for using this strategy are:

- The pricing procedure conforms to government, military, or construction regulations.

- There are unpredictable total costs owing to ongoing new product development and testing phases.

- A project or product moves through a series of start-and-stop sequences.

Cost-plus pricing, unless mandated by government procedures, is product-based pricing. Such an approach contrasts with market-based pricing, which takes into consideration the following:

- Corporate, divisional, or product-line objectives concerning profits, competitive inroads, market share and market stability.

- Target-market objectives dealing with desired market position, profile of customer segments, current demand for product and future potential of the market.

Slide-Down Pricing

The purpose of slide-down pricing is to move prices down to tap successive layers of demand. The conditions for considering this strategy are:

- The product would appeal to progressively larger groups of users at lower prices in a price-elastic market.

- The organization has adopted a low-cost producer strategy by adhering to learning curve concepts and other economies of scale in distribution, promotion and sales.

- There is a need to discourage competitive entries.

Slide-down pricing is best utilized in a proactive management mode rather than as a reaction to competitors' pressures. If you anticipate the price movements and do sufficient segmentation analysis to identify price-sensitive groups, you can target those groups with specific promotions to preempt competitors' actions.

Skim pricing, as previously noted with the electronics industry, begins with high pricing and then evolves to slide-down pricing. The downward movement of price usually coincides with such events as new competitors entering to buy market share through low price and then waits for economies of scale to begin taking effect.

Segment Pricing

Segment pricing involves pricing essentially the same products differently to various groups. The conditions for considering this strategy are:

- The product is appropriate for several market segments.

- If necessary, the product can be modified or packaged at minimal costs to fit the varying needs of customer groups.

- The consuming segments are non-competitive and do not violate legal constraints.

Examples abound for segment pricing. The most visible ones are airlines that offer essentially one product, an airplane seat between two locations. Yet this 'same' product may serve different segments, such as business people, clergy, students, military, senior citizens, each at different prices. Then, there is further segmentation according to time of day, day of week, or length of stay at one destination.

To best take advantage of this pricing strategy, search out poorly served, unserved, or emerging market segments.

Flexible Pricing

Pricing to meet competitive or marketplace conditions is known as flexible pricing. The conditions for considering this strategy are:

- There is a competitive challenge from imports.

- Pricing variations are needed to create tactical surprise and break predictable patterns.

- There is a need for fast reaction against competitors' attacking your market with penetration pricing.

As organizations downsize to become more competitive, field managers familiar with the dynamics of their respective markets usually are handed greater pricing authority and accountability. The intent is to allow a flexible pricing strategy when appropriate. In contrast, the opportunity to react is missed where there is a long chain of command from field managers to executive levels, with the detrimental effect of consuming excessive response time.

Pre-emptive Pricing

Pre-emptive pricing is used to discourage competitive market entry. The conditions for considering this strategy are:

- You hold a strong position in a medium to small market.

- You have sufficient coverage of the market and sustained customer loyalty (that is, customer satisfaction) to cause competitors to view the market as unattractive.

Pre-emptive pricing, as with flexible pricing, requires close contact with the field. That means tuning into customers, competitors, market and economic conditions, and any other factors that would influence pricing decisions.

Phase-Out Pricing

Phase-out pricing means pricing high to remove a product from the line. The conditions for considering this strategy are:

- The product has entered the down side of the product life-cycle, but it is still used by a few customers.

- Sudden removal of the product from the line would create severe problems for your customers and create poor relations,

Phase-out pricing does not mean dumping a product. Rather, it is intended for use with a select group of customers who are willing to pay a higher price for the convenience of a source of supply.

Loss-Leader Pricing

Pricing a product low to attract buyers for other products is called loss-leader pricing. The conditions for considering this strategy are:

- Complimentary products are available that can be sold in combination with the loss leader at normal price levels.

- The product is used to draw attention to a total product line and increase the customer following. The strategy is particularly useful in conjunction with impulse buying.

Loss-leader is one of the most common forms of pricing strategy. It is prevalent in all ranges of businesses, from department stores to auto dealers to industrial product lines. You should remember, however, to consider the profitability of the total product line.

Summary

Your overriding purpose in all of the above strategies is to void or postpone price wars. You can begin by locating untapped market segments and focusing on product improvements. You can also preempt and discourage new competitors by gradually sliding down prices, thereby making the market seem unprofitable. You can always price according to the flexibility of demand and your production economies.

Consider six strategies to avoid the dire consequences of a price war:

1. Look for viable acquisitions or possible joint relationships with firms that offer services to complement your own.

2. Devote time and energy to develop value-added services. For instance, initiate emergency delivery, offer private-label packaging, install computerized inventory control systems and ordering procedures, reduce time to resolve complaints, connect a '24/7' hot-line for technical assistance, and other customized services.

3. Work jointly with suppliers to find new applications for products that would open up new market niches.

4. Examine opportunities for multiplex marketing. That is, search for opportunities to add new segments with innovative distribution approaches.

5. Make use of new technologies. Look to the immense opportunities to create a competitive edge and unstick yourself from the commodity/price problem. For instance reach for high performance with computerized order-entry systems or warehouse automation.

6. Hone your marketing efficiency with direct-response, telemarketing and Internet breakthroughs.

Promotion Strategies

9.1 Developing Promotion Strategies

Promotion is incorporated in SBP Section 2 (Growth Strategies) and Section 8 (Tactics). To develop effective promotion strategies, you need to shape a program that combines advertising and sales promotion (including the Internet) into a totally integrated force. Keeping these activities separate leads to vague advertising and ineffective sales support. Let's begin with advertising and how to develop a successful advertising campaign.

The purpose of the details that follow is to acquaint you with the process and arm you with guidelines for evaluating the promotional strategies. It is in your best interest to understand the approaches, since the output becomes an integral part of the strategic and tactical portions of the SBP – and ultimately is your responsibility.

9.2 Advertising

Advertising is only one part of the communications mix; communications is only one part of promotion; promotion is only one component of the marketing mix. Thus, advertising – as with all the other components – is never created in isolation.

Initially, you should know what you want advertising to accomplish. For example, it can support personal selling, inform a target audience about the availability of your product, or persuade prospects to buy. Then, you can choose media and copy themes to match those objectives. As a result, your advertising becomes realistic, measurable and results-oriented.

How to Develop a Successful Advertising Campaign

If you are responsible for implementing an overall advertising strategy through an advertising department or an outside advertising agency, here are **key points** you need to know:

- First, advertising is aimed at informing your target audience about the availability and features of your product or service.

- Second, once that audience has been informed, advertising should persuade your prospects to buy your offering.

In this process, advertising interacts closely and continuously with the other elements of your marketing mix, such as your product, pricing and distribution. More specifically it reinforces personal selling efforts. In turn, its impact is enhanced by sales promotion activities.

Table 9.1 details the steps involved in developing an advertising campaign. It shows that continuous marketing research is the foundation of a sound campaign.

CAMPAIGN STEP	ADVERTISING ACTIVITIES	RESEARCH ACTIVITIES
	Pre-Campaign Phase	
1. Market analysis		Study competitive products, positioning, media, distribution and usage patterns
2. Product research		Identify perceived product characteristics and benefits
3. Customer research		Conduct demographic and psychographic studies of prospective customers; investigate media, purchasing and consumption patterns
	Strategic Decisions	
4. Set advertising objectives	Determine target markets and identify user profile, exposure goals	
5. Decide on level of appropriation	Determine total advertising spending necessary to support objectives	Investigate competitive spending levels and media costs necessary to reach objectives
6. Formulate advertising strategy	Develop creative approach and prepare 'shopping list' of appropriate media	Examine audience profiles, reach, frequency and costs of alternative media
7. Integrate advertising strategy with overall marketing strategy	Make sure that advertising supports and is supported by other elements of the marketing mix	
	Tactical Execution	
8. Develop detailed advertising budget	Break down overall allocation to spending on media categories and individual media	

CAMPAIGN STEP	ADVERTISING ACTIVITIES	RESEARCH ACTIVITIES
9. Choose message content and mode of presentation	Develop alternative creative concepts, copy and layout	Conduct concept and copy tests
10. Analyze legal ramifications	Choose copy reviewed by legal staff or counsel	
11. Establish media plan	Determine media mix and schedule	Conduct media research, primarily from secondary sources
12. Review agency presentation	See entire planned campaign for approval	
	Campaign implementation	
13. Production and traffic	Finalize and reproduce advertisement(s), buy media time and space, and deliver ads	
14. Insertion of advertisements	Actually run ads in selected media	Check whether changes yielded desired results
	Campaign Follow-Through	
15. Impact control		Get feedback on consumer and competitive reaction
16. Review and revision	Adjust advertising execution or spending levels to conditions	Check whether ads appeared as agreed and directed

TABLE 9.1: **DEVELOPING AN ADVERTISING CAMPAIGN**

Pre-Campaign Phase

Sound planning techniques call for a careful assessment of overall market conditions before formulating an advertising campaign. The individual(s) in charge of this function should do the following:

STEP ONE

Conduct a market analysis that surveys the competitive field. For instance, this analysis should examine the range of competitive offerings and related market trends, their positioning and media choices, and their distribution and usage patterns.

You will want to find out who competitors' customers are and when, where and for what purpose they make purchases. This background information will provide the necessary perspective for choosing appropriate strategies.

STEP TWO

Subsequent product research should focus more intensively on your own product. You want to find out from actual or potential users of the product which features they consider desirable and what benefits they associate with its use.

Such information will help you make the right positioning decision and formulate effective appeals. In this context, study the usage patterns in depth.

STEP THREE

Finally, the pre-campaign research should concentrate on the customer. Here, you attempt to develop demographic and psychographic (behavioral) profiles of actual or prospective buyers.

For instance, recognize who are the frequent and infrequent users of your product, how old they are, where they live, how much money they have at their disposal, their educational backgrounds, their occupations, their marital status and family size. To the extent you are able, attempt to find out their buying behavior and what factors influence buying decisions.

You can gain additional insights by looking at consumption patterns. At that point, you can determine who ultimately consumes your product, when, how much, how often and under what circumstances. Only after all of this preliminary information has been gathered, interpreted and internalized should the advertising planning be initiated.

Strategic Decisions

Once you assemble and examine the relevant data, then you are ready to make a number of strategic decisions that will guide the detail work that follows. As in all planning activities, the first major decision is to set advertising objectives for SBP Section 7.

Advertising Objectives

You could say that the basic objective of all advertising is to sell something — a product, service, idea, or company. To that end, advertising is effective communication, resulting in positive attitudes and behavior on the part of the receivers of the message that results in increased sales.

However, the objective of increasing sales is too broad to be implemented effectively in an advertising program. Rather, you, or those responsible for implementing advertising campaigns, should formulate more specific aims that pinpoint with greater precision and measure with accuracy. For example:

- Support a personal selling program.

- Achieve a specific number of exposures to your target audience.

- Address prospects that are inaccessible to your salespeople.

- Create a specified level of awareness, measurable through recall or recognition tests.

- Improve dealer relations.

- Improve consumer attitudes toward your product or company.

- Present a new product and generate demand for it.

- Build familiarity and easy recognition of your company, brand, package, or trademark.

The list illustrates some of the possibilities and identifies the need for precision to derive maximum guidance from objectives. Because objectives imply accountability for results, they often lead to an evaluation of individual or advertising agency performance.

Advertising Appropriation

Having determined where you want to go, you must now decide how best to get there. You can choose from a number of alternative approaches for setting the level of total advertising spending.

- **Affordable Method**: Ignores your objectives and is simply an expression of how much you think you can afford to spend. This viewpoint makes your level of appropriation subject to whim and may grossly over- or under-estimate the amount in relation to your needs.

- **Percentage of Sales Approach**: Probably the most widely used because of its simplicity. That is, it ties your advertising allowance to a specified percentage of current or expected future sales. This procedure, with its built-in fluctuations, not only discourages long-term advertising planning but also neglects current business needs and opportunities.

- **Competitive Parity Method**: Proposes that your company match competitive spending levels. This simplistic outlook is no more sophisticated or justifiable than the two preceding approaches.

- **Objective and Task Method**: Produces the most meaningful results. You proceed in three steps: (1) define your advertising objectives as specifically as possible; (2) identify the tasks that must be performed to achieve your objectives; and (3) estimate the costs of performing these tasks.

The sum total of these costs represents your level of appropriation. While this approach does not examine or justify the objectives themselves, it nevertheless reflects a reliable assessment of your perceived needs and opportunities, which you can translate into a workable budget.

Tactical Execution

At this point, tactical execution deals with selecting those appeals most likely to stimulate prospects' purchasing decisions in your favor. Product appeal is defined in terms of price, importance to the consumer, frequency of purchase, competitive edge and utility.

While the creative process at this stage involves a considerable amount of intuition, the quality and reliability of the data available to copywriters and designers significantly affect the outcome of their efforts. Therefore, besides selecting appeals, you must understand the basic method by which messages are conveyed. This means considering audience profiles, style and costs of alternative media.

Making Your Advertising Investment More Productive

Advertising is a key element in a total communications package. In terms of creating widespread awareness and exposure of your product, it certainly is your best buy. Remember, however, no matter how good your agency or advertising department is, you bear the ultimate responsibility for results. Therefore, it pays to be sceptical, independent and not be intimidated by the creators of your advertising.

You can work more intelligently and effectively with your advertising people, and offer more precise guidance as to what they should stress. The following cardinal guidelines pertain primarily to print advertising:

1. **Be aware of your product's positioning in the marketplace**. You may choose to offer it as an alternative to an exciting way of doing things or to the competing product in the field. Also, emphasize a major customer benefit that is unique, meaningful, and competitive – and one that can truly and convincingly be delivered by your product.

2. **Maintain a personality for your brand**. Use your advertising to make a positive contribution to the brand image. If you want your ads to command attention and produce results, try for a uniqueness that makes them stand out from the flood of competing messages. It is helpful to use a symbol, logo, or other repetitious element that will be remembered by customers.

3. **Don't bore your audience and don't be impersonal**. Innovate, don't imitate. Start trends instead of following them. The risks are high, but so are the potential rewards.

4. **Solve a problem**. Choose a problem that your prospects can relate to and show how your product or service can solve it.

5. **Formulate effective headlines**. Use simple, understandable language. Department store advertising research has shown that headlines of ten or more words sell more merchandise than do shorter ones. (This guideline about number of words is still open to debate by advertising professionals. It needs to be tested in your marketplace.)

6. **Visually reinforce your advertising with illustrations, particularly of demonstrations**. Also, pictures with story appeal awaken the curiosity of the readers and tempt them to read the text. In some markets, photographs pull better than drawings. Here, too, you will have to test your audience for best response.

7. **Use captions, the capsule explanations beneath pictures, to sell**. Include your product's brand name and the major benefit you promise.

8. **Generate an informative atmosphere**. Filling your ads with solid information is most often the approach to take rather than relying on using elaborate 'creative' layouts. However, there is a current trend in using unrelated story-lines and illustrations with only minimal reference to the features and benefits of the product. Again, know your audience and test your advertising.

9. **Be aware that readership falls off rapidly in ad copy of up to 50 words but shrinks only insignificantly in copy of 50 to 500 words**. Although relatively few people read long copy, those people generally represent genuine prospects. Studies show those business-to-business ads with more than 350 words are read more thoroughly than shorter ones.

10. **Don't replace your advertisements before they have a chance to develop their full potential**. The most basic learning theories stress the importance of repetition in affecting behavior. Repeat your winners until their effects start to wear off.

9.3 Sales Promotion

Used primarily in SBP Sections 7 and 8, attempt to integrate sales promotion with your advertising and sales-force objectives and strategies. Your intent is to use sales promotion to encourage more product usage, induce dealer involvement, and stimulate greater sales-force efforts.

Here are some characteristics of effective sales promotion: Use sales promotion as an incentive to buy, whereas advertising offers a reason to buy. Also, while sales promotion is part of an overall tactical program, it involves a variety of company functions to make it work effectively. Sales promotion permits tremendous flexibility, creativity and application.

Consider the following applications:

- **Consumer promotions**: consists of samples, coupons, cash refunds, premiums, free trials, warranties and demonstrations.

- **Trade promotions**: includes buying allowances, free goods, cooperative advertising, display allowances, push money for sales people, video conferencing and dealer sales contests.

- **Sales-force promotions**: employs bonuses, contests and sales rallies.

As indicated with advertising, sales promotion is not a stand-alone activity. Instead, make it a component of the tactical portion of your SBP. Further, establish your sales promotion objectives to support the broader vision of your strategic direction.

Such objectives include:

- Entering new market segments
- Gaining entry into new channels of distribution
- Encouraging purchase of larger size units
- Building trial usage among non-users
- Attracting switchers away from competitors
- Building brand loyalty
- Stimulating off-season sales
- Winning back customers.

How to Use Sales Promotion to Stimulate Sales

Sales promotion is a potentially powerful tool that is often poorly understood, planned, and applied, leading to considerable waste and inefficiency. Yet, it can be an effective component of almost any promotion mix with creative applications from consumer goods, to industrial goods and even services. It supplements and complements the more sophisticated advertising and personal selling efforts.

What is sales promotion? It consists of all those promotional efforts of a firm that cannot be grouped under the heading of advertising, personal selling, publicity, or packaging. More precisely:

> *'Sales promotion refers to activities or objects that attempt to encourage salespeople, resellers and ultimate buyers to cooperate with a manufacturer's plans by temporarily offering more value for the money or providing some special incentive related to a specific product or service.'*

While somewhat lengthy, this definition points to a number of essential features:

- Sales promotion includes both *activities* – such as demonstrations and contests and *objects* – such as coupons, premiums and samples.

- It may be directed at one or any combination of three distinct audiences: a company's own sales-force; middlemen of all types and levels, such as wholesalers and retailers (for simplicity sake, they will be referred to as dealers); and consumers or business-to-business buyers.

- In contrast with the continuous, long-term nature of the other elements of the promotion mix (legendary advertising guru, David Ogilvy said "an advertisement is a long-term investment in the image of a brand"); sales promotion campaigns are *temporary measures* that should be used with discretion.

However, unless used wisely, sales promotion can easily become self-defeating and counterproductive. While there are no hard and fast rules, a brand, for example, that is 'on deal' one-third of the time or more is likely to suffer image problems. In fact, if yours is a leading brand in a mature market, you should use sales promotion most sparingly because it is unlikely that you will gain any lasting advantage from a more generous application.

It is important to remember that sales promotion is costly and should thus be judged from a cost/benefit point of view. So, don't overuse it – even if the temptation is great to yield to external competitive challenges.

Some important external reasons for the increased use of sales promotion include:

- The number of products in the business-to-business and consumer marketplaces have proliferated, leading to intensified competition and the need to create more 'noise' at the point of purchase.

- There is a need to respond to competitive increases in promotion spending, although clearly accompanied by the danger of escalation into a 'war' in which all sides lose.

- In a recessionary economy, manufacturers are more willing to use rebates to shrink inventories and improve liquidity, just as consumers are more responsive to sales stimulation measures.

- The growing power of and pressure from the trade produce more promotional allowances and support from suppliers.

- There is a certain degree of disenchantment with advertising, which many managers feel has declined in efficiency and effectiveness owing to a disproportionate rise in cost and in competing messages.

Beginning a Sales Promotion Campaign

To develop a planned approach to sales promotion over a haphazard one, you will find it profitable to follow a series of logical steps for maximum impact and efficiency. This can be achieved only if you make a sales promotion campaign an integral part of your SBP, carefully coordinated with the other elements of your firm's promotion mix and, ultimately, with its marketing mix.

As already stated, sales promotion complements, supplements and often amplifies other promotional tools; and it should always be used in concert with them. For example, displays that tie in with TV commercials produce more sales than unrelated ones.

The following steps are involved in the evolution of a sales promotion campaign:

1. Establish your objectives.
2. Select appropriate techniques.
3. Develop your sales promotion program.
4. Pretest your sales promotion program.
5. Implement and evaluate your campaign.

Establish Sales Promotion Objectives

While the main purpose of sales promotion is to increase the sales volume of a product or to stimulate traffic in a retail outlet, more specific objectives can be identified, depending upon the type of audience and the nature of the task involved.

For instance, sales promotion efforts directed at your company's own sales-force aim to generate enthusiasm and zeal. It is important, then, that you offer your salespeople special incentives to excel and provide the desired support.

A second targeted group is your company's dealers or distributors, without whose active cooperation your entire marketing effort and, more specifically, a sales promotion campaign would falter.

Lastly, while the support and loyalty of your sales-force and dealer/distributor network are certainly crucial, a sales promotion campaign would hardly be complete if it failed to stimulate buyer action.

Consider these objectives:

- Identify and attract new buyers.
- Encourage more frequent and varied usage of current products.
- Motivate trial and purchase of new products.
- Educate users and non-users about improved product features.
- Suggest purchases of multiple and/or larger units of your product.
- Win over buyers of competitive products.
- Reinforce brand loyalty and purchase continuity.
- Create customer enthusiasm and excitement leading to word-of-mouth recommendations and referrals.
- Diminish fluctuations by encouraging off-season usage.
- Counter competitive raiding.
- Generate more traffic at your dealers' outlets.

Although sales promotion campaigns represent short-term stimulation, they are most effective when used in a long-term framework. Further, sales promotion objectives cannot and should not be developed in a vacuum, but rather should tie in with overall strategies and tactics. In addition, your sales promotion objectives should be audience-specific and should be spelled out in quantitative form to facilitate later evaluation.

Select Appropriate Techniques

Once you have decided which market segments you want to address, you can select specific techniques for motivating the dealer, introducing new products and promoting existing products.

MOTIVATING THE DEALER

With dealers (or any intermediary in the business-to-business, consumer and service sectors), the most powerful language to speak is still money, that is, profit. Among many available techniques, sales promotion to motivate dealers can include buying allowances, cooperative advertising, dealer listings, sales contests, specialty advertising and exhibits at trade shows.

INTRODUCING NEW PRODUCTS

Another meaningful way to break down the variety of approaches is to group them according to their major application area. Sales promotion techniques particularly well suited to the introduction of new products include free samples or trial offers, coupons and money refunds.

PROMOTING EXISTING PRODUCTS

You may want to use one or more different tools when attempting to promote established brands, such as: premiums, price packs, contests and sweepstakes, trading stamps and demonstrations. These tools aim to attract competitors' customers and build market share, introduce new versions of established brands and reward buyer loyalty.

Table 9.2 will aid your selection process by presenting the pros and cons of these sales techniques.

TECHNIQUE	ADVANTAGES	DISADVANTAGES
Free samples	Induce trial Attract new customers Speed up adoption	Expensive Lacks precision Cumbersome
Free trial	Overcomes market resistance	Costly to administer
Door-to-door couponing	Very selective High redemption rate	Time consuming Needs careful supervision Lead time needed
Direct-mail couponing	High targetability At-home coverage High redemption rate	Needed Costly Dependent upon list quality
Newspaper couponing	Quick and convenient Geographically targetable Low cost	Low redemption rate Retailers may balk Requires careful planning
Magazine/supplement couponing	Targeted audience Effective coverage Increases in readership	Can become expensive Consumers neglect to clip Slow redemption rate
Money refund	Generates new business Reinforces brand loyalty	Results can be slow Modest impact
In-or-near pack premiums	Increases product sales Modest distribution cost	Bonus to loyal buyers Pilferage problem
Self-liquidating premiums	Low cost Boosts brand image	Modest sales impact May be too popular
Price pack	Moves merchandise Keeps up visibility	Not selective May cheapen brand image
Contests/sweepstakes	No purchase required Increases brand awareness	Expensive Modest participation
Trading stamps/promotional games	No extra expense for consumer Creates store preference	Consumer boredom Expensive
Point-of-purchase displays	Effective stimulation	Requires dealer cooperation

TABLE 9.2: **ADVANTAGES AND DISADVANTAGES OF VARIOUS SALES PROMOTION TECHNIQUES**

Develop Your Sales Promotion Program

A critical point is deciding on the length of your campaign. If the promotion is too short, neither you nor your target audience will derive sufficient benefit from it. On the other hand, if it is too long, your brand's image is likely to be cheapened and your campaign's 'act now' urgency will be diluted.

A related issue is, of course, frequency – that is, how often you should promote a given product. Generally, the rules are not too often, not too short and not too long. Other issues to maximize the effectiveness of your campaign include the following:

PRETEST YOUR SALES PROMOTION PROGRAM

Having further determined when to run your campaign, make sure your schedule ties in smoothly with the other elements of your SBP. You should also proceed to pretest your campaign on a limited scale. This activity will help reassure you that you have chosen the most appropriate device and incentive, and are delivering it in the most effective manner.

IMPLEMENT AND EVALUATE YOUR CAMPAIGN

Once your campaign has been fine-tuned and fully orchestrated, put it into effect. If you are introducing a new product, you may want to demonstrate it at a national sales meeting to motivate your sales-force to go out and excel. For an established product, you may instead send your salespeople kits that spell out the objectives of your campaign and its operational details, as well as the nature and size of the incentives offered to them, your dealers and your consumers.

MONITOR THE PROGRESS OF YOUR CAMPAIGN

You can measure the extent of goal attainment and campaign effectiveness in various ways; the essential ones,   example, are product movement or market-share figures. But it is here that you must keep in mind the limitations of your sales promotion campaign, namely: Sales promotion is a short-term tool that can support long-term goals only in a supplementary capacity. It cannot build a consumer franchise. To the contrary, if it is used too often, it can destroy the image of a brand. Thus, it should be used not as a substitute for advertising, but rather as a complementary effort.

9.4 Marketing Over The Internet

Spanning the networks of retailers to brokers and manufacturers, a remarkable marketing tool, the Internet, is transforming the way individuals buy and the methods by which companies conduct business. Its usage is as far-reaching as the World Wide Web itself, with applications as sweeping as trading stocks, obtaining information on autos, subscribing to book and music clubs, getting price quotes on mortgages and purchasing airline tickets.

Let's track the workings of a particular transaction where a computer maker is searching for the best price and delivery of a memory chip in an open-market networking system:

1. A computer maker needs 10,000 memory chips to assemble one of its new models.

2. The purchasing department logs on to the Internet network and enters information about the chip. The system shows a list of available chips with price, quantity and other specifications.

3. The computer maker puts in a price. E-mail notifies the suppliers and other buyers interested in the same part of the bid.

4. The seller indicates its selling price. The buyer is alerted by e-mail and accepts the price.

The ability to utilize the Internet is not confined to the large organizations, small companies with limited sales resources can establish a home page as a way to communicate a product message, offer special deals, announce a new service, or launch into foreign markets.

Having established your Internet presence, the next step is to market your on-line service and have customers and prospects visit your site. The following guidelines will assist you in gaining visibility:

-   Promote your web site in all advertising media, including sales promotion brochures, technical manuals, letterheads and business cards.

-   Display your web address on packages, in-store displays and counter tops.

-   Use your web address on press releases and any articles written for or about your firm.

- Develop dedicated promotions that 'sell' the recipient on the advantages of visiting your web site. This goes together with the guidelines of offering genuine information to the visitor.

- Register with web search engines, the means by which individuals locate sites that interest them. You can also buy a banner ad in a popular search engine in a particular section in which your company is classified. Interested users can then link or connect to your site, thereby increasing your traffic at a modest cost. The major search engines include Yahoo, Google, Excite, Infoseek, WebCrawler, Alta Vista, Lycos and OpenText.

This exciting medium is still in its infancy and with the projected revenue growth into the 21st Century projected to skyrocket into the billions, establishing a solid presence on the Internet will pay off in sales growth and market expansion.

The bottom line: Make the Internet an integral component of your promotion effort in SBP Sections 7 and 8.

Distribution Strategies

10.1 Developing Distribution Strategies

The ultimate success of your business strategy depends on moving your product to its intended market. Accordingly, you should take considerable care in selecting distribution strategies and considering the far-reaching impact of channel decisions.

Such decisions involve (1) the long-term commitment to the distribution channel; (2) the amount of geographic coverage needed to maintain a competitive advantage; and (3) the possibility of competitive inroads.

10.2 Channel Size

Your initial step in developing a channel strategy is to review the categories of products being sold by your company and their market coverage. In your review consider these criteria:

- Speciality products do best with exclusive (restricted) distribution.

- Convenience products do best with intensive (widespread) distribution.

- Shopping products do best with selective (high sales potential) distribution.

Next, determine if existing channels provide adequate market coverage and if there are possibilities for expansion. Enhancing your present distribution network or creating a new one affords a prime opportunity to unseat a channel leader or deter a challenger.

First, begin by tailoring distribution to each major market segment, weighing up the following alternatives:

- **Direct versus distributors**. Consider selling direct. Eliminating the middlemen permits faster, more efficient access to product users. The rapid growth of direct response marketing through telephone, mail and the expanding use of the Internet, permit flexible response to customers' demands by circumventing traditional space and time barriers. With this in mind, determine whether you can deliver service that distributors normally offer.

- **Distributors versus brokers**. Whereas distributors typically carry inventory and brokers do not, question how each would serve market niches in light of customers' need for critical delivery schedules, immediate customer assistance and storage needs.

- **Distributors versus retailers**. Pinpoint how each of these two options is efficient, taking into account quantities purchased, services rendered and access to technical backup.

- **Exclusive versus non-exclusive outlets**. Weigh up the pros and cons: Exclusivity may constrict a channel's breadth of coverage; yet provide compensating service and commitment benefits. On the other hand, non-exclusive outlets may broaden overall availability, but impair the level of commitment required for your product line.

Also, look for potential possibilities for enhancing your distribution strategy by infusing value-added services that may provide enough differentiation to save your product from becoming a commodity. For example, employing value-added services can strengthen customer relationships by:

- Making use of greater mobility as it follows customers into growth segments, thereby serving buyers' needs at various locations.

- Developing one-stop-shopping that allows buyers to order a variety of related products with ease, convenience and volume discounts. The combined effect makes it harder for competitors to gain a foothold in the distribution network.

- Centralizing the delivery of technical training, customer service and reliable after-sales support provides an infrastructure from which to launch into new segments.

- Installing a computerized ordering and stocking system ties customers to supplier, thereby creating an electronic stronghold from which it is difficult for competitors to disengage a customer.

Choosing Channels of Distribution

There are at least three reasons why distribution channel size should rank high in importance as you develop your firm's SBP:

1. CHANNEL DIMENSIONS INVOLVE LONG-TERM COMMITMENTS TO OTHER FIRMS

Once chosen, distribution channels typically develop a great deal of inertia against change. Your choice of a channel type associates your brand in the consumer's mind with a certain kind of store or outlet, thus creating an image that is difficult to alter.

Signing up individual wholesalers or retailers often involves substantial up-front outlays. This money is needed for the following: field training of sales personnel, granting of easy terms for initial stock, advertising and promotional support, and field sales support through missionary salespeople. These and many other investments and commitments would be wasted if you decide to abandon these channel partners.

Remember, too, that it would hardly sit well with the trade if you walked away from your commitments. Your channel partners would also resent any infringement on their franchise if you adopted a multiple-channel strategy for the same brand.

2. CHANNEL DIMENSIONS DELIMIT THE PORTION OF THE MARKET YOU CAN REACH

Your selection of channel members restricts the kinds and numbers of ultimate buyers you can reach through them. In effect, you could be cut off from that part of the market that does not patronize those outlets. Conversely, your selection of outlets may coincide with your target market, in which case neglecting the remainder of the market is deliberate.

But what if you can't attract the kinds of stores or outlets that cater to the group of consumers you wish to reach? Then you have to settle for what you can get. To avoid this trap, your product, price and support must satisfy the intermediaries you want to win over.

3. CHANNEL DIMENSIONS AFFECT ALL OTHER STRATEGY DECISIONS

The interdependence of marketing mix decisions is most evident when choosing distribution channels. If you choose a pattern of exclusive distribution, your product often becomes a luxury item requiring high prices and high dealer margins. If, on the other hand, you go after intensive market coverage, you characterize your product as mass merchandise, which often necessitates a low-price policy.

Choice of advertising approaches, themes, messages, and media will vary with your product's distribution channels. Also, product and packaging design must reflect the characteristics of your selected channels.

For instance, merchandise suited for self-service outlets have to be presented differently from goods requiring the advice and explanation of knowledgeable sales personnel. Consequently, don't make channel decisions in a void, since they have repercussions on every other strategy decision you make and thus affect your entire planning effort.

Distribution and Market Exposure

Adequate market coverage is interconnected to the product being promoted. Depending on the degree of market exposure desired, you can choose from exclusive, intensive and selective distribution strategies (see Table 10.1).

DISTRIBUTION CONSIDERATIONS	EXCLUSIVE	SELECTIVE	INTENSIVE
Degree of coverage	Limited	Medium	Saturation
Degree of control	Stringent	Substantial	Virtually nil
Cost of distribution	Low	Medium	High
Dealer support	Substantial	Limited	Very limited
Dealer training	Extensive	Restricted	None
Type of goods	Specialty	Shopping	Convenience
Product durability	Durable	Semi-durable	Non-durable
Product advertising	Yes	Yes	No
Couponing	No	No	Yes
Product example	Automobile	Suit	Chewing gum

TABLE 10.1: **CONSIDERATIONS IN CHOOSING YOUR DEGREE OF MARKET EXPOSURE**

EXCLUSIVE

If you sell a prestige product, you are likely to grant exclusive rights covering a geographic area to a specific wholesaler or retailer, protecting this firm against territorial encroachments by other companies carrying your products. This policy severely limits the number of middlemen handling your products and should be adopted only if you want to exercise substantial control over your intermediaries' price, promotion, presentation and service. It results in a stronger commitment on the part of your dealers and, thus, in a more aggressive selling effort.

INTENSIVE

Intensive distribution is the direct opposite of exclusivity. Popular among producers of convenience items, this policy aims to make these goods available in as many outlets as possible.

As the category name suggests, buyers of such products expect them to be conveniently accessible and will not expend much shopping effort. Products in this category are frequently purchased, low-ticket non-durables, such as cigarettes and chewing gum.

SELECTIVE

Selective distribution falls between the extremes of exclusive and intensive distribution. This policy involves setting up selection criteria and deliberately restricting the number of retailers that will be permitted to handle your brand. More than one, but less than all applicants in an area will be selected. This approach implies quality without the restrictions of exclusivity.

Direct Versus Indirect Distribution

A very basic distribution decision that you have to make relatively early in your planning is whether you want to handle the distribution of your product alone or you want to enlist expert help. Your decision is direct distribution or indirect distribution.

DIRECT DISTRIBUTION

Direct distribution involves a direct transfer of ownership from the producer to the consumer. This method does not preclude various types of facilitators from entering into the picture. As long as they do not assume title separate and distinct from the manufacturer, the channel still remains direct.

Thus, producers can sell through the mail, over the phone, door to door, the Internet, through a factory outlet, through their own retail stores, or even through an independent agent, and still be involved in a direct transaction. Direct distribution obviously involves a greater degree of control than indirect distribution, but it cuts a producer off from the widespread coverage that the latter approach can offer.

INDIRECT DISTRIBUTION

On the other hand, indirect distribution always incorporates middlemen or resellers, who are basically of two types: distributors and retailers.

In the direct distribution channel there is never a third party who takes title to the goods in question. For indirect distribution, the opposite situation is clearly the case, even though the manufacturer is likely to have a sales-force to call on intermediaries of the middleman variety.

Function versus Institution

In differentiating between direct and indirect distribution, a basic distinction ought to be made between the functions and institutions of wholesaling and retailing. The function of wholesaling is to sell those items necessary for use in the conduct of a business (for example, word processors) or for resale.

The function of retailing, in contrast, is to sell for personal, non-business use. In a retailing transaction the buyer of an item is a consumer who intends it for private use or consumption.

The reason for drawing these rudimentary distinctions between function and institution is that *institutions can be eliminated, their respective functions cannot.* When you first enter a new market, it is generally advisable to go the indirect route, involving wholesalers who can deliver a variety of quick and reliable services at little or no cost.

Later, though, as your product moves into the maturity stage of the life-cycle, you may want to eliminate your wholesalers in order to gain more immediate access to your retailers and better control over the selling effort. It is at this point that you often discover that one can eliminate the institution but not the function of wholesaling (or retailing, for that matter). The question, therefore, is not whether to perform these functions, but who is to perform them.

Making the Decision

When the time comes to make the channel decision for your product, you should consider several factors. Initially, an important consideration is where does the customer expect to find your product or service?

Therefore, the industry's prevailing distribution pattern is a powerful guide in making such a channel decision. If your current sales-force has related experience and appropriate business contacts, you may want to follow established routes.

Other factors you should take into account can be grouped as company, competitive and customer factors.

- **Companies** that are strong financially have the option of direct distribution, while weaker firms have to use middlemen. If your product line is broad, you are in a better position than a specialized supplier to consider going direct. In keeping with the market-based credo of staying close to the customer, the fewer intermediaries you will want to have.

- **Competitive** practices will often encourage you to meet competitors head-on in the very same outlets they use.

- **Customer** characteristics include the number of buyers, their geographic location and their buying patterns. You are better off going direct when you have a limited number of prospects. Again, if they are concentrated in only a few areas, you can send your own sales-force out to do the job. Should they buy often and in small quantities, you had better let others handle the selling.

Channel members are a vital link in your effort to satisfy distant customers. By making them your partners and serving their best interests, you will find that they will help you achieve your goals.

As discussed in the promotion section of Help Topics, there is still another factor that is beginning to make a significant impact on channel-related decisions: the Internet.

As a channel of distribution, doing business via the Internet shows cost savings averaging 5% to 10% of sales. For instance, chipmaker National Semiconductor Corp. reported saving its distributors $15 million in one year. Boeing Co. booked $60 million in spare parts orders from airlines in one year through its web site, and networking giant Cisco Systems Inc. booked $7 million in orders each day from resellers.

10.3 Channel Control

Channel control considers four sets of circumstances that dictate the search for new distributors:

1. New marketing efforts, for example, the introduction of a new product or entry into new markets.
2. Desire to intensify market coverage.
3. Need to replace existing distributors.
4. Industry changes or your strategy changes in methods of distribution.

After you've developed a channel control strategy that involves distributors, you need to know how to select and evaluate them. Use the following guidelines:

Selecting Distributors

Only with the appropriate distribution mix can you satisfactorily achieve your market-based goals. For instance, as you introduce new products, you may find that your current distributors are ill equipped to sell and service them; or that it already handles competitive products from other manufacturers.

Or you may be addressing a new kind of clientele not serviced by your current network. If you enter into new geographic markets, the need for appropriate representation may become self-evident.

As you review your share of the business in a given segment, you may conclude that your firm is under-represented. Or you may determine that your present distributor network is not going after the business aggressively enough to satisfy you. As a result, you may need to add or replace more distributors in the territory, based on population, sales, buying potential, or other relevant considerations.

By far the most frequent reason for appointing new distributors is the turnover of existing outlets. These changes may be due to natural attrition, the death or retirement of principals, or the sale or collapse of a distributor. The recent trend toward more specialization or limited-line selling has also led many distributors to drop a certain manufacturer's line.

Often, changes in your distributor mix come about by inadequate distributor performance that leaves the manufacturer, or even both sides, dissatisfied. In some instances, you may try to rekindle an existing relationship, as long as there is a willingness to recognize the dynamic changes of the market place, and consequently the changes required in strategy.

LOOKING AT YOUR DISTRIBUTION STRUCTURE

Rarely should you have to revamp your entire distribution structure. In some situations, however, you may want to add or eliminate an intermediary step in distributing your company's products, requiring the selection of new distributors.

Once you establish a need for a new or additional distributor representation, your next task is to develop a list of candidates. You usually have a number of sources for this list, including your own field sales-force, your manager of distributor sales, trade associations, and present distributors and dealers.

Table 10.2 highlights the selection criteria most often mentioned by some 200 leading manufacturers in a study on this subject. Look at how the numerous considerations are classified and summarized into a limited number of categories that can apply to any distributor selection task. You have the option of modifying or adding criteria to the list to suit your particular needs.

CRITERIA	INTERPRETATION
Financial aspects	Only a distributor of solid financial strength and practices can assure you of adequate, continuous representation
Sales organization and performance	The sales strength and record of a prospect is essential to your potential relationship
Number of salespeople	The general rule: the more salespeople, the more sales and the more effective the market coverage
Sales and technical competence	Salespeople with inadequate technical and sales skills are a liability
Sales performance	Accomplishments speak for themselves
Product lines carried	Pick your partners carefully
Competitive products	Generally avoid, sometimes okay
Compatible products	Tend to be beneficial
Quality level	The higher, the better
Number of lines	Will your line get enough attention
Reputation	You are judged by the image you project
Market coverage	Exposure means sales
Geographic coverage	Avoid overlap and conflicts
Industry coverage	Major user groups must be covered
Intensity of coverage	Infrequent calls mean lost business
Inventory and warehousing	Ability to deliver is often crucial
Kind and size of inventory	You want the right mix and a willingness to maintain adequate stock
Warehousing facilities	Storage and handling must be appropriate
Management	Proper leadership spells success
Ability	You want competent leadership
Continuity	Succession should be assured
Attitudes	Look for enthusiasm and aggressiveness

TABLE 10.2: **CRITERIA FOR SELECTING DISTRIBUTORS**

Evaluating Distributors

Once you have secured the services of a sought-after distributor candidate, you must then ensure that your association brings maximum benefit to both parties. You need to perform periodic evaluations designed to keep you continually informed about the relative performance of your various distributors.

These evaluations may be in the nature of current operating appraisals or may take on the form of overall performance reviews. If they are simple and limited in scope, you could conduct them monthly. Thorough analyses, however, should be undertaken only at infrequent intervals: annually, biannually, or even triannually.

If you engage in selective rather than exclusive distribution, the amount of evaluative input that you can obtain from your distributors is quite limited, forcing you to rely mostly on your own records, observations and intelligence. If your product is a high-volume, low-cost item with little need for after-sale servicing, you can restrict yourself to a more limited evaluation than in the case of complex systems installations.

If your team is composed of many hundreds of multi-line distributors, you will tend to take a closer look at a particular reseller only if its sales trends are way out of line. This procedure is called evaluation by exception.

If, in contrast, your firm employs only a moderate number of outlets, you analysis can be more thorough. You may not even need a formal evaluation if you have a close, continuous working relationship.

Whether you are a distributor or manufacturer, here are some broad guidelines:

IF YOU ARE A DISTRIBUTOR

Take control of the distribution channel by becoming more than just a conduit for supplying products from manufacturer to customer. Utilize technology to manage customers' inventories, improve delivery times, solve customers' problems, and reduce costs in order processing and shipping.

IF YOU ARE A MANUFACTURER

Recognize that if you decide to bypass the middleman, you will have to deliver the above services. With distributors taking the initiative, it may be a prudent alternative to select a distributor and provide maximum support, even to the extent of supplying capital to purchase or update the distributor's technology.

Such an alliance accepts the middlemen not as a weak link in a distribution chain, but as a powerful coupling to activate a marketing strategy.

Regardless of your position in the distribution chain, there are key functions you have to deal with in shaping a distribution strategy:

- **Information**: Collect, analyze and disseminate market intelligence about potential and current customers, competitors and other forces affecting the market.

- **Communication**: Combine various forms of communication including literature, videos and workshops to attract and retain customers.

- **Negotiation**: Seek agreement on price, terms of delivery and other value-added services as they relate to a preferred-customer status and long-term relationships.

- **Ordering**: Set-up procedures for the efficient transmission of ordering information, e.g., using the Internet.

- **Financing**: Develop the means to fund a managed inventory system.

- **Risk taking**: Assume the responsibility for risks associated with the expanded role and activities of the middleman.

- **Physical possession**: Develop a suitable capability to store additional varieties of products for customers and manage increases in inventory turnover.

- **Payment**: Design an effective system for payment – including the selective financing of inventories for the buyer.

- **Title**: Develop a system to pinpoint the transfer of ownership from seller to buyer. In some situations, inventory is held at the buyer's location and title changes only when usage occurs.

With the backward and forward flow of activities throughout the distribution channel, different participants in the channel assume distinct functions. Therefore, whether manufacturer or distributor, when forming a relationship clearly define the role of each channel member.

Creating Global Strategies

11.1 Creating a Global Perspective

A global business perspective goes well beyond geography and, in its broader dimensions, focuses on fresh applications of competitive strategies. Exhibiting a global perspective requires the mind of a strategist and the scope of thinking of a senior-level executive.

It boils down in pragmatic terms to opportunistic thinking. Such thinking is expressed in how you select and target markets and then penetrate for market-share leadership (based, of course, on your company's capabilities and resources). Such a perspective is the central aim behind developing your SBP.

11.2 Achieving a Global Perspective

More specifically, a global perspective means acquiring a mindset to assist you in successfully managing today's customer-oriented business, such as:

- Exhibiting expertise in competitive strategies.

- Encouraging sound strategic business planning.

- Fostering product innovation.

- Encouraging entrepreneurship.

- Committing to total product quality.

- Driving for product differentiation.

- Pursuing target (niche) marketing.

- Maintaining a complete global perspective.

Applying that orientation must play out against tough barriers, including aggressive competition from an increasing number of countries worldwide. Then, there are the fighting-back attitudes from domestic companies, as well as the growing protectionist feelings from some world governments.

Overseas Markets Offer Attractive Potential

There is no denying, however, that international markets present a challenging and steadily growing opportunity for global expansion, particularly as you develop SBP Section 4. It is likely that there are many people and companies around the world in need of what you have to offer, regardless of your industry.

More and more, the world is becoming a global marketplace. To stop your business activities at your geographic borders is not only arbitrary, but also short-sighted. Such an expansive orientation is not confined only to large organizations. Smaller companies are able to expand globally using some of the techniques listed below.

Developed countries generally provide an easier place to break into international markets, because they usually have fully developed communications, distribution and transportation systems, to name but a few facilitating factors.

In developing countries, on the other hand, you will need a more flexible approach, since they tend to be more jealous of their national prerogatives and less advanced in their infrastructure. Nevertheless, their sales potential is quite substantial. It can be tapped successfully if you are willing to adapt.

The entry strategies that follow show the choices available to your firm in its attempt to penetrate markets abroad and to establish a presence in them. While representing alternative possibilities, they can also be thought of as stages in a sequential process of increasing commitment. For example:

1. Products have to be tailored for local markets. Setting up such a strategy requires coordination at many levels. Sometimes termed 'mass customization', local marketing involves full cooperation from product developers, producers and local users in finding applications and solutions to customers' problems.

2. Employ country nationals in key positions, where possible. Cultural, language and local market barriers are more likely to be overcome by the sensitive responses of management familiar with the local markets.

3. Participate with distributors that can create effective linkages to specific customer groups.

4. Monitor the image your company and product line projects to target segments. When completed, the next step is to determine what changes are needed in product quality, performance, or service to improve the image that is consistent with the culture and practices of individual market segments.

11.3 Entry Strategies for International Markets

Strategies for entering foreign markets are conveniently classified into five basic categories: *exporting, licensing, joint venture, wholly owned subsidiaries* and *management contract.*

Table 11.1 presents these approaches in a systematic form for comparison. These alternatives differ from one another in intensity of commitment, amount of investment, extent of control and degree of profitability.

The choice from among them is often dictated by circumstances such as insufficient funds, inadequate knowledge of a foreign environment and host country restrictions on ownership. The intent here is to present an overview of the benefits and drawbacks of each category to enable you to make more informed decisions when considering the possibilities open to you on the international scene.

STRATEGY	DEFINITION	INTENSITY OF COMMITMENT	AMOUNT OF INVESTMENT	EXTENT OF CONTROL	DEGREE OF PROFITABILITY
Exporting	Marketing in one country those goods produced in another	Typically very limited	Possible investment in inventory	Rather limited, except in the case of exclusive distribution	Moderate, due to transportation cost, import duties, middlemen cost
Licensing	Licensor grants licensee right to use patent, know-how	Own marketing effort precluded until expiration of license	Virtually none	Very restricted; spelled out in license agreement	Fixed royalties dependent on licensee effort
Joint venture	Sharing ownership and control of foreign operation with at least one partner	Generally provide know-how and equity capital portion	Dependent on equity share	Dependent on ownership ratio and power play	Varies according to circumstances
Wholly owned subsidiary	Firm abroad 100% owned by own company	Strong commitment of all kinds of resources	Substantial investment in plant, etc.	Complete control over all phases of operation	Can be highly profitable
Management contract	Managing a foreign facility under contract	Only human resources	Facility not owned by managing firm	Restricted by contract; typically quite limited	Moderate, due to its fee character

TABLE 11.1: **COMPARISON OF ENTRY STRATEGIES FOR GLOBAL MARKETS**

Exporting

Your company may want to begin exporting and take best advantage of selling into markets that may be more responsive than domestic ones. If your productive capacity is not fully utilized, international markets can provide outlets that enable you to get extra mileage out of your plant.

Many firms consider revenues produced by exporting as 'found money', because domestic sales and the profit margin have already covered the plant's fixed costs.

Also, your firm may stumble onto the international scene because of excess production capacity and need stop-gap measures to bring utilization up to a more desirable level. You may not be serious about continuing export activities, but are attracted by the ratio of considerable sales potential to limited commitment and risk.

At the outset, for instance, you might not be inclined to invest in inventories abroad. Rather, you would want to minimize exposure by initially restricting activities to representation or distribution arrangements in a given country without committing funds for inventory, advertising and so forth. There is a price to pay, of course, for this lack of initial commitment.

If you leave everything to agents or distributors, you will have very little control over what happens. With inexperience, costs tend to be somewhat higher than they are otherwise, thus cutting into profit potential. In international trade, cost categories include transportation, import duties and middleman expenses. The paperwork involved in exporting should not be underestimated either.

Licensing

In one way, the simplest way to enter international markets is through licensing. In this setup, a licensor grants the right to exploit patents, trademarks, or proprietary technological know-how to a licensee (usually one per country) on an exclusive basis. Thus, without additional investment, your company could benefit from the efforts of others, based on its specialized knowledge and proprietary rights.

Relationships with individual licensees are arranged in licensing agreements. Such agreements generally stipulate the responsibilities of each party, the rights transferred, markets to be served, payments to be made, control procedures and termination circumstances. Protective clauses relate to the maintenance of proprietary rights, to protection against disclosure of information and to arbitration or litigation procedures.

On the surface, licensing looks like the ideal way for reaping effortless rewards. You can penetrate overseas markets with virtually no investment. There is no need to make capital outlays and send key personnel abroad, as in other entry strategies. Your licensee is likely to be a firm that is well established in the field and can give maximum support and exposure to your product.

Licensing offers you a source of additional earnings with little risk and minor demands on executive time. It gives you a chance to meet the needs of foreign prospects, overcome trade barriers, build-up goodwill and protect your patents and trademarks through usage. Sometimes, licensor and licensee cross-license each other, thus mutually benefiting from present and future know-how in a field.

Licensors are compensated for granting the license in the form of royalties. The royalty rate depends on the value of the rights being made available, the bargaining power of each party and the prevailing rate level. The amount of these royalties is, naturally, the direct outcome of the level of effort expended by the licensee.

This is the crux of the matter – once you have gained a license, you are at the mercy of your licensee. Though your agreement may provide for quality inspections and audits, you really cannot control the day-to day operations of your licensee and the extent of market development.

Should the licensee's efforts prove unsatisfactory or the licensed property's international potential grows, a license agreement can turn out to be a stranglehold, effectively restricting you from using your own property and quite possibly creating a strong international competitor. So, be cautious at the onset.

Joint Venture

If you want an active manufacturing presence in a host country transcending the amount of involvement and impact that you can have with exporting or licensing, a joint venture can prove an attractive possibility. In essence, a joint venture means that your firm establishes a subsidiary abroad that is jointly owned with at least one individual or company native to the country in question.

This approach may be advisable for a number of reasons:

- A joint venture may provide valuable help in gaining a foothold in a host country.
- It may reduce the risk of failure or expropriation.
- It provides additional capital or personnel you may lack to expand into this market on your own.
- It provides access to a local partner's distribution system or know-how.
- The law of the land may prevent setting up wholly owned subsidiaries.

In co-owning and co-controlling your common subsidiary, your firm and its overseas partner may share patents, trademarks and control over manufacturing or marketing. Joint ventures prove to be an excellent vehicle for entering international markets if the local partner has the marketing expertise to complement your firm's technological know-how.

A well-established local partner can provide your firm with physical facilities, a labor force, and contacts with businesses and officials, while your company may offer capital, technology and managerial talent.

The most obvious disadvantage of joint ventures is the reduced control of the foreign co-owner. Points of view may differ as to the policies and practices of the joint venture operation. Differences in culture, language and business philosophy may be difficult to overcome. While the potential for conflict is substantial, a well-chosen and well-motivated partner could result in great value.

Wholly Owned Subsidiaries

The greatest form of commitment abroad is a subsidiary that is wholly owned by your firm. The underlying idea is that ownership equals control and that complete control is necessary to meet corporate objectives. When demand and the competitive situation justify the substantial investment involved, this strategy can provide substantial benefits to the parent company. Your company may want to manufacture abroad in order to:

- Capitalize on low-cost labor.

- Avoid high import taxes or quotas.

- Reduce transportation cost.

- Gain access to raw materials.

- Export preferentially to related markets.

If your products are labor-intensive, you may want to locate plants in low-wage nations or areas, subsequently exporting the finished goods to more developed countries. Some countries and markets have erected high, even prohibitive, import duty barriers in an effort to preserve precious hard currency and foster local industry.

Less developed countries are concerned about possible exploitation of local resources if foreign firms within their borders do not have local partners. Thus, almost without exception, they require joint ownership and no longer permit wholly owned subsidiaries.

Increasingly, even in developed nations, firms may insist on taking local partners into their overseas subsidiaries. Doing so avoids criticism and improves their ability to cope with union demands and the complex requirements of the host government.

Management Contract

A management contract involves managing an overseas facility for its owner. It is entered into when the local owner does not possess, and cannot obtain, sufficient management expertise locally to run the facility efficiently.

Such a contract may be connected with the building of a sophisticated new facility, such as an airport or an oil refinery in a less developed country. The general contractor of such a turnkey facility often provides the talent to run it under a management contract.

Yet management by contract can represent the ultimate humiliation for the contractee when developing countries expropriate major industrial complexes and then ask the former owners to run these facilities under contract. At one time, this happened in the 'friendly' takeover of oil producing facilities by the Venezuelan government. Being pragmatic, the firms affected agreed to manage their former properties in return for special considerations in addition to their management fees.

Summary

You can feel out a selected market through exporting. If you are successful, the need may arise for local production. If you are not ready for direct investment, licensing provides a reasonable substitute. In order not to have to go it alone from the financial and marketing angles, you may instead (or subsequently) choose a joint venture arrangement.

Where permitted, wholly owned subsidiaries put you fully in charge. Management contracts offer a solution when a host country seeks your company's expertise, without allowing it to acquire ownership of the managed properties.

Whichever entry strategy your firm chooses to penetrate a foreign market, going global will increase your potential for growth and profit.

PART 12

The Team Approach – Thinking Like A Strategist

12.1 Thinking Like a Strategist

This final part of Help Topics concerns people interaction; that is, the mind of the strategist and the human will. These human factors intensify whenever there is a conflict of human wills, whenever there is an effort to grow, expand, or achieve objectives.

The purpose of this section is to show how you can coordinate the diverse talents of individuals into a cohesive force for developing your SBP. Therefore, the focus will be on (1) the role of strategy teams in developing your SBP; (2) broadening the perspective of teams to look at new developments that can be incorporated into the SBP; and (3) guidelines to thinking like strategists.

12.2 The Roles and Responsibilities of Strategy Teams

The mind of the manager, the human factors, and the people interactions are all key ingredients in organizing the input of market and competitive analyses into your SBP. Now let's overlay that concept with a definition of conducting strategic business operations in a market-driven environment, as a:

> 'Total system of interacting business activities designed to plan, price, promote and distribute want-satisfying products and services to household and organizational users at a profit in a competitive marketplace.'

You can effectively blend people interaction with the market-driven concept through strategy teams consisting of individuals from all functional areas of the organization (for example, manufacturing, product development, R&D, finance, distribution and sales/marketing). These functions may vary in some organizations.

Nonetheless, the key idea is that individuals from those major functions must be present in the strategy team to fulfill the strategic direction or vision (SBP Section 1) and the tactical day-to-day objectives (SBP Section 7) within a competitive environment.

One of the most notable users of strategy teams is Dow Chemical Co. It has employed an organizational structure for over 25 years that permits strategy teams to operate for individual products and markets, and at various levels throughout its worldwide operations. At any given time there may be as many as 40 strategy teams at work within Dow.

These teams have the various designations of Product Management Team (PMT), operating at a product manager level for a product line; Business Management Team (BMT) at the next level up, dealing with a business unit or major market; and Industry Management Team (IMT), operating on a still broader dimension.

Looking, for example, at the BMT, the team is usually chaired by a product/marketing manager and staffed by individuals representing such functional activities as manufacturing, finance, technical management and marketing/sales. This arrangement not only allows for the dynamics of team members working together, but also defuses traditional adversarial relationships – for example, between marketing and manufacturing.

Team members may change from time-to-time, and the frequency of meetings may vary with teams. Yet, the key element is that the permanency of the team as part of the organizational structure exists and can be called into action at any time.

In establishing a strategy team in your organization, take the lead in educating the team members to the key corporate concepts, SBP requirements and strategy techniques illustrated in this book. Further, brief the members (with the active endorsement of senior management) on the team's roles and responsibilities, which follow.

The strategy team, business management team, or product management team – whichever designation you select – is one of the most successful organizational formats for conceiving and delivering innovative and entrepreneurial thinking to the organization. Such a team should be initiated at every operational level by adopting role and responsibility guidelines.

For our purposes, let's designate the team as a Business Management Team (BMT) and establish its duties and responsibilities.

Team Duties

The Business Management Team serves as a significant functional contributor to the strategic business planning process with the following leadership responsibilities:

- Define the business or product strategic direction. (SBP Section 1.)
- Analyze the environmental, industry, customer and competitor situations. (SBP Sections 1 and 5.)
- Develop long-term and short-term objectives, strategies and tactics. (SBP Sections 2, 7 and 8.)
- Define product, market, distribution and quality plans to implement competitive strategies. (SBP Section 3, 4 and 8.)

Team Responsibilities

- Create and recommend new or additional products.
- Approve all alterations or modifications of a major nature.
- Act as a formal communications channel for field product needs.
- Plan and implement strategies throughout the product life-cycle.

- Develop programs to improve market position and profitability.
- Identify market or product opportunities in light of changing consumer demands.
- Coordinate activities of various functions to achieve short-term and long-term objectives.
- Coordinate efforts for the inter-divisional exchanges of new market or product opportunities.
- Develop a Strategic Business Plan.

12.3 Identifying Business-Building Opportunities

A team should enjoy a clear-cut mandate to create opportunities or to tackle competitive threats. More specifically, the team should actively look for opportunities and take action. The following opportunities are presented as examples.

Opportunity 1

Search for opportunities in unserved, poorly served, or emerging market segments.

ACTIONS
- Penetrate and expand niches.
- Improve products and services.
- Stretch product lines.
- Position products to the needs of customers and against competitors.

Opportunity 2

Identify ways to create new opportunities.

ACTIONS
- Seek new product or market niches.
- Participate in new technology, innovations and manufacturing.
- Pioneer something new or unique.

Opportunity 3

Look for opportunities through marketing creativity.

ACTIONS

- Promote image through quality, performance and training.
- Promote creativity in sales promotion, advertising, personal selling and the Internet.

Opportunity 4

Monitor changing behavioral patterns and preferences.

ACTIONS

- Practice segmenting markets according to behavioral patterns.
- Identify clusters of customers who might buy or utilize different services for different reasons.

Opportunity 5

Learn from competitors and adapt strategies from other industries.

ACTIONS

- Understand how competitors conduct their respective businesses.
- What products they sell.
- What strategies they pursue.
- How they manufacture, distribute, promote and price.
- What their weaknesses, limitations and possible vulnerabilities are.

Opportunity 6

Help your organization develop into an active, 21st century customer-driven organization.

ACTIONS

a) Show customers revenue-expansion opportunities:

- Reduce returns and complaints from the end user.

- Speed-up production and delivery.

- Improve the customer's market position and image.

- Add brand-name value for the customer (where appropriate).

- Add customer benefits through additional services.

- Create areas of differentiation that gives a customer a competitive advantage.

- Improve a customer's re-ordering procedure.

b) Show cost-reduction opportunities:

- Cut the customer's purchase costs.

- Reduce the customer's production costs.

- Absorb all or part of a customer's product development function.

- Reduce the customer's delivery costs.

- Lessen the customer's administrative overhead.

- Maximize the customer's working capital.

Internalize these guidelines and you will master the essence of Strategic Business Planning.

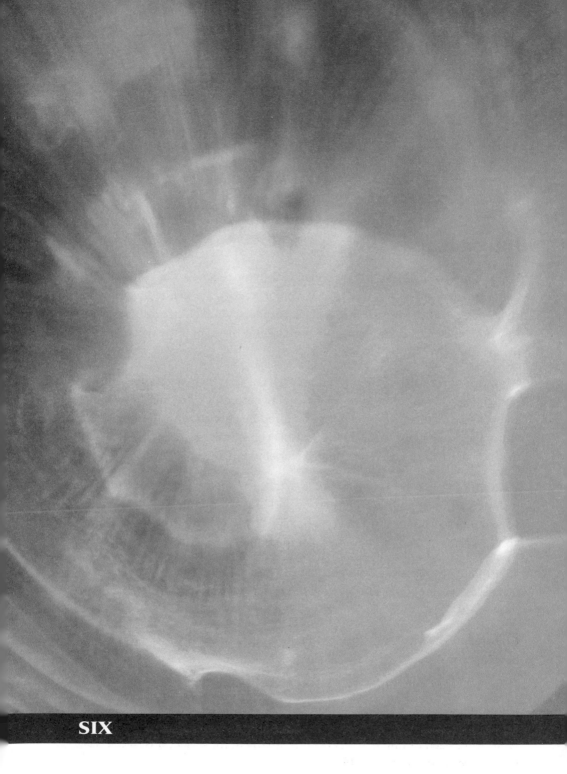

Appendix: Forms and Guidelines

Appendix:
Forms and Guidelines

Introduction

You can now develop your personalized Strategic Business Plan (SBP) using the forms and guidelines that follow. That means you have the flexibility to customize the forms by inserting specific vocabulary and unique issues related to your industry and company, while retaining the planning structure of a proven format.

Also, you can make the SBP a permanent part of your management operating system by scanning this entire planning format into your computer. Doing so permits you to add special forms required by your organization or insert any of the commercially available spreadsheet programs, as well as the growing number of Customer Relationship Management (CRM) programs.

Further, you can rely on substantial assistance as you develop your SBP. For instance, to hone your planning skills and improve the quality of the plan you submit to management or to an outside financial institution for funding, you can refer to the following parts of the book:

Chapter 1: The Strategic Business Plan: Strategic Section, illustrates through actual case examples how to develop the visionary 3 to 5-year strategic section of the SBP.

Chapter 2: The Strategic Business Plan: Tactical Section, describes how to develop a realistic 1-year tactical section, also using a real case example to illustrate each planning guideline.

Chapter 3: Business Problem Solver: the Strategic Business Plan in Action, shows how successful companies solved severe competitive problems and won. After each example, references are made to those sections of the SBP that address the specific problem.

Chapter 4: Checklists for Developing Competitive Strategies, includes numerous forms to help you evaluate the potential of a market and develop competitive strategies. It is particularly valuable in adding greater precision to your SBP and improving the overall performance of your company.

Chapter 5: Help Topics, provides a comprehensive reference on most subjects related to developing your SBP.

Overview of the Strategic Business Plan: Strategic Section

You can obtain optimum results for your SBP by following the process diagrammed in Figure 6.1. As you examine the flowchart, notice that the top row of boxes represents the *strategic* portion of the plan and covers a 3 to 5-year timeframe.

The second row of boxes displays the *tactical* 1-year plan. It is the merging of the *strategic* plan and *tactical* plan into one unified SBP that makes it a complete format and an operational management tool to energize your company's potential.

You will find that following the SBP process will add an organized and disciplined approach to your thinking. Yet, the process in no way confines your thinking or creativity. Instead, it expands your flexibility, extends your strategy vision and elevates the creative process. In turn, the strategy vision results in providing you with a choice of revenue-building opportunities expressed through markets, products and services.

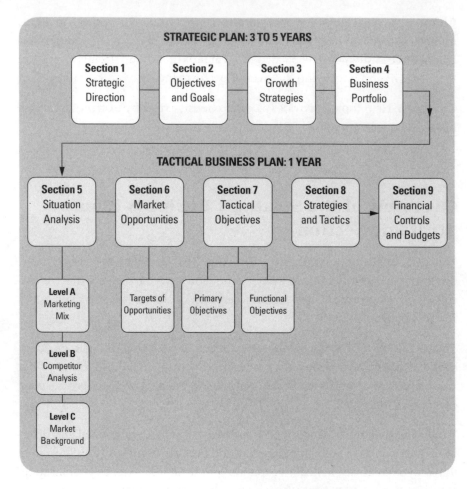

FIGURE 6.1: **STRATEGIC BUSINESS PLAN**

Section 1: Strategic Direction

The first box in Figure 6.1, Section 1, *Strategic Direction,* allows you to visualize the long-term direction of your company, division, product, or service.

Planning Guidelines

The first step is to use the following questions to provide an organized approach to developing a strategic direction. Answering the questions below will help you shape the ideal vision of what your company, business unit, or product/service will look like over the next 3 to 5 years.

More precisely, it should echo your (or your team's) long-term outlook, as long as if conforms to overall corporate objectives and policies. To develop your strategic direction, fill in your answers to the following six questions.

1. What are your firm's distinctive areas of expertise? This question refers to your organization's (or business unit's) competencies. You can answer by evaluating the following:

    *   Relative competitive strengths of your product or service based on customer satisfaction, profitability and market share.

    *   Relationships with distributors and/or end-use customers.

    *   Existing production capabilities.

    *   Size of your sales-force.

    *   Financial strength.

    *   R&D expenditures.

    *   Amount of customer or technical service provided.

    Fill in: _____

    _____

    _____

2. What business should your firm be in over the next 3 to 5 years? How will it differ from what exists today?

    Fill in: _____

    _____

    _____

3. What segments or categories of customers will you serve?

    Fill in: _____

    _____

    _____

4. What additional functions are you likely to fulfill for customers as you see the market evolve?

Fill in: _____

_____

_____

5. What new technologies will you require to satisfy future customer market needs?

Fill in:_____

_____

_____

6. What changes are taking place in markets, consumer behavior, competition, environmental issues, culture and the economy that will impact on your company?

Fill in: _____

_____

_____

Now compress your answers to the above six questions into one statement that would represent a realistic Strategic Direction for your company, business unit, or product. (See Part 1 for an example of how a Strategic Direction is written.)

Fill in: _____

_____

_____

Section 2: Objectives and Goals

Planning Guidelines

State your objectives and goals both quantitatively and non-quantitatively (the second box in the top row in Figure 6.1). Your primary guideline: take a strategic focus covering a timeframe of 3 to 5 years. That means, look again at how you defined your Strategic Direction, so that you can develop objectives that will have the broadest impact on the growth of your business.

Quantitative Objectives

Indicate, in precise statements, major performance expectations such as sales growth, market share, return on investment, profit and any other quantitative objective required by your management.

With the longer timeframe, your objectives are generally broad and relate to the total business or to a few major market segments. (In the tactical section these objectives will be more specific for each product and market.)

Fill in: _____

_____

_____

Non-quantitative Objectives

Think of these objectives as setting a foundation from which to build on to your organization's existing strengths or core competencies, as well as to eliminate any internal weaknesses.

Use the following examples to trigger objectives for your business. Above all, keep your objectives specific, actionable, realistic and focused on achieving a sustainable competitive advantage.

- Upgrade distribution channels.
- Expand secondary distribution or enhance your product's position on the supply chain.
- Build specialty products for market penetration.
- Establish or improve business intelligence.
- Focus training actions to improve skills and performance of employees.
- Launch new and reposition old products.
- Upgrade field services.
- Improve marketing mix (product, price, promotion and distribution) management.

Fill in: _____

_____

_____

Section 3: Growth Strategies

Planning Guidelines

This section outlines the process you can use to secure your objectives and goals. Think of *strategies* as actions to achieve your longer-term objectives; tactics as actions to achieve shorter-term objectives.

Since this timeframe covers 3 to 5 years, strategies are indicated here. The 1-year portion, illustrated later in the plan, identifies tactics.

In practice, where you have developed broad-based, long-term objectives you should list multiple strategies for each objective. In instances where you find it difficult to apply specific strategies, it is appropriate to use general strategy statements.

Suggestion: How you write your strategies can vary according to your individual or team's style. For example, you have the option of merging the objectives and strategies sections by re-stating each objective from Section 2 followed by a listing of corresponding strategies. Still another option is to write a general strategy statement followed by a detailed listing of specific objectives and strategies. (See Part 1 for examples.)

Overall, your thinking about strategies boil down to actions related to the following:

- Growth and mature markets.
- Long-term brand development and product positioning.
- Product quality and value-added options.
- Market share growth potential.
- Distribution channel and supply chain options.
- Product, price and promotion mix.
- Asset allocations.
- Specific marketing, sales, R&D and manufacturing strengths to be exploited.

Fill in: _____

_____

_____

Section 4: Business Portfolio Plan

Planning Guidelines

The business portfolio includes listings of *existing* products and markets and *new* products and markets. Following a logical progression, it is based on the strategic direction, objectives and goals, and growth strategies outlined in the previous sections.

Suggestion: The content of your portfolio should mirror your strategic direction. That is, the broader the dimension of your strategic direction, the more expansive the range of products and markets in the portfolio. Conversely, the narrower the dimension of your strategic direction, the more limited the content of products and markets.

Use the following format and guidelines to develop your own business portfolio:

Existing Products/Existing Markets (Market Penetration)

List those *existing* products you currently offer to *existing* customers or market segments. In an appendix of the SBP, you can document in numerical or graphic form sales, profits and market share data. From such information you can determine if your level of penetration is adequate and if possibilities exist for further growth.

After identifying new opportunities, it may be necessary for you to revisit Section 3 (Growth Strategies) and list actions you would take to implement the opportunities.

Fill in: _____

_____

_____

New Products/Existing Markets (Product Development)

Use this section to extend your thinking and list potential *new* products you can offer to *existing* markets. Again, recall the guideline that the broader the dimension of your Strategic Direction the broader the possibilities for the content of your portfolio. Also, you should be thinking in a timeframe of 3 to 5 years.

Fill in: _____

_____

_____

Existing Products/New Markets (Market Development)

Now list your existing products into *new* markets. Explore possibilities for market development by identifying emerging, neglected, or poorly served segments in which existing products can be utilized.

Fill in: _____

_____

_____

New Product/New Markets (Diversification)

This portion of the business portfolio is visionary, since it involves developing *new* products to meet the needs of *new* and yet-untapped markets. Consider new technologies, global markets and potential strategic alliances to provide input into this section.

Once again, interpret your Strategic Direction in its broadest context. Do not seek diversification for its own sake. Rather, the whole purpose of the exercise is for you to develop an organized framework for meaningful expansion.

Fill in: _____

_____

_____

The grid in Figure 6.2 is a useful format to fill in your business portfolio of products and markets, both existing and new.

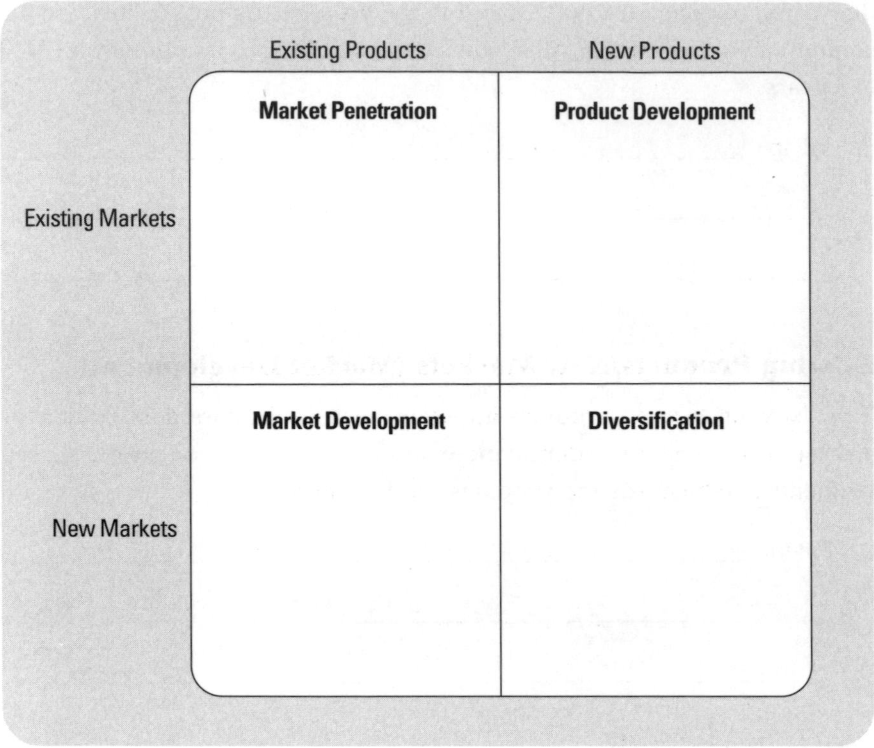

	Existing Products	New Products
Existing Markets	**Market Penetration**	**Product Development**
New Markets	**Market Development**	**Diversification**

FIGURE 6.2: **BUSINESS PORTFOLIO PLAN**

The Business Portfolio competes the strategic portion of your SBP. Now you are ready to proceed to the 1-year tactical plan.

Overview of the Strategic Business Plan: Tactical Section

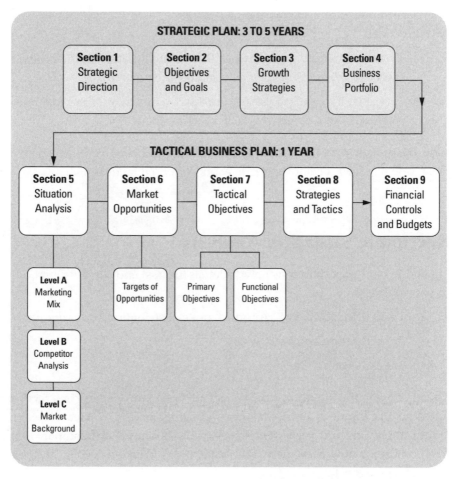

STRATEGIC PLAN: 3 TO 5 YEARS

Section 1	Section 2	Section 3	Section 4
Strategic Direction	Objectives and Goals	Growth Strategies	Business Portfolio

TACTICAL BUSINESS PLAN: 1 YEAR

Section 5	Section 6	Section 7	Section 8	Section 9
Situation Analysis	Market Opportunities	Tactical Objectives	Strategies and Tactics	Financial Controls and Budgets

Level A Marketing Mix

Targets of Opportunities   Primary Objectives   Functional Objectives

Level B Competitor Analysis

Level C Market Background

FIGURE 6.3: **STRATEGIC BUSINESS PLAN**

The tactical plan, the second row of boxes designated as Sections 5 through to 9, is not a stand-alone plan. It is an integral part of the total SBP.

Where commonalties exist between products and markets, one tactical plan can work as long as you make the appropriate changes in such areas as the sales-force and the communications mix (advertising, sales promotion, Internet and publicity). Where you face substantial differences in the character of your product and markets, then develop separate tactical plans.

Suggestion: Avoid the temptation to develop a plan for a business, division, or product line by jumping into the middle of the SBP and beginning the process with the 1-year tactical plan.

There are no suitable short cuts. Reason: Input to the tactical plan flows from two directions:

1. From the strategic portion of the SBP (top row) containing the strategic direction, objectives, strategies and business portfolio;

2. From the situation analysis (second row), which progresses to opportunities, annual objectives, tactics and budgets.

Also, the thought process that went into the strategic portion of the plan now flows down to feed the shorter-term, action-oriented tactical plan.

Section 5: Situation Analysis

The following 3-part situation analysis details the past and current situations of your business:

*   Level A: Marketing Mix (product, price, distribution and promotion).

*   Level B: Competitor Analysis.

*   Level C: Market Background.

The purpose of the Situation Analysis is to define your business in a factual and objective manner. Compile historical data for a period of at least 3 years. Doing so provides an excellent perspective about where your company has been, where it is now, and where you want it to go as defined in your Strategic Direction (Section 1).

Planning Guidelines

- Objectively describe the performance of your product or service by: sales history, profitability, share of market and other required financial data; where appropriate, you can graphically chart sales history with spreadsheets or your company's forms.

  Fill in: _____

  _____

  _____

- Current position in the industry related to market share, reputation, product life-cycle (introduction, growth, maturity, or decline) and competition.

  Fill in: _____

  _____

  _____

- Future trends related to environment, industry, customer and competitive factors that may affect the position of your product.

  Fill in: _____

  _____

  _____

- Intended purpose of your product in terms of its application or uniqueness.

  Fill in: _____

  _____

  _____

- Features and benefits of your product as related to quality, performance, safety, convenience, or other factors important to customers.

  Fill in: _____

  _____

  _____

- Other pertinent product information such as expected product improvements and additional product characteristics (size, model, price, packaging); recent features that enhance the position of your product; competitive trends in features, benefits, technological changes; and changes that would add superior value to the product and provide a competitive advantage.

  Fill in: _____

  _____

  _____

Level A: Marketing Mix – Pricing

History of Pricing

Examine the history of pricing policies and strategies for each market segment and/or distribution channel. Consider their impact on the market position of your product.

Fill in: _____

_____

_____

Future Pricing Trends

Product pricing trends as they pertain to product specification changes (including formulation and design), financial constraints and expected market changes (trade/consumer attitudes, and competitive responses to price changes).

Fill in: _____

_____

_____

Level A: Marketing Mix – Distribution Channels and Methods

Current Channels

Describe your current distribution channels. Identify the function performed for each stage in the distribution system (distributor, dealer, direct, e-commerce). Indicate levels of performance (sales volume, profitability and percentage of business increases).

Where appropriate, analyze your physical distribution system, such as warehouse locations, inventory systems, or just-in-time delivery procedures.

Fill in: _____

_____

_____

Effectiveness of Coverage

Characterize the effectiveness of coverage by the programs and services provided for each channel.

Comment on effectiveness of distribution systems (distributors, dealers, direct). Specify the key activities performed at each point and indicate any areas that require corrective action. Also comment on the impact of future trends in distribution channels and methods, such as e-commerce.

Fill in: _____

_____

_____

Special Functions

Indicate special functions performed by your company's sales-force for a particular distribution channel and what effect it had on the targeted market segments. Also include your distributors' sales-forces, if applicable. Comment, too, on such approaches as 'push' strategy (through distributors) or 'pull' strategy (through consumers).

Fill in: _____

_____

_____

Target Accounts

List target accounts and their level of performance related to sales and quantity. Add comments related to special needs of any customer.

Fill in: _____

_____

_____

Future Trends

Indicate future trends in distribution methods and channels. Project what growth is expected in each major market segment. Also identify how this growth will affect your need for different distribution channels or methods of physical distribution.

Fill in: _____

_____

_____

Level A: Marketing Mix – Advertising, Sales Promotion, Internet and Publicity

Analyze your efforts directed at each market segment or distribution channel based on the following elements: expenditures, creative strategy, media, types of promotion and other forms of communications unique to your industry.

Fill in: _____

_____

_____

Competitive Trends

Identify and evaluate competitive trends in the same categories as above. Your advertising agency (or advertising department) and the sales-force may prove helpful in compiling this information.

Fill in: _____

_____

_____

Strategies

Identify your company's past and current communications strategies by product and market segment and describe trends in these areas.

Fill in: _____

_____

_____

Other Support Strategies

Identify other support programs (publicity, educational, professional, trade shows, literature, films/videos, the Internet) that you have used and evaluate their effectiveness.

Fill in: _____

_____

_____

Level B: Competitive Analysis – Market Share

Planning Guidelines

List all your competitors in descending-size order along with their sales and market shares. Include your company's ranking within the listing. Show at least three competitors, more if the information is meaningful. (If unable to provide useable information for this portion, and the others that follow, you should give very high priority to developing a business intelligence initiative, of which competitor intelligence is a key component.)

Fill in: _____

_____

_____

Competitors' Strengths and Weaknesses

Identify each competitor's strengths and weaknesses related to such factors as product quality, distribution, pricing, promotion, management leadership and financial condition. Also indicate any significant trends that would signal unsettling market situations, such as aggressiveness in growing market share or excessive discounting to maintain market position.

Attempt to make your competitive analysis as comprehensive as possible. The more competitive intelligence you gather, the more strategy options you have open to you. (To assist you in developing a quality analysis, go to Part 4, Checklist for Developing Competitive Strategies.)

Fill in: _____

_____

_____

Product Competitiveness

Identify competitive pricing strategies, price lines and price discounts, if any. Identify those competitors firmly entrenched in low-price segments of the market, those at the high end of the market, or competitors that are low-cost producers.

Fill in: _____

_____

_____

Product Features and Benefits

Compare the specific product features and benefits with those of competitive products. In particular, focus on product quality, design factors and performance. Evaluate price/value relationships for each, discuss customer preferences (if available), and identify unique product innovations.

Fill in: _____

_____

_____

Advertising Effectiveness

Identify competitive spending levels and their effectiveness, as measured by awareness levels, competitive copy test scores and reach/frequency levels (if available).

Such measurements are conducted through formal advertising research conducted by your advertising agency, independent marketing research firms, or some publications. Where no reliable quantitative research exists, use informal observation or rough measurements of advertising frequency and type.

Fill in: _____

_____

_____

Effectiveness of Distribution Methods

Compare competitive distribution strengths and weaknesses. Address differences in market penetration, market coverage, delivery time and physical movement of the product by regions or territories. Also identify major accounts where competitors' sales are weak or strong.

Fill in: _____

_____

_____

Packaging

Compare the package performance, innovation and preference of competitive products. Also review size, shape, function, convenience of handling, ease of storage and shipping.

Fill in: _____

_____

_____

Trade/Consumer Attitudes

Review both trade (distributor or dealer) and consumer attitudes toward product quality, customer/technical service, company image and company performance.

Fill in: _____

_____

_____

Competitive Share of Market Trends

While market share was previously included as a way of determining overall performance, the intent here is to specify trends in market share gains by individual products, as well as by market segments.

Further, you must identify where each competitor is making a major commitment and where it may be relinquishing control by product and segment.

Fill in: _____

_____

_____

Sales-force Effectiveness and Market Coverage

Review effectiveness as it relates to sales, service, frequency of contact and problem-solving capabilities, by competitor and by market segment. Look to all sales-force performance within the distribution channel. For example, if you are a manufacturer, look at your distributors' market coverage. Then examine distributors' coverage of *their* customers, which could be dealers and/or end users.

Fill in: _____

_____

_____

Planning Guidelines

This last part of the situation analysis focuses on the demographic and behavioral factors of your market. Doing so helps you determine market size and customer preferences (both trade and consumer) in a changing competitive environment.

You can derive data from primary market research (market segmentation studies, awareness levels and product usage studies) or from secondary sources (trade and government reports). See extensive information on this subject in Part 5, Help Topics.

If you give careful attention to compiling accurate information, you will benefit from reliable input for developing the following parts of the SBP: Section 6, Opportunities; Section 7, Objectives; and Section 8, Strategies/Tactics.

This information also highlights any gaps in knowledge about markets and customers and thereby helps you determine what additional market intelligence is needed to make more effective decisions.

The following categories are considered part of the market background:

Customer Profile

Define the profile of present and potential end-use customers that you or your distributors serve. Your intent is to look further down the distribution channel and view the end-use consumer. Examine the following factors:

MARKET SEGMENTS DISTRIBUTORS/DEALERS SERVE

Address this factor from your distributors' point of view.

Fill in: _____

_____

_____

DISTRIBUTORS' OVERALL SALES

Concentrate on classifying the key customers that represent the majority of sales.

Fill in: _____

_____

_____

OTHER CLASSIFICATIONS

Profile your customers by such additional factors as type of products used, level of sophistication, price sensitivity and service. Also indicate any target accounts that you can reach directly, thereby bypassing the distributor.

Fill in: _____

_____

_____

FREQUENCY AND MAGNITUDE OF PRODUCTS USED

Define customer purchases by frequency, volume and seasonality of purchase. Additional information might include customer inventory levels, retail-stocking policies, volume discounts. Also look at consumer buying behavior related to price, point-of-purchase influences, or coupons.

Fill in: _____

_____

_____

GEOGRAPHIC ASPECTS OF PRODUCTS USED

Define customer purchases regionally or territorially (both trade and consumer). Segment buyers by specific geographic area (e.g., rural, urban) or by other factors relevant to your business.

Fill in: _____

_____

_____

MARKET CHARACTERISTICS

Assess the demographic, psychographic (life style) and other relevant characteristics of your customers. Also examine levels of product technology in use; purchase patterns and any distinctive individual or group behavioral styles; and attitudes toward the company's products, services, quality and image.

Fill in: _____

_____

_____

DECISION-MAKER

Define who makes the buying decisions and when and where they are made. Note the various individuals or departments that may influence the decision.

Fill in: _____

_____

_____

CUSTOMER MOTIVATIONS

Identify the key motivations that drive your customers to buy the product. Why do they select one manufacturer (or service provider) over another? Customers may buy your product because of quality, performance, image, technical/customer service, convenience, location, delivery, access to upper-level management, friendship, or peer pressure.

Fill in: _____

_____

_____

CUSTOMER AWARENESS

Define the level of consumer awareness of your products. To what extent do they:

- Recognize a need for your type of product?

- Identify your product, brand, or company as a possible supplier?

- Associate your product, brand, or company with desirable features?

Fill in: _____

_____

_____

SEGMENT TRENDS

Define the trends in the size and character of the various segments or niches. (A segment is a portion of an entire market; a niche is part of a segment.) A segment should be considered if it is accessible, measurable, potentially profitable and has long-term growth potential.

Segmenting a market also serves as an offensive strategy to identify emerging, neglected, or poorly served markets that can catapult you to further sales growth.

You can also consider segments as a defensive strategy to prevent inroads of a potential competitor through an unattended market segment.

Fill in: _____

_____

_____

OTHER COMMENTS/CRITICAL ISSUES

Add general comments that expand your knowledge of the market and customer base. Also identify any critical issues that have surfaced as a result of conducting the situation analysis – ones that should be singled out for special attention.

Fill in: _____

_____

_____

Section 6: Marketing Opportunities

Planning Guidelines

In this section, you examine marketing strengths, weaknesses and options. Opportunities will begin to emerge as you consider the variety of alternatives.

Try to avoid restricted thinking. Take your time and brainstorm. Dig for opportunities with other members of your planning team. If one doesn't exist, then put together a team representing different functional areas of the business (or persuade senior management to approve its formation).

Consider all possibilities for expanding existing market coverage and laying the groundwork for entering new markets. Also consider opportunities related to your competition. For instance, offensively, which competitors can you displace from which market segments? Defensively, which competitors can you deny entry into your market?

As you go through this section, revisit your strategic portion of the SBP (top row of boxes in Figure 6.1). While that portion represents a 3 to 5 year period, work must begin at some point to activate the strategic direction, objectives, growth strategies and business portfolio sections.

Further, you should refer to the situation analysis in the last section, specifically the competitive analysis, for voids or weaknesses that could represent opportunities.

Note the two-directional flow used to create opportunities: (1) the visionary thinking you used to shape the strategic portion of the SBP now flows down to focus on 1-year opportunities, and (2) the situation analysis that exposes voids and weaknesses also represents opportunities.

Now review the following screening process to identify your major opportunities and challenges. Once you identify and prioritize the opportunities, convert them into objectives and tactics, which are the topics of the next two sections of the SBP.

Present Markets

Identify the best opportunities for expanding present markets through:

- Cultivating new business and new users.
- Displacing competition.
- Increasing product usage or services by present customers.
- Redefining market segments.
- Reformulating or repackaging the product.
- Identifying new uses (applications) for the product.
- Repositioning the product to create a more favorable perception by consumers and to develop a competitive advantage over rival products.
- Expanding into new or unserved market niches.

Fill in: _____

_____

_____

Targets of Opportunity

List any areas outside your current market segment or product line not included in the above categories that you would like to explore. Be innovative and entrepreneurial in your thinking. These areas are opportunistic. Therefore, due to their innovative and risky characteristics, they are isolated from the other opportunities. Those you select for special attention are placed in a separate part of the objectives section of the SBP.

Fill in: _____

_____

_____

Section 7: Tactical Objectives

At this point, you have reported relevant factual data in Section 5, Situation Analysis; you have interpreted their meaning and business-building potential of your product line in Section 6, Opportunities. You must now set the objectives you want to achieve during the current planning cycle – generally defined as a 12-month period to correspond with annual budgeting procedures.

Once again, you will find it useful to review Sections 5 and 6. Also, it will be helpful to review the strategic portion of the plan. You want to be certain that actions related to your long-range strategic direction, objectives and strategies are incorporated into your tactical 1-year objectives.

This section consists of three parts:

1. **Assumptions**: projections about future conditions and trends.

2. **Primary objectives**: quantitative measurements related to your responsibility, including targets of opportunity.

3. **Functional objectives**: operational goals for various parts of the business.

Assumptions

Planning Guidelines

For objectives to be realistic and achievable, you must first generate assumptions and projections about future conditions and trends. List only those major assumptions that will affect your business for the planning year as it relates to the following:

- Economic assumptions: comment on the overall economy, local market economies, industrial production, plant and equipment expenditures, consumer expenditures and changes in customer needs. Also document market size, growth rate, costs and trends in major market segments.

    Fill in: _____

    _____

    _____

- Technological assumptions: include depth of research and development efforts, likelihood of technological breakthroughs, availability of raw materials and plant capacity.

  Fill in: _____

  _____

  _____

- Sociopolitical assumptions: indicate prospective legislation, political tensions, tax outlook, population patterns, educational factors and changes in customer habits.

  Fill in: _____

  _____

  _____

- Competitive assumptions: identify activities of existing competitors, inroads of new competitors and changes in trade practices.

  Fill in: _____

  _____

  _____

Planning Guidelines

Focus on the primary financial objectives that your organization requires. Also include targets of opportunity that you initially identified as innovative and entrepreneurial in Section 6.

Where there are multiple objectives you may find it helpful to rank them in priority order. Be sure to quantify expected results where possible. You can separate your objectives into the following categories:

Primary objectives: Current and projected sales, profits, market share, return on investment and other quantitative measures. (Use Table 6.1, a form provided by your organization, or any spreadsheet software.)

Fill in:

PRODUCT GROUP BREAKDOWN	Current				Projected			
	SALES ($)	UNITS	MARGINS	SHARE OF MARKET	SALES ($)	UNITS	MARGINS	SHARE OF MARKET
Product A								
Product B								
Product C								
Product D								

TABLE 6.1: **PRIMARY OBJECTIVES**

Targets of opportunity objectives

State the functional objectives relating to both product and non-product issues in each of the following categories. (You can alter the list of objectives to fit your business and industry.)

PRODUCT OBJECTIVES

Quality: Identify quality objectives that would achieve a competitive advantage by exceeding industry standards in some or all segments of your market.

Fill in: _____

_____

_____

Development: Deal with new technology through internal R&D, licensing, or joint ventures.

Fill in: _____

_____

_____

Modification: Deliver major or minor product changes through reformulation or engineering.

Fill in: _____

_____

_____

Differentiation: Enhance competitive position through function, design, or any other changes that can differentiate a product or service.

Fill in: _____

_____

_____

Diversification: Transfer technology or use the actual product in new applications, or diversify into new geographic areas, such as developing countries.

Fill in: _____

_____

_____

Deletion: Remove a product from the line due to unsatisfactory performance, or keep it in the line if the product serves some strategic purpose, such as presenting your company to the market as a full-line supplier.

Fill in: _____

_____

_____

Segmentation: Create line extensions (adding product varieties) to reach new market niches or defend against an incoming competitor in an existing market segment.

Fill in: _____

_____

_____

Pricing: Include list prices, volume discounts and promotional rebates.

Fill in: _____

_____

_____

Promotion: Develop sales-force support, sales promotion, advertising, Internet and publicity to the trade and consumers.

Fill in: _____

_____

_____

Distribution channel: Add new distributors to increase geographic coverage, develop programs or services to solidify relationships with the trade, remove distributors or dealers from the channel, or maintain direct contact with the end user.

Fill in: _____

_____

_____

Physical distribution: Identify logistical factors that would include order entry, physical movement of a product through the supply chain and eventual delivery to the end user.

Fill in: _____

_____

_____

Packaging: Use functional design and/or decorative considerations for brand identification.

Fill in: _____

_____

_____

Service: Broaden the range of services, from providing customers access to key executives in your firm to providing on-site technical assistance.

Fill in: _____

_____

_____

Other: Indicate other objectives as suggested in Targets of Opportunities.

Fill in: _____

_____

_____

Non-product Objectives

Although most activities eventually relate to the product or service, some are support functions that you may or may not influence. How much influence you can exert depends on the functions represented on your planning team.

Target Accounts: Indicate those customers with whom you can develop special relationships through customized products, distribution or warehousing, value-added services, or participation in quality improvement programs.

Fill in: _____

_____

_____

Manufacturing: Identify special activities that would provide a competitive advantage, such as offering small production runs to accommodate the changing needs of customers and reduce inventory levels.

Fill in: _____

_____

_____

Marketing research: Cite any customer studies that identify key buying factors and include competitive intelligence.

Fill in: _____

_____

_____

Credit: Include any programs that use credit and finance as a value-added component for a product offering, such as rendering financial advice or providing financial assistance to customers in certain situations.

Fill in: _____

_____

_____

Technical sales activities: Include any support activities, such as 24/7 hot-line telephone assistance that offers on-site consultation to solve customers' problems.

Fill in: _____

_____

_____

R&D: Indicate internal research and development projects as well as joint ventures that would complement the Strategic Direction identified in Section 1 of the SBP.

Fill in: _____

_____

_____

Training: List internal training programs, as well as external end-user programs.

Fill in:_____

_____

_____

Human resource development: Identify specialized skills required by those individuals who would make the SBP operational.

Fill in:_____

_____

_____

Other: Include specialized activities that may be unique to your organization.

Fill in:_____

_____

_____

Section 8: Strategies and Tactics

Strategy is the art of coordinating the means (money, human resources, materials) to achieve the ends (profits, customer satisfaction, growth) as defined by company policy, strategic direction and objectives. From another perspective: strategies are actions to achieve long-term objectives; tactics are actions to achieve short-term objectives.

Therefore, in this section strategies and tactics have to be identified and put into action. Responsibilities are assigned, schedules set, budgets established, and checkpoints determined. Make sure that the members of the planning team actively participate in this section. They are the ones who have to implement the strategies and tactics.

Planning Guidelines

Restate the functional product and non-product objectives from Section 7 and link them to the strategies and tactics you will use to reach each objective.

One of the reasons for restating the objectives is to clarify the frequent misunderstanding between objectives and strategies. Objectives are what you want to accomplish; strategies are actions that indicate how you intend to achieve your objectives.

Note: If you state an objective and don't have a related strategy, you may not have an objective. Instead, the statement may be an action for some other objective.

Fill in:

Objective 1: _____

Strategy/Tactic: _____

Objective 2: _____

Strategy/Tactic: _____

Objective 3: _____

Strategy/Tactic: _____

Summary Strategy

Summarize the basic strategies for achieving your primary objectives. Also, include alternative and contingency plans should situations arise to prevent you from reaching your objectives. Be certain, however, that such alternatives relate to the overall SBP.

As you develop your final strategy statement, use the following checklist to determine its completeness:

- Changes needed to the product or package, including differentiation and value-added features.
- Strategies to create a competitive advantage, along with contingency plans to counter competitors' aggressive moves.
- Changes to price, discounts, or long-term contracts to address market share issues.

- Changes to advertising strategy, such as the selection of features and benefits, or copy themes to special groups.

- Strategies to reach new, poorly served, or unserved market segments.

- Promotion strategies related to private-label products; dealer and/or distributor, consumer and sales-force incentives.

Fill in: _____

_____

_____

Section 9: Financial Controls and Budgets

Planning Guidelines

Having completed the strategy phase of your SBP, you must decide how you will monitor its execution. Therefore, before implementing it, you have to develop procedures for both control (comparing actual and planned figures) and review (deciding whether planned figures should be adjusted or other corrective measures taken).

This final section incorporates your operating budget. If your organization has reporting procedures, you should incorporate them within this section.

Included below are examples of additional reports or data sheets designed to monitor progress at key checkpoints of the plan and to permit either major shifts in strategies or simple midcourse corrections:

- Forecast models.
- Sales by channel of distribution
    - Inventory or out-of-stock reports.
    - Average selling price (including discounts, rebates, or allowances) by distribution channel and customer outlet.
- Profit and loss statements by product.
- Direct product budgets.
- R&D expenses.

- Administrative budget.
- Spending by quarter.

As an overall guideline – regardless of the forms you use – make certain that the system serves as a reliable feedback mechanism. Your interest is in maintaining explicit and timely control so you can react swiftly to impending problems. Further, it should serve as a procedure for reviewing schedules and strategies.

Finally, the system should provide an upward flow of fresh market intelligence that, in turn, could impact on broad policy revisions at the highest levels of the organization.

The only other part left in your SBP is an appendix. It should include the following items: pertinent industry data and market research; additional data on competitors' strategies, including information on their products, pricing, promotion, distribution and profiles of management leadership (if available); and details about new product features and benefits. (Various computer-based data bases, CRM and other software programs can assist to strengthen your plan.)

Thorogood publishing

Thorogood publishes a wide range of books, reports, special briefings and psychometric tests. Listed below is a selection of key titles.

DESKTOP GUIDES

The marketing strategy desktop guide	*Norton Paley* • £16.99
The sales manager's desktop guide	*Mike Gale and Julian Clay* • £16.99
The company director's desktop guide	*David Martin* • £16.99
The credit controller's desktop guide	*Roger Mason* • £16.99
The company secretary's desktop guide	*Roger Mason* • £16.99
The finance and accountancy desktop guide	*Ralph Tiffin* • £16.99
The commercial engineer's desktop guide	*Tim Boyce* • £16.99
The training manager's desktop guide	*Eddie Davies* • £16.99
The PR practitioner's desktop guide	*Caroline Black* • £16.99
Win new business – the desktop guide	*Susan Croft* • £16.99

MASTERS IN MANAGEMENT

Mastering business planning and strategy	*Paul Elkin* • £14.99
Mastering financial management	*Stephen Brookson* • £14.99
Mastering leadership	*Michael Williams* • £14.99
Mastering negotiations	*Eric Evans* • £14.99
Mastering people management	*Mark Thomas* • £14.99
Mastering personal and interpersonal skills	*Peter Haddon* • £14.99
Mastering project management	*Cathy Lake* • £14.99
Mastering marketing	*Ian Ruskin-Brown* • £16.99

BUSINESS ACTION POCKETBOOKS

Edited by David Irwin

Building your business pocketbook	£6.99
Developing yourself and your staff pocketbook	£6.99
Finance and profitability pocketbook	£6.99
Managing and employing people pocketbook	£6.99
Sales and marketing pocketbook	£6.99
Managing projects and operations pocketbook	£6.99
Effective business communications pocketbook	£6.99
PR techniques that work	*Edited by Jim Dunn* • £6.99

OTHER TITLES

The John Adair handbook of management and leadership	*Edited by Neil Thomas* • £24.99
The pension trustee's handbook (3rd edition)	*Robin Ellison* • £25
Boost your company's profits	*Barrie Pearson* • £12.99
Negotiate to succeed	*Julie Lewthwaite* • £12.99
The management tool kit	*Sultan Kermally* • £10.99
Working smarter	*Graham Roberts-Phelps* • £14.99
Test your management skills	*Michael Williams* • £15.99
The art of headless chicken management	*Elly Brewer and Mark Edwards* • £6.99
EMU challenge and change – the implications for business	*John Atkin* • £11.99
Everything you need for an NVQ in management	*Julie Lewthwaite* • £22.99

Customer relationship management	*Graham Roberts-Phelps* • £14.99
Sales management and organisation	*Peter Green* • £10.99
Telephone tactics	*Graham Roberts-Phelps* • £10.99
Companies don't succeed people do!	*Graham Roberts-Phelps* • £12.99
Inspiring leadership	*John Adair* • £15.99
The book of ME	*Barrie Pearson and Neil Thomas* • £14.99
The complete guide to debt recovery	*Roger Mason* • £12.99
Janner's complete speechmaker	*Greville Janner* • £10.99
Gurus on business strategy	*Tony Grundy* • £14.99
Dynamic practice development	*Kim Tasso* • £19.99
Successful selling solutions	*Julian Clay* • £12.99
High performance consulting skills	*Mark Thomas* • £14.99
The concise Adair on leadership	*edited by Neil Thomas* • £9.99
The inside track to successful management	*Gerry Kushel* • £12.99
The concise time management and personal development	
	John Adair and Melanie Allen • £9.99
Gurus on marketing	*Sultan Kermally* • £14.99
The concise Adair on communication and presentation skills	
	edited by Neil Thomas • £9.99
The dictionary of colour	*Ian Paterson* • £19.99

Thorogood also has an extensive range of reports and special briefings which are written specifically for professionals wanting expert information.

For a full listing of all Thorogood publications, or to order any title, please call Thorogood Customer Services on 020 7749 4748 or fax on 020 7729 6110. Alternatively view our website at www.thorogood.ws.

Focused on developing your potential

Falconbury, the sister company to Thorogood publishing, brings together the leading experts from all areas of management and strategic development to provide you with a comprehensive portfolio of action-centred training and learning.

We understand everything managers and leaders need to be, know and do to succeed in today's commercial environment. Each product addresses a different technical or personal development need that will encourage growth and increase your potential for success.

- Practical public training programmes
- Tailored in-company training
- Coaching
- Mentoring
- Topical business seminars
- Trainer bureau/bank
- Adair Leadership Foundation

The most valuable resource in any organisation is its people; it is essential that you invest in the development of your management and leadership skills to ensure your team fulfil their potential. Investment into both personal and professional development has been proven to provide an outstanding ROI through increased productivity in both you and your team. Ultimately leading to a dramatic impact on the bottom line.

With this in mind Falconbury have developed a comprehensive portfolio of training programmes to enable managers of all levels to develop their skills in leadership, communications, finance, people management, change management and all areas vital to achieving success in today's commercial environment.

WHAT FALCONBURY CAN OFFER YOU?
- Practical applied methodology with a proven results
- Extensive bank of experienced trainers
- Limited attendees to ensure one-to-one guidance
- Up to the minute thinking on management and leadership techniques
- Interactive training
- Balanced mix of theoretical and practical learning
- Learner-centred training
- Excellent cost/quality ratio

FALCONBURY IN-COMPANY TRAINING

Falconbury are aware that a public programme may not be the solution to leadership and management issues arising in your firm. Involving only attendees from your organisation and tailoring the programme to focus on the current challenges you face individually and as a business may be more appropriate. With this in mind we have brought together our most motivated and forward thinking trainers to deliver tailored in-company programmes developed specifically around the needs within your organisation.

All our trainers have a practical commercial background and highly refined people skills. During the course of the programme they act as facilitator, trainer and mentor, adapting their style to ensure that each individual benefits equally from their knowledge to develop new skills.

Falconbury works with each organisation to develop a programme of training that fits your needs.

MENTORING AND COACHING

Developing and achieving your personal objectives in the workplace is becoming increasingly difficult in today's constantly changing environment. Additionally, as a manager or leader, you are responsible for guiding colleagues towards the realisation of their goals. Sometimes it is easy to lose focus on your short and long-term aims.

Falconbury's one-to-one coaching draws out individual potential by raising self-awareness and understanding, facilitating the learning and performance development that creates excellent managers and leaders. It builds renewed self-confidence and a strong sense of 'can-do' competence, contributing significant benefit to the organisation. Enabling you to focus your energy on developing your potential and that of your colleagues.

Mentoring involves formulating winning strategies, setting goals, monitoring achievements and motivating the whole team whilst achieving a much improved work life balance.

For more information contact Kate Jackson on: +44 (0)20 7729 6677

Falconbury Business Seminars
10-12 Rivington Street, London EC2A 3DU, UK